WITHDRAWN

BOONE COUNTY PUBLIC LIBRARY
BURLINGTON, KY 41005
wwwbcpl.org

MAR 0 9 2020

WITHDRAWN

PRIVILEGED VICTIMS

Advance Praise for *Privileged Victims*

"How did everyone in America get so unhappy all of a sudden? In part, because it pays. Eddie Scarry lays out the scam in this infuriating and fascinating book. It'll make you never want to complain again, just for the sake of being countercultural."
—Tucker Carlson, Host of *Tucker Carlson Tonight* on Fox News and Author of *Ship of Fools*

"What I love about Eddie is his courage. He knows the outrage mob is constantly coming and he doesn't care. Some of us call that being a First Amendment advocate. Count me as a fan and a reader."
—Megyn Kelly

"According to Eddie Scarry, there is little justice associated with the term 'social justice.' And in *Privileged Victims*, Scarry proves his point while naming names and exposing cons. There's no safe space in this book!"
—Bill O'Reilly, author of the bestselling *Killing* series and former Fox News host

"Eddie Scarry holds up the mirror to the 'woke' Left with a book that exposes the self-contradictions and delusions at the heart of intersectional insanity."
—Buck Sexton, radio host of *The Buck Sexton Show*

Also by Eddie Scarry

Fraud and Fiction: The Real Truth Behind Fire and Fury

PRIVILEGED VICTIMS

HOW AMERICA'S CULTURE FASCISTS HIJACKED THE COUNTRY AND ELEVATED ITS WORST PEOPLE

BY EDDIE SCARRY

BOMBARDIER
BOOKS

A BOMBARDIER BOOKS BOOK
An Imprint of Post Hill Press
ISBN: 978-1-64293-145-7
ISBN (eBook): 978-1-64293-146-4

Privileged Victims:
How America's Culture Fascists Hijacked the Country
and Elevated Its Worst People
© 2020 by Eddie Scarry
All Rights Reserved

Cover Design by Cody Corcoran

No part of this book may be reproduced, stored in a retrieval system, or transmitted by any means without the written permission of the author and publisher.

Post Hill Press
New York • Nashville
posthillpress.com

Published in the United States of America

To Michael and Marcela, who taught me that life isn't fair and that the universe owes me nothing.

Contents

CHAPTER 1

PRESENT-DAY AMERICA, WHERE THE CRAP RISES TO THE TOP

"If I had a world of my own, everything would be nonsense. Nothing would be what it is, because everything would be what it isn't. And contrary wise, what is, it wouldn't be. And what it wouldn't be, it would."—Lewis Carroll, *Through the Looking-Glass*

As we have it right now, so-called social justice infects every single part of our society. It dominates every corner of American life, positioning the aggrieved against the "privileged."

You have probably heard, at least in passing, about social justice. If you haven't, you will have certainly seen its corrosion on everything you once thought was normal. That's because it's a disease and it runs through our most vital cultural arteries: academia, the national media, Hollywood, and most of political Washington.

These areas dominate American life. Social justice rules about "privilege" and victimhood have set the tone. It's a whole system that now governs our national discourse and the way we live.

The system has its enforcers: professors cloistered on their campuses, liberal journalists in the media representing only one perspective, and entertainment figures who advocate on behalf of the social justice movement. They're America's culture fascists, and they keep social justice alive by repeating its dogma and by shaming those who stray from it. As a consequence, we all have to share in its misery, regardless of whether we recognize it.

At any one of hundreds of college campuses to visit around the country, you'll hear of students violated by opinions they simply didn't want to hear. It's "violence" to be exposed to certain views, they say. University money is then poured into sensitivity trainings, cultural diversity offices, and "safe spaces" for the purpose of reaffirming the self-worth of the delicate victims.

Pick up an issue of the *New York Times* and there will invariably be a story on the plight of illegal immigrants crammed into holding cells—a complete distraction from the fact that there are more important problems with our immigration system than the wait time migrants endure at detention facilities before being unleashed into our neighborhoods (like all of the violent crime and drugs pouring across the border).

Buy a ticket to a movie theater and relax in your seat as you're inundated with messages about "body positivity" (applicable to fat people and no one else), racism (because slavery never ended for Hollywood), and the intolerance of the religious (unless it concerns Islam, which is, we're endlessly reminded, "a religion of peace").

Most Americans have a vague sense of what's going on. They see that political correctness has gone too far. They see that there are kids who are now too sensitive. They see that everyone gets a trophy.

But that misses the mark. There's a lot more to it than that and it's a lot worse than realized.

Social justice isn't so simple, even if it's a fairly simple concept. It's not something that happened by accident. It's not a trend. It's not a generational problem. It's not at all incidental.

And the problem isn't going away. It's growing.

Social justice is a deliberate, systematic attempt to reorganize the country in such a way that anyone who claims to have been aggrieved and victimized due to their race, gender, or sexuality has absolute power over their oppressors, the so-called privileged. It's an erasure of American traditions, conventions, and foundations. It's a reversal of what is, at least for now, our way of life. Social justice has it that the lowest among us rise to the top and those currently at the top are expected to step aside, succumb, and submit. It's an ideology that shapes the entire world in terms of race, gender, and sexuality, and then frames it in grievance, oppression, and victimhood.

It's everywhere, and it's closing in on all of us.

I had heard in recent years about "social justice," "white privilege," "toxic masculinity," and "snowflakes." But like a lot of you, I ignored it or dismissed it as a weird internet thing, some ridiculous hobby the fringes of society had busied themselves with, like when kids were eating Tide pods. I thought it must have been something we would all eventually look back on and laugh. Then I heard about it again. And again. I heard of college professors who resigned because their students aggressively objected to being confronted with opposing ideas and concepts. I read news reports about celebrities who saw their careers collapse because they offended a "marginalized" group.

And I saw the rise of a new spawn of people who advanced in our society by claiming to have been oppressed, aggrieved, and victimized simply by living as their own individual race, gender, or sexuality.

I thought that was odd. Why wasn't I among them? I'm a Latino. I'm gay. I'm from the working-class South. I'm the only one in my immediate family to have obtained a four-year college degree. My father, otherwise, is a retired Marine and my mother is a Mexican immigrant brought here as a child by her mother.

You would think, under social justice rules, that my background must count for something. Shouldn't I get the right to be heard or seen or even just a complimentary pack of pretzels for my own situation?

Why didn't anyone defer to *me* on anything? Where was *my* guaranteed platform? Why hadn't anyone in a more "privileged" position asked *me* how they could help compensate for *my* lack of fortune? When would *I* be recognized as a victim of circumstance?

I never was and I never would be.

That's because I never thought to claim victimhood based on my own personal identity. Instead, I decided what I wanted and figured out how to get there. That meant foregoing a lot of things I wanted to do in college, taking on an internship after I graduated, taking my first full-time job (which I didn't want) and another internship on top of that, and then finally getting a break in political writing.

If I've never gotten ahead by using my race, gender or sexuality, why should anyone else? But a lot of people do. I'm just one person. Social justice doesn't have to worry about me when it has a vice grip on the entire culture.

⌘ ⌘ ⌘

The campus rape written about in *Rolling Stone* magazine, the biggest media hoax of the last decade, was made possible entirely by the insufferable atmosphere created by social justice.

In November 2014, journalist Sabrina Rubin Erdely told the story of Jackie Coakley, a college freshman who suffered a horrific gang rape by frat boys at the University of Virginia.

"'Shut *up*,' she heard a man's voice say as a body barreled into her, tripping her backward and sending them both crashing through a low glass table," wrote Erdely, recounting Jackie's story in harrowing detail. "There was a heavy person on top of her, spreading open her thighs, and another person kneeling on her hair, hands pinning down her arms, sharp shards digging into her back, and excited male voices rising all around her. When yet another hand clamped over her mouth, Jackie bit it, and the hand became a fist that punched her in the face. The men surrounding her began to laugh…. 'Grab its motherfucking leg,' she heard a voice say. And that's when Jackie knew she was going to be raped."[1]

The nine-thousand-word article went on to describe a pervasive culture on college campuses that excuses, or even permits, the rape of young women. It held up UVA as the pinnacle of so-called campus rape culture, the notion that there's rampant sexual violence committed by young men against women at universities across America.

It was certainly a riveting tale, but like all stories of privilege and victimhood told by today's news media, it turned out to be bullshit. A smart reporter at the *Washington Post* and another at the *Daily Caller* led the way in dismantling Jackie Coakley's tale and Erdely's negligence in properly corroborating it.

Coakley made it up, and Erdely and *Rolling Stone* were both sued multiple times for defamation by the fraternity named in the story, UVA's dean, and even some of the fraternity's individual members.

In court, Coakley claimed that she remembered nothing of what she relayed to Erdely in their interview about the rape; not a thing of the gruesome, violent, unforgettable rape she claimed to endure:

Counsel for former UVA dean Nicole Eramo: Did you tell Ms. Erdely that your date on Sep. 28, 2012, was a Phi Kappa Psi brother?

Jackie Coakley: I don't remember.

Counsel: Did you tell Ms. Erdely that you had met your date, the person who later orchestrated your assault, while working as a lifeguard shift at the UVA pool?

Coakley: I don't remember.

Counsel: Did you tell Ms. Erdely that this coworker had invited you to a date function at Phi Kappa Psi on Sep. 28, 2012?

---

1   Sabrina Ruben Erdely, "A Rape on Campus: A Brutal Assault and Struggle for Justice at UVA," *Rolling Stone*, Nov. 19, 2014: http://web.archive.org/web/20141119200349/http://www.rollingstone.com/culture/features/a-rape-on-campus-20141119.

Coakley: I can't recall. I don't know.

Counsel: Did you tell Ms. Erdely that you left Phi [Kappa] Psi at 3 a.m. barefoot and splattered with blood?

Coakley: I don't remember.

Counsel: Did you tell Ms. Erdely details of what happened to you inside the fraternity on the night of your assault?

Coakley: I don't remember specifically what I told her.[2]

Is there anything that Jackie *could* remember?

The *Rolling Stone* article was retracted in April 2015, and Erdely and the magazine lost or settled each of the lawsuits against them for millions of dollars.[3, 4, 5]

This isn't a tragedy. The tragedy would be if Coakley and *Rolling Stone* had gotten away with it. The tragedy is that a once respected publication and Erdely, a journalist, so desperately bought into social justice ideology that they eagerly published a lie, defaming a number of innocent people in the process.

---

2   T. Rees Shapiro, "Hear U-Va.'s 'Jackie' testify about Rolling Stone's gang rape story," *Washington Post*, Oct. 26, 2016: https://www.washingtonpost.com/news/grade-point/wp/2016/10/26/hear-u-va-s-jackie-testify-about-rolling-stones-gang-rape-story/?utm_term=.301235cc18c9.

3   "Rolling Stone Settles Last Remaining Lawsuit Over UVA Rape Story," *Hollywood Reporter*, Dec. 21, 2017: https://www.hollywoodreporter.com/thr-esq/rolling-stone-settles-last-remaining-lawsuit-uva-rape-story-1069880.

4   T. Rees Shapiro, "Fraternity chapter at U-Va. to settle suit against Rolling Stone for $1.65 million," *Washington Post*, June 13, 2017: https://www.washingtonpost.com/local/education/fraternity-chapter-at-u-va-to-settle-suit-against-rolling-stone-for-165-million/2017/06/13/35012b46-503d-11e7-91eb-9611861a988f_story.html?utm_term=.8f5aa5b73746.

5   T. Rees Shapiro and Emma Brown, "Rolling Stone settles with former U-Va. dean in defamation case," *Washington Post*, April 11, 2017: https://www.washingtonpost.com/local/education/rolling-stone-settles-with-u-va-dean-in-defamation-case/2017/04/11/5a564532-1f02-11e7-be2a-3a1fb24d4671_story.html?utm_term=.d4f093198762.

Jackie Coakley's story was the social justice system functioning just as intended. Coakley is a woman and therefore it was assumed she had been aggrieved. *Believe her.*

As Erdely proved, some journalists are all too ready to believe and to print the lie in a national magazine.

The disease is everywhere.

Without the social justice movement, Amy Schumer would have never had her turn as a Hollywood It Girl. She's not beautiful. She's not funny. I'd also add that she can't act, but that's a matter of personal taste.

When Schumer was featured on the cover of *GQ* magazine in July 2015, Matt Drudge of the Drudge Report asked on Twitter, "Why is she being force-fed on [the] population?"[6] Social justice, oppression, and "privilege" are why. Schumer is an unattractive, unfunny woman, otherwise known in the mainstream entertainment industry as a "victim" of those who have "privilege." Social justice dictates that she *should* get attention, and that she *should* be a celebrity for her shortcomings, including her lack of talent.

Some people, naturally, may enjoy Schumer. But they have little choice when she's foisted on their lives in a slew of big-money rom-coms, magazine covers, and network TV interviews. Hollywood studios, celebrity tabloids, and entertainment shows, all run by culture fascists in their own right, want you to *want* Schumer and "victims" like her. They make it happen with hundreds of millions of dollars in publicity, TV, movie, and book deals, for the express purpose of advancing the social justice ideology.

This is like presenting a starved Ethiopian child with canned peas and enthusiastically asking him how they taste. He's been living in a desert for all his life, famished, and so it's safe to assume the rave review he might offer won't reflect the reality that he's eating a bunch of wet seeds.

At least Schumer is in on the social justice scam. While promoting her movie *I Feel Pretty* (2018) on ABC's *The View*, she said that she

---

6 Matt Drudge, Twitter.com, July 16, 2015.

regretted her whiteness and that her starring role in the movie didn't instead go to a darker woman. "I think it's fair to say that it's a lot harder for other people," she said. "And I recognize that I am a Caucasian. I would love if this movie were starring a woman of color who's had it way harder than me, and I think—I hope we get there." She added that she hoped that her role was "just a step in the right direction."[7]

This is social justice in its purity: a hefty, talentless white woman starring in a major production, yet still pretending to humble herself because she didn't have as hard a life as a black lesbian who uses a wheelchair.

As Amy Schumer proves, social justice is the advancement of the worst among us. It's the spotlighting of the undeserving. It's the elevation of our worst people.

Social justice no doubt gave us *New York Times* columnist Charles M. Blow. Before Blow was given the most prestigious job in journalism—his own space in the world's most important paper—he had no discernible experience in journalism. The *Times* gave Blow, who is black, the column in 2008. All indications are that he had no history in actual writing before that, which explains his clunky prose. Before Blow got his *Times* column, he designed graphics.

Hey, graphics guy, wanna write your uninformed opinions twice per week in the paper of record?

Journalists around the country work for decades to get the opportunity to become an opinion writer, even in just a *local paper*. Most of them will never get it, but there is Blow sitting on high.

Blow bragged in an August 2019 column that he has "been in journalism all my adult life, 26 years."[8]

---

7   Amy Schumer, *The View*, ABC, April 20, 2018.
8   Charles Blow, "Yearning for more Yang," *New York Times*, Aug. 1, 2019: https://www.nytimes.com/2019/08/01/opinion/2020-andrew-yang.html.

Wow, that sounds like a lot of years in journalism. The truth is that Blow never wrote until the *Times* inexplicably allowed him a twice-per-week column, accompanied by a hefty salary and even more opportunities, like a CNN contract, which Blow has. How exactly did Blow get the job? It's a mystery. His own *New York Times* bio gives no clue. It says that Blow joined the *Times* in 1994 as a graphics editor and then "quickly became the paper's graphics director." The bio says he left in 2006 to become *National Geographic* magazine's art director, and then at some point held the same job at the *Detroit News*.[9]

How, then, might a person who makes charts and pictures suddenly become an opinion writer for the gold standard of journalism, the *New York Times*? Social justice is the only plausible answer.

If anyone deserved that boost, according to social justice, it's Blow. He's not only the klutziest writer you've ever read, but he suffers every form of oppression, grievance, and victimization on this planet: He's black; he's nonheterosexual (bisexual, he says); he was molested as a child by his cousin, according to his first memoir (he's written two, because he apparently has a lot of memories about himself to share); and his college-age son was held up at gunpoint by campus police at Yale at the peak of the Black Lives Matter movement, because he had matched the description of a suspect (though when Blow publicized that incident, he neglected to mention that the officer who confronted his son was also black).[10]

Blow's inexplicable advancement may be the blackest mark on journalism. There is no discernible merit, talent, or reason to justify his abrupt move from being a graphics person to being a prestigious columnist. He rose to the top anyway.

---

9   "Charles M. Blow," *New York Times*: https://www.nytimes.com/by/charles-m-blow.

10   Eddie Scarry, "N.Y. Times' Charles Blow said nothing about cop who arrested his son being black," *Washington Examiner*, Jan. 27, 2015: https://www.washingtonexaminer.com/ny-times-charles-blow-said-nothing-about-cop-who-arrested-his-son-being-black.

Jayson Blair, former *New York Times* journalist, was at least creative when it came to his own undeserved attention. He may have fabricated a bunch of stories but that takes *some* effort. Blow, on the other hand, writes something like, "I prefer the boot of truth to slam down to earth like thunder, no matter the shock of hearing its clap," and, well, that's the standard for being a columnist at the *Times*.[11]

The hysterical Trump v. "The Squad" controversy is an exquisite illustration of how social justice has infected our politics. In July of 2019, just a few months after Democrats had taken control of the House and sworn in a group of first-term, social media-preoccupied women representatives, President Trump put out some nonsensical tweets suggesting that they "go back" to their "countries" and "help fix the totally broken and crime infested places from which they came."

The congresswomen in question were Representatives Ayanna Pressley of Massachusetts, Alexandria Ocasio-Cortez of New York, Rashida Tlaib of Michigan, and Ilhan Omar of Minnesota. I'm not going to assume there was any coherent or consistent meaning to Trump's tweets, given that three of the congresswomen were born in America, but since the media leaped at the chance to call his missives "racist," I'll at least acknowledge that he was right as his tweets pertained to Omar.

The tweets were, if anything, a truncated version of a *Washington Post* profile on Omar from just days before they were posted.

The story said that in Omar's view, "America wasn't the bighearted country that saved her from a brutal war and a bleak refugee camp [in Kenya]. It wasn't a meritocracy that helped her attend college or vaulted her into Congress." The *Post* said that instead, for Omar, America "was the country that had failed to live up to its founding ideals, a place that

---

11   Charles M. Blow, "Trump Isn't Hitler. But the Lying …" *New York Times*, Oct. 19, 2017: https://www.nytimes.com/2017/10/19/opinion/trump-isnt-hitler-but-the-lying.html?smid=tw-nytopinion&smtyp=cur.

had disappointed her and so many immigrants, refugees and minorities like her."[12]

Another gem in the story recounted the time Omar, on the day she was elected as a state representative in 2016, wrote a letter to a judge who was about to sentence men in the United States who had been convicted of attempting to aid the Islamic State terrorist network. "The desire to commit violence is not inherent in people," she wrote in defense of the convicts. "It is the consequence of systemic alienation." For context, the problem of Minneapolis locals (Somalis) attempting to join the Islamic State is so pervasive that Minnesota U.S. Attorney Andrew Luger said in 2015 that "Minnesota has a terror recruiting problem." And the *New York Times* reported that year that "Federal prosecutors have charged more than 20 people in Minnesota in relation to Al Shabaab, a Somali terrorist organization. At least 10 more have been charged with supporting the Islamic State.[13]

No matter what anybody says about America being "multicultural" and "a nation of immigrants," I'll go out on a limb and say that Omar's views aren't shared by the typical native-born American, or even the typical immigrant, for that matter.[14]

We should expect Omar's view of America to be, for lack of a more perfect word, alien. She only got here as a child and then moved to "Little Mogadishu" in Minneapolis, where there are more Somalis than anywhere else outside of actual war-torn Somalia.

---

12 Greg Jaffe and Souad Mekhennet, "Ilhan Omar's American story: It's complicated," *Washington Post*, July 6, 2019: https://www.washingtonpost.com/politics/2019/07/06/ilhan-omar-is-unlike-anyone-who-has-served-congress-this-is-her-complicated-american-story/?arc404=true.

13 Christina Capecchi and Mitch Smith, "Minneapolis Fighting Terror Recruitment," *New York Times*, Sept. 9, 2015: https://www.nytimes.com/2015/09/10/us/minneapolis-fighting-terror-recruitment.html.

14 Eddie Scarry, "Tying Ilhan Omar's anti-Semitism to her overseas roots," *Washington Examiner*, March 7, 2019: https://www.washingtonexaminer.com/opinion/tying-ilhan-omars-antisemitism-to-her-overseas-roots.

She's a foreign-born Muslim with views shaped by a foreign experience as she lived in a foreign country. And when she got to the U.S., her family immersed her in an area with people who shared that same foreign backstory. Democrats and their liberal friends in the media can carp all they want about Trump's tweets, but they can't pretend he didn't have a point about Omar.

In response to Trump's tweets, "the squad" held a press conference to address them, though it more closely resembled a battered women's group therapy session. They hugged each other and smiled encouragingly at one another while each went up to a podium to say how brave they felt. This, by the way, is what counts as bravery in the social justice movement: confronting tweets.

A few days later, Trump hosted one of his campaign mega rallies in North Carolina, where his supporters broke out in chants of "Send her back! Send her back!" It was obnoxious, but so is Omar. She was generously allowed into the United States by its good graces so that she and her family could escape the dump she was born into, she speaks with a foreign accent because her family never fully assimilated, and yet her entire political career has been nothing but one long criticism of everything that's wrong with America. Why wouldn't someone whose family history here dates back at least one generation feel like saying, "If you hate everything about it, then leave"?

Omar makes a bunch of inflammatory remarks against the country, but because she's a woman and she's not white, she's assumed to be the victim, and the "privileged"—i.e. anyone who disagrees with her—should have no recourse. If anyone criticizes her, they're immediately labeled racist by the media.

That's the effect that social justice has had on our politics.

Living under this passive dictatorship is hell. Most people know it, but they're too polite to speak up, ever conscious that they might further offend the supposedly aggrieved. Instead, they sit quietly, many of them convinced that they must be missing something or that there's a new reality which sprung up overnight, leaving them behind.

The truth is that they're not missing anything. The truth is that over the course of four decades, a toxic ideology has slowly spread throughout the country, creating what is now lovingly referred to as social justice. A deadly cocktail of grievance on the basis of race, gender, and sexuality make up its movement.

Incidentally, there is no justice involved. There are only the people and ideas representing the worst of society put on a fast track to the top. They're rewarded for their mediocrity because more important than merit are their "grievance" and "oppression" on account of their gender, sexuality, and race.

It's everywhere and it's corrosive. It has ruined nearly all of the entertainment industry, the news media, politics, and academia.

This is the modern culture war. Social justice fights by publicly shaming its critics, angrily mobbing its opponents, and most crucially, seizing control of America's cultural arteries, the institutions that dictate the direction in which our country moves.

There can only be one winner in that battle: social justice or you. Right now, social justice is ahead and it has a massive lead.

Oppression is the new "privilege" and social justice is rapidly elevating America's worst people.

CHAPTER 2

PRIVILEGE FOR DUMMIES

"When I use a word," Humpty Dumpty said, in rather a scornful tone, "it means just what I choose it to mean—neither more nor less."

"The question is," said Alice, "whether you can make words mean so many different things."—Lewis Carroll, *Through the Looking-Glass*

"Social justice" as a concept is like if Tyler Perry made another one of those *Madea* movies: You can see it as a cruel, intimidating atrocity and assume it must be an unfortunate accident of history. But when you look closely, you find that, like a *Madea* movie, social justice is actually a deliberate production, delicately crafted with time and patience.

Privilege is an outgrowth of the social justice movement, that branch of political activism that asserts there's an inherent unfairness and prejudice rooted in American life. That unfairness manifests itself in the oppression, grievance, and victimization of women, nonwhites, gays, lesbians, and even transsexuals. It's an ideology that demands that the country's very foundations, customs, and norms be reordered to right all of its wrongs. The goal of the movement isn't always clear because it frequently changes, depending on which set of people is deemed to

14

have adequately suffered and which set is guilty of some form of privilege. Because the movement operates largely by using shame, it can sometimes seem that shame is in itself the objective.

Check your privilege! Mansplaining! My culture is not your costume! Microaggression! You're perpetuating the patriarchy! Toxic masculinity!

Admittedly, to refer to social justice as a kind of political activism is exceedingly generous. It's not as though it's just another special interest group. It's not another niche lobby organization like the Association for Renaissance Martial Arts. Social justice is more like an incurable cancer. With aggressive treatment, you might keep it at bay. You might even shrink it for a while. But it will always be there, waiting for the right time to come roaring back the moment you get comfortable.

Dr. Michael Rectenwald, who until recently was a liberal studies professor at New York University, is the foremost critical authority on the social justice movement—its history and the ideology that fuels it. He has a doctorate in literary and cultural studies from Carnegie Mellon University and a master's in English literature from Case Western Reserve University in Ohio. His memoir, *Springtime for Snowflakes: 'Social Justice' and Its Postmodern Parentage*, recounts his own horrendous run-in with social justice at New York University.

Rectenwald was, until recently, a political leftist. He studied Russian literature and philosophy and considered himself to be a "libertarian communist." That changed in late 2016, when he said that he noticed a "politically correct authoritarianism" taking hold at NYU and other universities. He created an anonymous Twitter account, @AntiPCnyuProf, that he used as an outlet to criticize college students who had shut down public speaking events, demanded "safe spaces" at their schools, and pressured college administrators to ban anything from campus that they declared offensive.

After Rectenwald revealed that he was behind the Twitter account in NYU's student paper, his colleagues revolted and he was asked to take paid leave for the purpose of his own "well being." He eventually left the school completely at the start of 2019. He now identifies as a political libertarian.

In his extensive body of work on the subject, Rectenwald traces the social justice movement to postmodernism. It is the spawn of postmodern philosophers like Jacques Derrida, Jean-François Lyotard, Jean Baudrillard, and Michel Foucault. They in turn were directly influenced by Karl Marx and Vladimir Lenin.

The origins of social justice date back to nineteenth- and twentieth-century theorists of Germany and France, the birthplaces of delightful and timeless ideas like class resentment and "*égalité*" (equality) through government force. Their ideas spread west, forming a worldview in present-day America that holds that words have no concrete meaning, the concept of truth is subject to individual perspective, and morality is subject to an individual's power.

The fundamentals started with Karl Marx and to some extent, Friedrich Nietzsche, both of the nineteenth century. Marx asserted that the people of any society can be truly equal only when the perpetual conflict between workers and owners of capital (capitalists) is eliminated and replaced with communism. The goal of communism was to see the laborers in possession of the means of production, even if it meant the complete destruction of the wealthier capitalist class. Wealth, Marx famously said, was to be distributed "from each according to their abilities, to each according to their needs." It was the original Bernie Sanders plan.

Unlike communism, social justice is not concerned with an outcome of equality. Whereas communism holds that society can be leveled by abolishing separate economic classes, social justice says that inequality is rooted in identity and the privilege or lack thereof that comes with belonging to a particular identity category.

The categories, like scenes from a Quentin Tarantino film, are endless. For our mental well-being, we'll largely stick to the basic three: race, gender, and sexuality, which also covers gender transformation. The social justice movement seeks to upend the established social hierarchy by demanding that the supposed grievance, oppression, and victimization stemming from those three areas be acknowledged and accounted for. That includes the punishment of those deemed to benefit from unearned privilege, meaning whites, men, heterosexuals, and the nontransgender.

Nietzsche directly influenced today's version of social justice by asserting that there is an inseparable link between morality and power. He wrote in his 1887 book *On the Genealogy of Morality* that those who wished to overthrow the established hierarchy intended to invert it so that the bottom would become the top and vice versa. This wasn't his prescription for society, but rather a severe criticism of the tendency of the time to view society's subordinates as inherently moral. "Only those who suffer are good," he wrote with acrimony, "only the poor, the powerless, the lowly are good; the suffering, the deprived, the sick, the ugly, are the only pious people, the only ones saved, salvation is for them alone, whereas you rich, the noble and powerful, you are eternally wicked, cruel, lustful, insatiate, godless, you will also be eternally wretched, cursed and damned!"[15]

Nietzsche was identifying and criticizing the notion that those at the bottom of civilized societies should be presumed virtuous and admirable simply by nature of their suffering and disadvantages. But that concept is precisely what forms the basis of the present social justice movement. According to the movement and its ideology, the good, virtuous, and admirable are those who claim to have been aggrieved on account of their race, gender, or sexuality. Under social justice, asserting

---

15 Friedrich Nietzsche, *On the Genealogy of Morality*, Cambridge Texts in the History of Political Thought, Revised Student Edition (Cambridge University Press, 2006), 17.

grievance and claiming oppression earns an individual a higher moral worth than those who are deemed "privileged."

Summing it up, there was Marx, who saw society's ultimate conflict as one of resentment between classes, and he believed it could be resolved only when the haves were reduced and the have-nots were elevated. And there was Nietzsche, who believed that the enduring fight is a struggle over who has the power to determine what is moral and just. Morality, then, is a matter of authority: Those viewed by society as possessing a higher morality and a greater moral worth are granted more authority.

When the two philosophies are put together and combined with the ideas of influential French postmodern theorists of the twentieth century, they form the nexus of social justice, the sprawling tentacles that make up its movement and those who enforce it. It's the feminists, the activist gays, the transgender lobby, the raging Black Lives Matter mob, the illegal-immigrant advocates, the news media, Hollywood, and academia. They have little in common. They don't share similar backgrounds or the same political self-interests. What they do have in common is a burning hatred for the "privileged," a desire to bring them down, and a demand that they themselves advance to the top of the social hierarchy for no other reason than that they claim to have been victimized. That's what drives their white-hot resentment for modern America, its institutions, conventions, and norms. Their bond is their ambition for a complete overhaul, a reordering of the country from top to bottom and, in effect, *reversing* who is at the top and who sits at the bottom.

Rectenwald writes that postmodernism "adopted Nietzsche's view that power and knowledge are inextricable, that values are historically contingent and socially constructed, that truth is a function of the most plausible narrative explanations as inflected by power."[16] In other words, truth is whatever the people in power say it is.

---

16 Michael Rectenwald, "A Critique of 'Social Justice' Ideology: Thinking through Marx and Nietzsche," CLG News, July 20, 2017: https://www.legitgov.org/Critique-Social-Justice-Ideology-Thinking-through-Marx-and-Nietzsche.

Who has the power in America's culture now? The social justice movement does, and that power is reinforced by Hollywood, the news media, academia, and much of the Washington political establishment. They are the culture fascists that support the social justice movement.

Seizing power in America was done through subversion of the country's cultural institutions and it happened relatively quickly, as far as disastrous revolutions go. Social justice ideology first spread through the universities and from there to the other hubs of American culture. It went from university academics, who taught it to their students, and then it flowed from screen writers and journalists.

What's seen in Hollywood entertainment and in national newspapers, on the TV news, and on the internet, becomes a piece of our collective culture. With enough repetition, it's then absorbed into the American mainstream. This is how social justice ended up everywhere.

> It's how grievance and oppression became synonymous
> with virtue and goodness. And how "privilege" became
> a sin.

The revolution took place over just a few decades and you may not have ever noticed. The goal has always been the same: It's the transfer of power from the "privileged" to the aggrieved, along with a complete reorganization of America. The method used to achieve it has never changed.

Social justice aggressively spreads by fostering resentments between men and women, blacks and whites, Latinos and whites, gays and straights, and the transgender and the cisgender (a social justice term for those who accept the gender that they were born with). Blacks are assumed to have been irreparably deprived by "white privilege." It's taken for granted that women are oppressed by men, "the patriarchy." Gays, lesbians, and transgender people (who, contrary to popular belief, are not natural associates) must have suffered at the hands of heterosexuals. The logical end is that all those who claim to have been aggrieved and oppressed on account of gender, race, or sexuality are assumed to retain a morally superior position, and an infallible perspective unclouded by privilege. They are the victims of society, and therefore their moral authority cannot be challenged. They've suffered, and therefore their "truth" on an individual basis is unimpeachable, admirable, and deserves to be seen, heard, and elevated.

The ridiculous notion that individuals hold their own truths, as reflected in the asinine "Live your truth" mantra, is a key feature of the social justice movement's ideology. It's traced back to the Marxist belief that the laborer has a unique viewpoint, and, as Rectenwald observes, is more explicitly linked to what early-twentieth-century Hungarian theorist Georg Lukács called "standpoint epistemology." Epistemology is the philosophy of understanding human knowledge. Standpoint epistemology, or standpoint knowledge, holds that the perspective of certain person can lend that individual access to a unique truth that others don't have and can never obtain. Lukács developed the concept in his 1923 work *History and Class Consciousness*, in which he refers to a kind of "knowledge" held by people of the working class that "stands on a higher scientific plane objectively."[17]

Rectenwald sums up the standpoint knowledge theory as adapted by social justice. It is, he writes, "the notion that particular social outlooks lend greater access to knowledge of reality." The nature of people's perspectives, with particular regard to those who claim to experience a form of oppression, "accords them an enhanced cognitive and perceptual grasp" of reality.[18]

In essence, depending on an individual's identity—race, gender, sexuality, or any combination thereof—he or she will have access to a

17 Georg Lukacs, "History and Class Consciousness," Marxist.org: https://www.marxists.org/archive/lukacs/works/history/hcc07_1.htm.
18 Michael Rectenwald, "A Critique of 'Social Justice' Ideology: Thinking through Marx and Nietzsche," July 20, 2017, LegitGov.org: https://www.legitgov.org/Critique-Social-Justice-Ideology-Thinking-through-Marx-and-Nietzsche.

truth unobtainable to anyone who doesn't share that identity. A black man's truth, then, is unknowable to a white man. A lesbian's truth is unknowable to a straight person. Furthermore, social justice dictates that these truths must be acknowledged as unchallengeable and are to be regarded with reverence for the "victims" who profess to hold them.

In America, the earliest signs of social justice in its current state began in the 1960s. Postmodern theories and ideas about class resentments and struggles made their way from Western Europe, spread among academics, and eventually gave birth to the third-wave feminist movement, according to Rectenwald. They spun off from there, creating the things that normal people in today's America now dread: political correctness, affirmative action, calls for reparations, identity politics, civil rights for infinite special classes of citizens, and on and on.

Because the social justice ideology, the movement, and its enforcers operate outside the purview of normal people, they have their own concepts and terms, some or all of which you might not have heard before. They include:

Postmodernism: A philosophical skepticism and theoretical criticism of modern Western society's foundation, structure, traditions, and conventions. When a feminist complains about the "patriarchy," for example, she is criticizing what she believes is a traditional way of life that was established from the start for the benefit of men and that is inherently biased against women. When a "gender-fluid" person asserts that there are more than two genders, despite all scientific evidence to the contrary, that person is assuming a postmodern view that what biology has told us for hundreds of years is simply a transphobic lie.

Deconstruction: The theory, developed by French theorist Jacques Derrida, that language and words have no concrete, universally understood meaning or structure, but only a meaning relative to whoever uses them. Deconstruction of the language is why the social justice movement insists that gender is not determined by biology but by the individual's naming of genders. The word "man" under social justice rules, then, does not solely refer to a person with a penis. It can also be a woman who *believes she is a man*, and if she believes she is, she must be treated by society as one, so long as she insists that she is one. The logic follows that an individual might feel like a "man" one day and not the next, rendering the term "man" in itself meaningless. Transgenderism, gender "fluidity," and "nonbinary" genderism are all made possible by the concept of deconstruction. The notion that words don't have to serve as concrete labels is why anything that is decidedly not racist can still be called racist. And it has made it possible to label nonviolent things, like free speech, as physical assaults.

Standpoint epistemology (standpoint knowledge): The theory that an individual's grasp of reality is dependent on his or her unique perspective, as introduced by Georg Lukács and heralded by French philosopher Jean-François Lyotard. Social justice ideology applies the concept to race, gender, and sexuality, fostering the notion that any individual can claim his or her own reality, their own truth. There is, then, no determinable, universal, objective truth. The very idea of objective truth has, in fact, been deemed an element of white supremacy by proponents of social justice.[19] Instead, there are endless variations of truth, dependent on an individual's life experience and guided by each person's race, gender, or sexuality. Recall that Supreme Court Justice Sonia Sotomayor said in a lecture at the University of California, Berkeley, in 2001 that "a wise Latina woman with the richness of her experiences would more often than not reach a better conclusion than a white male who hasn't lived that life."[20] Her view is that a person's gender, race and sexuality can give the individual access to a different, even better, level of knowledge. The truth under social justice is colored by grievance, oppression, and victimhood.

---

19 Robby Soave, "Pomona College Students Say There's No Such Thing as Truth, 'Truth' Is a Tool of White Supremacy," Reason.com, April, 17, 2017: https://reason.com/2017/04/17/pomona-college-students-say-theres-no-su/.

20 Frank James, "Sotomayor's 'Wise Latina' Line Maybe Not So Wise," npr.org, May 27, 2009: https://www.npr.org/sections/the two-way/2009/05/sotomayors_wise_latina_line_ma.html.

Intersectionality: The overlapping of race, gender, and sexuality that creates countless layers of identity and, therefore, countless variations of oppression and grievance that an individual can claim. It is the social justice hierarchy of victimhood, a way to rank the various forms of hardship endured due to race, gender, and sexuality. Two white women, for example, can be understood by the social justice standard to have been oppressed, generally, by men. If one of them is a lesbian, however, that's yet another layer of victimhood, placing her at least one notch above the other on the intersectionality hierarchy.

Struggle session: A form of mass manipulation exercised in the form of shaming and ostracizing of individuals who stray from established orthodoxy. The technique is rooted in the Maoist Cultural Revolution in China, where those who were deemed insufficiently loyal to the state-party ideology were verbally and physically abused in public so as to intimidate other potential political defectors. Rectenwald observes that the social justice movement has adapted the procedure, as recognized in the insufferable "check your privilege" catchphrase. "Check your privilege" is the social justice command for an individual to acknowledge his perceived, unearned advantages supposedly bestowed upon him by his whiteness, maleness, or heterosexuality. A white male, for example, may be told to check his privilege by declining to speak on subjects involving racism and defer instead to the lived experience of an ethnic minority. This shouldn't be confused with taking turns in a given discussion. The purpose of the mandate is to entirely silence those with "privilege" and shame them into withdrawing from any particular conversation, debate, or event.

Discursive violence: The spoken word interpreted as physical harm, a concept championed by French theorist Michel Foucault. As noted by Rectenwald, social justice holds that speech and expression alone can function as assault. The concept is most prolific on university campuses, where students who find offense in a speech or an idea decry it as violence or even consider it an assault. This is what led to the demand for "safe spaces" at universities, areas carved out on campus where specific ideas, speech, or even people are forbidden if they don't adhere to social justice orthodoxy.

Woke: Used to describe a person who is enlightened, aware of, and sensitive to all of the previous terms and all things related to social justice. That includes the ability to identify individuals who possess "privilege," and the grievance, oppression, and victimization experienced by those who don't on account of their race, gender, or sexuality. The woke concept is also used as a form of affirmation for adherents to the ideology. If a person is "woke," they're good in the eyes of the social justice movement.

An infusion of these ideas brings you to modern-day social justice, a system, a worldview, and a movement that bears no semblance to actual justice.

According to Rectenwald, "social justice" as a well-intentioned remedy to economic societal problems traces back to the 1840s, when Italian Catholic Jesuit priest Luigi Taparelli d'Azeglio used the term to describe "the glaring lack of an adequate Catholic response to industrialism and urbanization, with their associated social and economic symptoms."[21] It was the "supplanting of guild-based cottage industries by urban factories [and] the displacement of workers" during the Industrial Revolution that moved d'Azeglio to state that a certain social justice was required to remedy the impact it had had on the laborers.

During that period, factories and advancements in machinery disrupted the working classes of Western Europe, just as automation has done to the Midwest in America today. The technological shift created economic opportunity for some at devastating expense to others.

"The original social justice," writes Rectenwald, "amounted to the protection and mobilization of small charitable and philanthropic organizations to address (but not eliminate) the recalcitrant social facts of individual, economic, and political inequality, which had been exacerbated under the new industrial economy."

---

21   Michael Rectenwald, "On the Origins and Character of 'Social Justice,'" *New English Review* (August 2018): https://www.newenglishreview.org/custpage.cfm?frm=189367&sec_id=189367.

In short, there were private charities that worked to ameliorate the effects of job displacement and poverty of the industrial age. That was considered social justice at the time.

It stands in contrast to today's social justice movement, which is only tangentially concerned with uplifting the impoverished. It instead trains its energy on bringing down the "privileged" and reordering America's social hierarchy around identity and grievance. It wants the moral superiority of the oppressed moved to the top and nothing less.

It's a societal subversion that began brewing in academia in the late 1960s with the feminist movement, and it gained prominence in the 1980s and 1990s.

American feminists of the 1980s did most of the work in bringing social justice from academia to the rest of America. In her 1986 book *The Science Question in Feminism*, influential feminist Sandra Harding writes that, "By starting from the lived realities of women's lives, we can identify the grounding for a theory of knowledge that should be the successor to both Enlightenment and Marxist epistemologies."[22]

In other words, Harding is asserting that women, simply by nature of their gender, possess a particular knowledge that should function as the viewpoint by which the world operates. And remember, only women can possess such perspective, so it follows that men should submit to the inherent superiority of all women without regard for merit or ability.

If standpoint knowledge functions as the brain of social justice ideology, its heart is intersectionality, an ever-shifting ranking system that determines who is more aggrieved than the next, who deserves more deference than the other. It's a hazy, nonconcrete way of measuring overlapping identities and their corresponding hardships and victimhood. The more cross sections of oppressed identities an individual can claim, the higher his or her status on the intersectionality scale.

---

22 Sandra Harding, *The Science Question in Feminism* (Cornell University Press, June 1986), 146.

It gets messy even within the movement. Who can say whether one person is more aggrieved than another? Is a black woman more or less oppressed than a white gay man? Is a Latino man more or less privileged than a Palestinian trans woman? Is an American Indian man more or less aggrieved than a lesbian Asian woman? (The answer for that one really depends on whether the Asian woman is hot, but the point remains.) It's all worked out through a type of never-ending oppression Olympics, a competition for the title of Most Aggrieved. The judges are the social justice enforcers, the culture fascists in academia, in Hollywood, in the news media, and in political Washington.

Black feminist author Gloria Watkins, better known by her pen name bell hooks, helped usher in the intersectionality ranking system in her 1984 book *Feminist Theory: From Margin to Center*, a critique of the feminist movement of the 1960s. In that book, she argues that the movement overlooked struggles against forms of oppression that fall outside of gender, and outside of white women in particular. She writes, "Within society, all forms of oppression are supported by traditional Western thinking…. Sexist oppression is of primary importance…[because] it is the practice of domination most people are socialized to accept before they even know that other forms of group oppression exist."[23] She continues, "Since all forms of oppression are linked in our society because they are supported by similar institutional and social structures, one system cannot be eradicated while the others remain intact."

Hooks maintains that the most discussed grievance of the time— the lack of women's sexual and economic independence—was only the first step in addressing other forms of oppression not yet acknowledged by society.

That observation was a prescient prediction of the situation in present-day America, where the well of grievance and oppression is bottomless.

---

23   bell hooks, *Feminist Theory: From Margin to Center*, third edition (Routledge, October 2014).

The most up-to-date idea of privilege—social justice theory's ultimate adversary—was pushed into the mainstream by Peggy McIntosh, who is famous for her 1988 essay "White Privilege and Male Privilege: A Personal Account of Coming to See Correspondences Through Work in Women's Studies." The essay builds on 1960s feminism but ventures into race by critiquing the privilege of white Americans in everyday life. Without ever using the phrase, McIntosh talks about the hierarchy of intersectionality. She refers to it instead as "interlocking oppressions." And without ever using the phrase, she introduces social justice ideology's most potent weapon: the modern-day struggle session—the command to "Check your privilege" in front of the masses.

"I have come to see white privilege as an invisible package of unearned assets that I can count on cashing in each day, but about which I was 'meant' to remain oblivious," she writes. "White privilege is like an invisible weightless knapsack of special provisions, assurances, tools, maps, guides, codebooks, passports, visas, clothes, compass, emergency gear, and blank checks."[24]

She goes on to give forty-six examples of white privilege she personally enjoys, an exercise that college students are now instructed to replicate at universities all over the country. (I personally went through it during a mandatory freshman-level course.)

Among McIntosh's examples of her white privilege are: "I can be reasonably sure that my neighbors in such a location will be neutral or pleasant to me," "I can go shopping alone most of the time, fairly well assured that I will not be followed or harassed by store detectives," and, "Whether I use checks, credit cards, or cash, I can count on my skin color not to work against the appearance that I am financially reliable."

24　Peggy McIntosh, "White Privilege and Male Privilege: A Personal Account of Coming to See Correspondences Through Work in Women's Studies," Wellesley Centers for Women, 1988: https://nationalseedproject.org/Key-SEED-Texts/white-privilege-and-male-privilege.

It's arguable that McIntosh's "knapsack" was full of experiences that were unique to her personally and not reflective of the color of her skin generally. Her assumption that all whites, based solely on their skin tone, are invariably trusted as honest, upstanding citizens belies the fact that the term "white trash" exists for a reason. (Contrary to popular belief, it wasn't invented solely for MSNBC's ever twangy and clueless Elise Jordan.)

Regardless, McIntosh's "knapsack of special provisions" might have simply served as an innocuous set of observations about unrecognized prejudices if it weren't for the second half of her essay. That half of the essay takes a maniacal nosedive and suggests that those who possess privilege feel a sense of shame and a sense of responsibility to atone for something they had no say in.

"[A] man's sex provides advantage for him whether or not he approves of the way in which dominance has been conferred on his group," McIntosh writes. "A 'white' skin in the United States opens many doors for whites whether or not we approve of the way dominance has been conferred on us." She says that "individual acts can palliate, but cannot end" the cycle. "To redesign social systems," she puts forth, "we need first to acknowledge their colossal unseen dimensions."

To redesign social systems. That's the entire purpose of the social justice movement. It's to remake American society from top to bottom—to, in fact, move the bottom of society *to* the top.

McIntosh concludes her essay by denouncing the "myth of meritocracy," which she says is kept alive by "[o]bliviousness about white advantage [and] obliviousness about male advantage" and is "kept strongly inculturated in the United States."

This is social justice. It's an ideology that says the America you understand today is fundamentally broken and that full equality is unobtainable without a complete overhaul of its current order and a total abandonment of what McIntosh called the "myth of meritocracy." Social justice maintains that there is no meritocracy, only identity, oppression, and privilege. Those assumed to hold an advantage due to their race, gender, or sexuality must submit to the aggrieved, in accordance with the new intersectionality hierarchy.

This worldview is reinforced by the culture fascists in academia, the national news media, Hollywood, and the established political class. It then moves by way of public signals, symbols, and shaming.

"Politics," says Rectenwald, "is reduced by social justice warriors to a series of … Facebook statuses, tweets, kneel-downs during the singing of the U.S. national anthem, and so forth."[25] This is called "virtue signaling"—overt gestures that communicate an adherence to the movement and its ideology.

When President Trump refers to violent Central American-born MS-13 gang members as animals, and John Harwood of CNBC reacts by tweeting that they should never be referred to as anything but human beings, that is virtue signaling.[26] When ABC News analyst Matthew Dowd bravely writes in an op-ed that white males like himself should "give up our seats at the table" so that minorities and women are more widely represented, that's virtue signaling.[27] When the media devote months of coverage to the shortcomings of the white males who made up the Republican Senate Judiciary Committee, in an effort to thwart the confirmation of an exceptionally qualified candidate for the Supreme Court, that's virtue signaling.

Social justice is centered on who can claim the highest form of oppression, grievance, and victimhood at any given moment. It's an endless competition in claiming to have been the most exploited, most subordinated, and most abused.

---

25 Michael Rectenwald, *Springtime for Snowflakes: 'Social Justice' and its Postmodern Parentage*, e-book (August 2018).

26 John Harwood, Twitter.com, May 17, 2018: https://twitter.com/johnjharwood/status/997068578116513793?lang=en.

27 Matthew Dowd, "Us white male Christians need to step back and give others room to lead: OPINION," ABCNews.Go.com, Sep. 30, 2018: https://abcnews.go.com/US/leadership-means-making-oneself-dispensable-opinion/story?id=58193412.

Social justice and its enforcers have created an ever-evolving, never-satisfied new class of Americans: the victims of privilege, who in turn become the privileged by victimization. They are our privileged victims.

CHAPTER 3

COLLEGE: WHERE FREE SPEECH IS LESS LIKELY TO OCCUR THAN A MASS SHOOTING

The sheer chaos that "privilege" and grievance have brought to college campuses would call for a proclamation of martial law if it weren't taken for granted that today's co-eds are just a bunch of melodramatic idiots.

The unfocused, unjustified student rage at universities and colleges across the country has turned these institutions into jungles.

Fox News and other conservative media tend to dismiss the boiling mess by calling naïve and overly sensitive college students "snowflakes," but the real problem is that these kids don't melt after graduation. Having been taught by America's higher education system (now thoroughly governed by social justice) that to get what you want, you need only become a kicking and screaming victim, the students are then unleashed on the general public, where they perform below standard, expect their professional superiors to tolerate, even accommodate, their bullshit, and, worse, vote in elections.

The Evergreen State College showed itself in 2017 to be an ideal petri dish for growing this special form of bacteria.

The school, based in Olympia, Washington, held an annual Day of Absence on April 12 of each year, during which nonwhite students would leave campus to participate in workshops and lectures on "race, equality, allyship, inclusion, and privilege."[28]

Though lectures on allyship and privilege sound about as riveting as a Lana Del Rey album played at half tempo, the day was nonetheless a tradition and presumably kept those at the school happy, functioning as a way for students and faculty with a privilege-guilt complex to feel good about themselves.

But on March 14, 2017, Rashida Love, the college's director of First Peoples Multicultural Advising Services (since updated to the more *inclusive* First Peoples Multicultural, Trans, and Queer Support Services), sent an email to faculty and staff with notice that the annual Day of Absence would come with a fun twist that year.

"Please note that in 2017, for the first time, we are reversing the pattern of previous years," Love wrote in the email. "Our day of absence program especially designed for faculty, staff and students of color will happen on campus this year, while our concurrent program for allies will take place off campus."[29]

The message was expertly crafted to obscure what Love was doing— asking all white students and faculty to leave school grounds rather than the usual tradition of having ·minorities participate in their seminars off campus.

Biology professor Bret Weinstein took notice of the subversion and, more importantly, of the severity of asking any group of people to leave the school premises based on race.

"There is a huge difference between a group or coalition deciding to voluntarily absent themselves from a shared space in order to highlight

28 Chloe Marina Manchester, "Day of Absence Changes Form," *Cooper Point Journal*, April 10, 2017: http://www.cooperpointjournal.com/2017/04/10/day-of-absence-changes-form/.
29 Walker Orenstein, "Read the email exchange that sparked protests against an Evergreen professor," *Olympian*, June 1, 2017: http://archive.is/uina0.

their vital and under-appreciated roles...and a group or coalition encouraging another group to go away," Weinstein replied to Love, faculty, and staff the next day. "The first is a forceful call to consciousness, which is, of course, crippling to the logic of oppression. The second is a show of force and an act of oppression in and of itself."

Weinstein further said his email should be viewed as "a formal protest" and that he was encouraging others to protest as well. "On a college campus," he said, "one's right to speak—or to be—must never be based on skin color."

Love replied to everyone later that day, explaining that the decision to reverse the tradition that year had been made largely because "many folks who identify as [persons of color] have found the national social and political climate discouraging." The shorter version: It's Donald Trump's fault.

Love added in the email, "In reversing the programming schedule, we are re-affirming the value of having [people of color] in higher education and specifically at Evergreen." (And what better way to reaffirm the value of minorities than by having white people leave them behind en masse?)

Love passively reminded Weinstein that while participation was voluntary, there were "many people in our campus community who believe it worthy to dedicate 8 hours of their lives to engaging in conversations around racism, equity and inclusion."

This is like being lectured by your mother on the importance of spending just one hour per week in church, but instead of the Immaculate Conception, you get intersectionality oppression.

The emails between Love and Weinstein were shortly thereafter published in Evergreen's student paper and the April 12, 2017, Day of Absence passed without incident.[30]

---

30   Bret Weinstein, "The Campus Mob Came for Me—and You, Professor, Could Be Next," *Wall Street Journal*, May 30, 2017: https://www.wsj.com/articles/ the-campus-mob-came-for-meand-you-professor-could-be-next-1496187482? ns=prod/accounts-wsj&ns=prod/accounts-wsj.

And yet, apparently working on a slight delay, the social justice beast raised its head more than a month later on May 23. A mob of angry students barged into one of Weinstein's classes to confront him over the emails.

A portion of the incident was uploaded on the internet, and it went viral, showing a hysterical horde of students screaming at the short and middle-aged Weinstein, who is seen hopelessly attempting to engage the mindless dopes in what was formerly known as a *discussion*. "I listen to you, and you listen to me," he says in the video, only to have one student scream back, "We don't care what you want to speak on. This isn't about you. We are not speaking on terms of white privilege."[31]

This was Weinstein's personal struggle session administered by social justice ideology's fiercest advocates, college students. And it was an example of standpoint knowledge theory, the inherent higher morality and virtue of the students by way of their having supposedly been aggrieved, and thus entitled to be seen and heard.

"You said some racist shit; now apologize," one student yells at Weinstein.

Another: "Fuck what you've got to say."

They begin chanting, "Hey, hey, ho, ho, Bret Weinstein's got to go."

"You do not control this conversation."

"You're acting like white supremacy." That's the social justice deconstruction of the language. "White supremacy" can mean anything, even the act of attempting to have a conversation.

The mobbing of Weinstein was a show of force to humiliate him and insist that he submit to the demands of social justice dogma.

It bore key traits exhibited by privileged victims. The student who mandated that Weinstein remain silent because of his white privilege

---

31 "Unedited - Bret Weinstein Tries To Reason With Angry Student Mob As They Call For His Resignation," YouTube.com, May 27, 2017: https://www.youtube.com/watch?v=LTnDpoQLNaY.

shows the reverence for standpoint knowledge, the belief that some people, purely on account of their race, gender, or sexuality, are to be treated with more reverence than others. The student who told Weinstein he was "acting like white supremacy" was deconstructing the language: He asserted that Weinstein is racist, so Weinstein must be racist, regardless of what the word "racist" means; definitions are only relative to the privileged victim.

As embarrassing as the Weinstein video was for the school, yet another online video thereafter showed more angry protests.[32] In that one, you see students conducting a sit-in at one of the campus facilities as Evergreen president George Bridges placates them.

Student: All of us are students and have homework and projects and things due.

Bridges: I know.

Student: What's—have you sent an email out to your faculty letting them know?

Bridges: No.

Student: What's been done about that? Because we're all here on our own time.

Bridges: That is the first thing I'll do. I have not done it yet. I will do it right now.

Student: So they [faculty] need to be told that these assignments won't be done on time, and we don't need to be penalized for that.

Bridges: I don't know the names of all the students here.

---

32 "Evergreen Top 20 Monstrous Moments," YouTube.com, June 2, 2017: https://www.youtube.com/watch?v=8YnSYvhSeyI. "Whiteness is the most violent fucking system to ever breed," a student says in one as others applaud. (Discursive violence)

Student: Well, just send it to all the faculty.

Bridges: I will do it as the first item.

In another life, these young adults would have looked to Bridges for guidance on how to emulate his leadership and how to conduct themselves as adults on the verge of entering professional careers. In this life, they make grubby, delusional demands and he readily concedes.

The Day of Absence at Evergreen was canceled in 2018.

This is what the miscreants have been taught to expect in college and, later on, in real life. As long as you claim to have ben aggrieved on account of your race, gender, or sexuality, everything else just falls into place. And if it doesn't, summon the mob and try, try again.

The social justice tyranny on college campuses would not exist if there weren't enough professors and school administrators advocating for it.

At Duke University in February 2017, professor Anathea Portier-Young at the college's religious school (Duke Divinity School) sent an email to her colleagues urging them to participate in one of those totalitarian, waste-of-time race-appreciation programs.[33]

"On behalf of the Faculty Diversity and Inclusion Standing Committee, I strongly urge you to participate in the Racial Equity Institute Phase I Training planned for March 4 and 5," wrote Portier-Young on May 7. Mind you, those two dates on that particular year were a Saturday and Sunday, and the seminars lasted each day from 8:30 a.m. to 5 p.m. You might devote that time to a loved one in the hospital emergency room, but to sitting in a race equality seminar with a bunch of professors with guilt complexes? MLK himself would have passed.

---

33 Rod Dreher, "Duke Divinity Crisis: The Documents Are Out," American Conservative, May 7, 2017: https://www.theamericanconservative.com/dreher/duke-divinity-crisis-griffiths-documents/.

Portier-Young wrote in her email that the workshop was "free to our community and we hope that this will be a first step in a longer process of working to ensure that DDS is an institution that is both equitable and anti-racist in its practices and culture." She helpfully affirmed that "ALL Staff and Faculty are invited to register for this important event," so that the college "can begin its own commitment to become an anti-racist institution." (Surely up until then, the institution had been pro-racist, or at least passively racist.)

Paul Griffiths, a professor of Catholic theology at the school at the time and an actual intellectual, made the mistake of engaging debate on an issue that the privileged victims have deemed undebatable.

"I exhort you not to attend this training," Griffiths replied to all faculty. "Don't lay waste your time by doing so. It'll be, I predict with confidence, intellectually flaccid: there'll be bromides, clichés, and amen-corner rah-rahs in plenty."

Because Griffiths' email was a work of beauty, notable for the balls it takes to put forth such truths in the intimidating face of social justice, here are some of its other memorable lines:

- "When (if) [the Faculty Diversity and Inclusion Standing Committee] gets beyond that, its illiberal roots and totalitarian tendencies will show. Events of this sort are definitively anti-intellectual."

- "(Re)trainings of intellectuals by bureaucrats and apparatchiks have a long and ignoble history."

- "We here at Duke Divinity have a mission. Such things as this training are at best a distraction from it and at worst inimical to it."

- "We have neither time nor resources to waste. This training is a waste. Please, ignore it. Keep your eyes on the prize."

All of what he said was true because that's exactly how social justice operates among academics: Faculty and staff are pressured to attend seminar after seminar, workshop after workshop on diversity, racial equality, and inclusion. To object is to out yourself as a bigot deserving of punishment, whether by professional reprimand or public shaming or ostracization on campus.

Tyrants who would like to force their education camps on the rest of us can't do it on their own. Their ideas are inherently repellent, so they move in mobs that reinforce one another. In that spirit, Elaine Heath, then the dean of the Divinity School, chimed in to support her sister in arms. "First, I am looking forward to participating in the [Racial Equity Institute] training, and I am proud that we are hosting it at Duke Divinity School," she wrote in an email to all. "Thea [Anathea Portier-Young], thank you for your part in helping us to offer this important event. I am deeply committed to increasing our school's intellectual strength, spiritual vitality, and moral authority, and this training event will help with all three."

As good as Heath must have felt about herself at that point, she was just getting started. Her note continued, "It is inappropriate and unprofessional to use mass emails to make disparaging statements—including arguments ad hominem—in order to humiliate or undermine individual colleagues or groups of colleagues with whom we disagree. The use of mass emails to express racism, sexism, and other forms of bigotry is offensive and unacceptable, especially in a Christian institution."

Where was the racism, sexism, or any other "forms of bigotry" found in Griffiths' email? He had voiced his opposition to the reeducation session, calling it a waste of time and resources. Based on Heath's email, you'd think he had called Anathea the N-word. But this is precisely what the privileged victims do: They shut down dissent by labeling critics as racists, sexists, and bigots.

You cannot disagree with these people. You cannot contradict, dispute, or argue. Miraculously, Griffiths was not alone on campus in believing the racial equity reeducation training was certain to be a time suck.

Thomas Pfau, a professor of English at Duke who also teaches at the Divinity School, replied to all on the email to say that he also had reservations about the efficacy of the training. Noting his current authority as a department chair and his past experience as a school director in both graduate and undergraduate studies, he said he was "fundamentally in agreement" with Griffiths that such trainings are largely proving worthless.

"Having worked at Duke for a long time for twenty-six years now, I have witnessed first-hand a dramatic increase [in] demands made on faculty time by administration-driven initiatives fundamentally unrelated to the intellectual work for which faculty were recruited by Duke," he said. "A seemingly endless string of surveys, memos, and 'training sessions' is by now a familiar reality for most faculty, and it is an altogether inescapable entailment (as I well know) of chairing a department or program, serving on a hiring committee, or chairing a review."

Pfau further pleaded that differing views on the value of yet more wasteful sensitivity training "be respected as a legitimate exercise of judgment and expression" rather than dismissed as bigotry. He argued that it was "intellectually irresponsible" to accuse Griffiths of expressing bigoted sentiments solely because he objected to the reeducation workshop.

That was that. The separate parties agreed to disagree and politely moved on.

Just kidding! That can never happen when confronting social justice freaks. Griffiths was shortly thereafter sanctioned by Dean Heath and then the subject of an official school complaint made by Portier-Young.

Griffiths wrote in a subsequent email to faculty and staff that Heath contacted him in February 2017 to request a meeting in which she intended to address his conduct, presumably in relation to his emails on the racial training thread. A meeting was scheduled for early March that would include Griffiths, Heath, and Dean of Faculty Randy Maddox, along with Pfau, whom Griffiths had asked to be allowed to attend.

The meeting was canceled, though, and Heath, according to Griffiths, scheduled a new one on the same matter, but stated that Pfau was no longer permitted to attend. Griffith then said he would participate in that meeting, but under the condition that Heath disinvite her hype man, Randy Maddox, given the new demands. Heath declined.

Thereafter, Heath sent Griffiths a printed letter formally reprimanding him, in the spiteful, gratuitously vengeful way that only a college administrator can.

The note read: "This letter is to inform you about a process that is in place in response to: 1) Your refusal to meet with me and Randy Maddox to discuss expectations for professional behavior as a faculty member and to abide by the agenda of the meeting which I have set 2) Your inappropriate behavior in faculty meetings over the past two years…. It is unacceptable for you to refuse to meet with me as Dean of the Divinity School."

We'll pause here to note that there was no refusal to meet Heath, Her Royal Heinous. There was only a dispute about the fairness of meeting two on one, as though Griffiths were up for parole, solely for having disagreed with a colleague in an email.

Heath's letter continued, "I cannot physically force you to meet with me, but your refusal to meet with me will have consequences. Beginning immediately you will not be permitted to attend or participate in faculty meetings or committee meetings…. Your continued refusal to meet with me will result in further consequences, including but not limited to the loss of travel and research funds."

To recap: A faculty member requested that her colleagues attend a racial seminar to prove they're in favor of antiracism; Griffiths rightly said it would be a waste of time and a distraction from otherwise valuable learning and teaching; Griffiths refused to attend a lopsided meeting with the dean to address his "conduct"; and, as a consequence, he was told his remaining time at the school could be made miserable.

Griffiths was not a fire-breathing, MAGA-hat-wearing right winger. He was one of 456 Catholic theologians in 2014 to sign a statement against racial injustice as it pertains to police shootings of unarmed black men. That statement read in part: "The killings of Black men, women and children…by White policemen, and the failures of the grand jury process to indict some of the police officers involved, brought to our attention not only problems in law enforcement today, but also deeper racial injustice in our nation, our communities, and even our churches.…We pledge to examine within ourselves our complicity in the sin of racism and how it sustains false images of White superiority in relationship to Black inferiority."[34]

That same year he published a review of *Darling: A Spiritual Autobiography*, by Richard Rodriguez, a gay man, and Griffiths wrote thoughtfully and approvingly. "On homosexuality and homosexual acts…I think Rodriguez much [sic] closer to being right than not," writes Griffiths. "Insofar as such acts are motivated by and evoke love, they are good and to be loved; insofar as they do not, not. In this, they are no different from heterosexual acts."[35]

That doesn't sound like the wild bigot that Griffiths was being portrayed as. But this is what academics mean now when they promote the "free exchange of ideas." Some things simply aren't up for debate, and dissenters like Griffiths are to be stripped of their dignity or even their jobs.

Portier-Young filed her complaint against Griffiths in early March with the school's Office of Institutional Equality (OIE). Griffiths then heard from OIE officer Cynthia Clinton, who said that Portier-Young had accused him of racist and sexist speech that contributed to a hostile working environment.

The OIE requested Griffiths' attendance at a meeting on March 30, 2017. He in turn requested that the office send him a "a written version of the allegation, together with its evidentiary support, in advance of

---

34 David Cloutier, "Statement of Catholic Theologians on Racial Justice," *Catholic Moral Theology*, Dec. 8, 2014: https://catholicmoraltheology.com/statement-of-catholic-theologians-on-racial-justice/.

35 Paul Griffiths, "Ulterior Lives: A Review of Darling," FirstThings.com, April 2014: https://www.firstthings.com/article/2014/04/ulterior-lives.

the scheduled meeting," according to Griffiths' account. His request was denied, and so he also declined to attend the meeting.

It's North Korea on college campuses. Due process is an alien concept to the privileged victims and their reinforcers, the culture fascists of academia. Evidence isn't necessary, and you're lucky if the reason for your persecution is coherently articulated at all.

But with the balls of a bull, Griffiths said in a written statement to the OIE that Portier-Young's complaint against him was "illiberal, anti-intellectual, and shameful." He called it "an attempt to constrain speech by blunt force rather than by free exchange," and said that attending the requested meeting "would be…to dignify a procedure that has no place in the life of a university."

Griffiths still resigned. Why wouldn't he? His administrators had come out against robust debate and in favor of the new standard: advancement by grievance.[36]

In November 2015, private liberal arts school Claremont McKenna College saw the resignation of its dean of students, Mary Spellman, after she made the grave mistake of attempting to comfort a Hispanic student who had complained about not feeling included by the school.

Lisette Espinosa, a senior at Claremont, wrote a column for the school newspaper on October 23, describing her lonely experience as a first-generation Latina student attending the school, which she said made her feel unwelcome.

"It was uncomfortable coming to CMC and seeing my home being better represented in the poorly paid, working-class staff rather than those more central to managing the school's trajectory and curriculum," she wrote. She also said she suspected that the school accepted her for admission in order "to fill a racial quota" and that she suffered from

---

36 Jane Stancill, "Duke divinity professor calls diversity training 'a waste,' faces discipline," *News & Observer*, May 9, 2017: https://www.newsobserver.com/news/local/education/article149462029.html.

"imposter syndrome" as well as depression by the end of her sopho-more year.[37]

In short: Espinosa applied to Claremont, a school she presumably wanted to attend, got accepted, and then resented the school for admitting her!

Much of Espinosa's column was absolutely incoherent, like her admission that "it was homophobia and transphobia on campus that encouraged me to complete a gender studies sequence." This is the type of nonsensical thinking that college professors and administrators should be stomping on so that these idiots aren't entering the world unprepared to deal with real things like learning from disappointment, embracing competition, and resolving conflict. But no, students are instead having their self-pity and narcissism enabled, and in the process, they're finding that there is a lot to gain in perpetual victimhood.

Dean Spellman was kind enough to reach out to the poor girl and see if she could be of any help. She sent an email to Espinosa two days after the op-ed published. It read in full: "Thank you for writing and sharing this article with me. We have a lot to do as a college and community. Would you be willing to talk with me sometime about these issues? They are important to me and the [dean of students] staff and we are working on how we can better serve students, especially those who don't fit our CMC mold. I would love to talk with you more. Best, Dean Spellman."

You could give the average American ten days to find the offense in this email and they would end up committed to a nuthouse, driven insane by the frustration of trying to sniff out the slightest hint of racism or any other transgression.

It was, in fact, the part about "our CMC mold" that set off raging protests and calls for Spellman to resign.

---

37 Lisette Espinosa, "Who Is the Happiest at the 'Happiest College in America'?," *The Student Life*, Oct. 23, 2015: https://tsl.news/opinions5116/>.

This was, according to reports, the climax of "months" of demands from the student body that predated the email from Spellman. The *Los Angeles Times* said that Spellman's email "appeared to be a tipping point for students who have pressed the campus for months for greater diversity among faculty and staff and more funding for multicultural services."[38]

"Multicultural services" were defined by the report as "a new resource center, funding for multicultural clubs, more diverse hiring, a mentoring program and an administrator to oversee diversity." When I was in college, I thought it was gutsy to argue with professors for a higher grade. Now, students think nothing of it to demand new buildings.

A factor leading up to the outbreak at Claremont was a photo that circulated on campus of two female students, both apparently white, who posed on Halloween as Mexican men, wearing ponchos, traditional sombreros, and fake mustaches. The photo also showed them holding maracas.

This was viewed by the school's privileged victims as a hate crime. A junior student posted it to her Facebook profile with precisely the kind of melodramatic, virtue-signaling caption that caused me to delete my own account two years ago. "Dear Claremont community," the post said, "For anyone who ever tries to invalidate the experiences of [people of color] at the Claremont Colleges, here is a reminder of why we feel the way we do. Don't tell me I'm overreacting, don't tell me I'm being too sensitive. My voice will not be silenced. I'm mentally drained from being a part of this community and I've had enough. If you feel uncomfortable by my cover photo, I want you to know I feel uncomfortable as a person of color every day on this campus."[39]

---

38 Teresa Watanabe and Carla Rivera, "Amid racial bias protests, Claremont McKenna dean resigns," *Los Angeles Times*, Nov. 13, 2015: https://www.latimes.com/local/lanow/la-me-ln-claremont-marches-20151112-story.html.

39 Shannon Miller, "Racially Insensitive Halloween Costumes Spur Discussion Online, in Student Senate," CMCForum.com, Nov. 9, 2015: https://cmcforum.com/2015/news/11102015-racially-insensitive-halloween-costumes-spur-discussion-online-in-student-senate.

It's not as if the photograph suggested in any way that Mexican men are lazy, or that they abuse their wives, or that they prefer tequila over their own children. The students had mustaches and maracas! There's nothing inappropriate about paying tribute to a culture using harmless stereotypes, unless you believe that mustaches, ordinary clothing, and musical instruments are inherently offensive.

After Spellman's email became public, two students went on a hunger strike to draw attention to it.

Spellman made the ill-fated decision to confront the mob during one of their mass protests on campus. It went over about as smoothly as a car ride with Beto O'Rourke after celebrating his twenty-sixth birthday.[40]

What took place was a shining example of the heightened, thoughtful discourse that college campuses are known for:

Student: Bring Spellman out.

Student: Where's Spellman?

Student: Wake up Spellman.

Spellman: I'm right here. And I will continue to be here to fight for students and to support students.

Students in chorus: How? How do we change your heart? What do you think of your vernacular?... Constantly been oppressive to others that don't look like you."

Spellman: The "CMC mold" is the thing that I talk with students about every day. They come to me and they tell me how they don't fit in and, "What do I do, Dean Spellman? I don't fit in here. I am not the perfect CMC-er." I can't tell my faculty—

---

40 "CMCers of Color Lead Protest of Lack of Support from Administration," YouTube.com, Nov. 11, 2015: https://www.youtube.com/watch?v=OlB7Vy-lZZ8.

Student (interrupting): Address "the mold."

This was yet another social justice-led struggle session for an insufficient believer.

Spellman: I am addressing it. That is what I am referring to as "the mold." A poorly worded email that was intended to support a student was poorly worded and I apologize again as I did in my email again.

Student: What else did you do to support that student?

Student: If you care about us, you'll resign.

This isn't a debate. It's not a dialogue. It's an untethered ideology nurtured by academics who have taught students that this is how you engage with the world when you want something. Students whine about being oppressed. They complain that they've been aggrieved. And then they demand that the "privileged" concede and submit.

One student at the protest asked Spellman whether she had personally spoken with Espinosa after the email episode.

"I did reach out to the student…. I am ready to speak with her if she is willing and ready to speak with me," Spellman said. "The 'CMC mold' is something students talk to me about. Students come to me in pain and suffering and they talk about how they need to transfer because they don't fit in here, and I work with them to figure out how they can be successful here, because there isn't a mold but it's this community that says there's the perfect CMC-er. We are all responsible for making students feel that they don't fit in that mold. That's what I'm talking about."

With the heightened critical thinking skills of a squirrel that can't decide whether it should run toward or away from an oncoming semi, yet another student blurted out, "It's our fault?…Take responsibility for what you said."

Spellman: No, no, I am not saying it's your fault—

Student: Then stop talking and leave.

This is more standpoint knowledge. Spellman had been deemed a beneficiary of privilege, so her perspective is worth less than that of the students claiming to have been victimized. She should "stop talking" and just "leave."

Spellman did leave, resigning on November 12, 2015, just days after her original sin of asking a student with low self-esteem how she could help her feel more included. When you understand the social justice ideology, you come to find that Spellman was naïve for thinking that any of them needed or wanted help in the first place. Privileged victims don't want help. They want absolute submission. They want power. This is how they get it. It works.

Yale found itself in the same sewer when childhood education professor Erika Christakis, who oversaw one of the residence halls, rebutted a campus-wide instruction to beware of insensitive Halloween costumes.

The ridiculous outrage over Halloween costumes captures a crucial element of the social justice ideology. It's a fake anger over something that's real only for those who buy into the hysteria.

On October 27, 2017, Yale's Intercultural Affairs Committee, an organization that includes the dean of student campus life, sent out a schoolwide email that cautioned students against donning potentially objectionable costumes.

The email said that Halloween is "unfortunately a time when the normal thoughtfulness and sensitivity of most Yale students can sometimes be forgotten and some poor decisions can be made including wearing feathered headdresses, turbans, wearing 'war paint' or modifying skin tone or wearing blackface or redface." It said that those "issues and examples of cultural appropriation and/or misrepresentation are increasingly surfacing with representations of Asians and Latinos."

The Intercultural Affairs Committee then offered the following questions to kick the festive spirit into high gear:

- "Wearing a funny costume? Is the humor based on 'making fun' of real people, human traits or cultures?

- "Wearing a historical costume? If this costume is meant to be historical, does it further misinformation or historical and cultural inaccuracies?

- "Wearing a 'cultural' costume? Does this costume reduce cultural differences to jokes or stereotypes?

- "Wearing a 'religious' costume? Does this costume mock or belittle someone's deeply held faith tradition?

- "Could someone take offense with your costume and why?"[41]

The point of a costume is that it isn't real and everyone's in on the joke. If I put on a turban and a fake beard and strap a ticking clock to my chest on Halloween, I should be able to safely assume that most people know that I am not a Muslim terrorist and that I'm mocking something that would otherwise be scary if it were worn in earnest. But the culture fascists at Yale and other college campuses want you to consult their rubric before any festivities take place to be sure that you're not in need of your own struggle session.

The reason, of course, isn't because there's actual harm inflicted by costumes. It's to reinforce the intersectionality aspect of social justice. It's a reminder that grievance and oppression as they relate to race, gender, and sexuality are not to be infringed upon and are, in fact, to be regarded with utmost reverence. To make light of them with a costume, even on a day intended for levity, would be blasphemous.

---

41 "Email From The Intercultural Affairs Committee," TheFire.org, Oct. 27, 2015: https://www.thefire.org/email-from-intercultural-affairs/.

On the day before Halloween, Christakis sent a follow-up email to students in Silliman College, the residence she supervised. "I don't wish to trivialize genuine concerns about cultural and personal representation, and other challenges to our lived experience in a plural community," she wrote. (It was as though she were a real professor about to give a lesson on engaging new ideas to young people!) "I know that many decent people have proposed guidelines on Halloween costumes from a spirit of avoiding hurt and offense. I laud those goals, in theory, as most of us do. But in practice, I wonder if we should reflect more transparently, as a community, on the consequences of an institutional (which is to say: bureaucratic and administrative) exercise of implied control over college students."[42]

Christakis added in her email that "American universities were once a safe space not only for maturation but also for a certain regressive, or even transgressive, experience; increasingly, it seems, they have become places of censure and prohibition. And the censure and prohibition come from above, not from yourselves!"

She said that her husband, Nicholas, a professor at the school and also a Silliman administrator, advised that "if you don't like a costume someone is wearing, look away, or tell them you are offended. Talk to each other. Free speech and the ability to tolerate offence are the hallmarks of a free and open society."

She concluded the note by asking, "Whose business is it to control the forms of costumes of young people?"

Once you have a grasp of the social justice sickness, Christakis' well-meaning attempt to get students to question their own thoughts on free expression seems quaint.

---

42 Email From Erika Christakis: "Dressing Yourselves," email to Silliman College (Yale) Students on Halloween Costumes, TheFire.org, Oct. 30, 2015: https://www.thefire.org/email-from-erika-christakis-dressing-yourselves-email-to-silliman-college-yale-students-on-halloween-costumes/.

Students of Silliman didn't appreciate the note. They responded by demanding that Christakis and her husband be removed from their positions.

On November 5, students gathered on campus to protest, calling for Yale dean Jonathan Holloway, who is black, to address Christakis' email and other perceived racial grievances.

"There was so much coded language in that e-mail that is just disrespectful," one student said.[43]

Nicholas Christakis showed up at the protest in an ill-fated attempt to converse with the students.[44]

One student, who identified herself as Makayla, lectured him on failing to remember her name. She added that she found it "incredibly depressing" that she no longer thought of Silliman as a "safe space" for her, in large part because Nicholas Christakis refused to accept the assertion that he and his wife had revealed racist sentiments in the Halloween email.

Another student chimed in on behalf of Makayla: "She wants an apology, yet you respond not with an apology. That's my question. I'm just saying, are you going to address the heart of her comment? That's all I want. Are you going to give an apology? Are you going to say you're hearing us?"

Christakis said he would need to think about what he was being asked to apologize for; though the little dandelions insisted their feelings were hurt, he wasn't aware that he bore any responsibility for it.

---

43 Isaac Stanley-Becker, "A confrontation over race at Yale: Hundreds of students demand answers from the school's first black dean," *Washington Post*, Nov. 5, 2015: https://www.washingtonpost.com/news/grade-point/wp/2015/11/05/a-confrontation-over-race-at-yale-hundreds-of-students-demand-answers-from-the-schools-first-black-dean/?utm_term=.48d2f34a1d90.

44 "Yale University - Full Version - New Videos of The Halloween Email Protest," YouTube.com, Sep. 20, 2016: https://www.youtube.com/watch?v=hiMVx2C5_Wg.

Student: I still think the phrase "hurt feelings" is—

Christakis: Okay, tell me the phrase you want me to use, and I'll use it.

Student: I don't know—"an expression of racism"? (This was Christakis' own struggle session administered by the privileged victims of Yale.)

Another student called the Christakis email "an act of violence." (Recall that discursive violence is the belief that spoken words can inflict physical harm, and the convenient logical end to that belief is that if an individual's speech is deemed to be "violent" in nature, that person should be silenced.)

At that point, students literally began publicly sobbing and consoling one another.

But then, yet another student set aside niceties and pierced the heart of the matter. "Let us define our own experience," she called out to Christakis. "Let *us* tell *you* if you're being a racist." It was more standpoint knowledge theory put into practice. A student claiming to have been aggrieved and oppressed also believes herself to be naturally endowed with a more virtuous perspective and life experience, and thus deserves deference from the privileged.

Student: This is my home and you came here. You adapt to me. (Struggle session.)

Student: What you did was create a space for violence to happen against us. (Discursive violence.)

Student: It doesn't matter whether you disagree or not. It's not a debate. (Standpoint knowledge.)

Student: You are not listening. You are disgusting.... I want your job to be taken from you. (Social justice.)

Struggle session. Discursive violence. Standpoint knowledge. Social justice.

The protest wasn't held for the purpose of resolving a conflict. It was held to affirm the new hierarchy on campus: The students as self-proclaimed victims were calling the shots, while the Christakises and anyone siding with them, the "privileged," were expected to assume a subservient role.

Over the course of the following month, anger swelled. Some students asked for advance notice of where and when the Christakises would be appearing in common campus areas so that those students could leave and wouldn't have to see them.[45] The pair was ostracized by much of Yale's faculty, apparently in the name of liberal tolerance. (It's worth noting some bit of tragic irony: Erika was a registered Democrat.)

Erika finally resigned in early December 2018, though apparently not at the behest of the Yale administration. She simply no longer wanted to be there. Who could blame her? Erika's husband Nicholas went on sabbatical but remains a professor at the school.

In an October 2016 column for the *Washington Post*, Erika revisited the episode, describing it in a way that should deeply embarrass the whole school and all of its alumni. "There was no official recognition that the calls to have us fired could be seen as illiberal or censorious," she wrote. "By affirming only the narrow right to air my views, rather than helping the community to grapple with its intense response, an unfortunate message was made plain: Certain ideas are too dangerous to be heard at Yale."

Ideas that are too dangerous for places of learning. Imagine.

---

45 Erika Christakis, "My Halloween email led to a campus firestorm—and a troubling lesson about self-censorship," *Washington Post*, Oct. 28, 2016: https://www.washingtonpost.com/opinions/my-halloween-email-led-to-a-campus-firestorm—and-a-troubling-lesson-about-self-censorship/2016/10/28/70e55732-9b97-11e6-a0ed-ab0774c1eaa5_story.html?utm_term=.c0329821cdcf.

It's not just at Yale. And it's not just in academia. Some ideas have become "too dangerous" *anywhere* in America. Our national discourse is now dictated based on who is deemed to have privilege, who has been victimized, and who ranks higher on the grievance scale known as intersectionality.

There are, at least, some signs of pushback.

At Claremont McKenna College, where Dean Mary Spellman was forced to resign over her email that referred to the CMC mold, students at the school's alternative newspaper penned an editorial expressing regret and shame over what had happened to Spellman.

"We are disappointed that you allowed a group of angry students to bully you into resignation," read the editorial directly addressing Spellman. "We are disappointed that you taught Claremont students that reacting with emotion and anger will force the administration to act. We are disappointed that when two students chose to go on a hunger strike until you resigned, you didn't simply say, 'so what?'"[46]

The editorial continued, "[W]e are disappointed in students like ourselves, who were scared into silence. We are not racist for having different opinions. We are not immoral because we don't buy the flawed rhetoric of a spiteful movement. We are not evil because we don't want this movement to tear across our campuses completely unchecked. We are no longer afraid to be voices of dissent."

---

46 Editorial Board, "We Dissent," *Claremont Independent*, Nov. 13, 2015: https://claremontindependent.com/we-dissent/.

CHAPTER 4

CAN'T GET AHEAD? FAKE IT (A HATE CRIME) TO MAKE IT

The Jussie Smollett saga revealed the social justice movement for what it is: a scam that gives those at the bottom a shortcut to the top.

On February 21, 2019, Chicago police superintendent Eddie Johnson laid out the shocking story of how thirty-six-year-old Smollett, an actor on the Fox series *Empire*, had staged a hate crime against himself, falsely claiming that he had been brutally assaulted in the predawn hours one morning by two men he identified as Trump supporters.

"This morning, I come to you not only as the superintendent of the Chicago police department, but also as a black man who has spent his entire life living in the city of Chicago," Johnson began the day's press conference. "…This announcement today recognizes that *Empire* actor Jussie Smollett took advantage of the pain and anger of racism to promote his career."

The scene was breathtaking, not only in Johnson's detailing of Smollett's brazen lie, but in his rebuke of the actor for attempting to use racism and homophobia for personal gain. He likely didn't know it at the time, but there has never been a more articulate dismantling of social justice and all of its toxicity than the statement delivered by Johnson.

"I'm left hanging my head and asking why," Johnson said. "Why would anyone, especially an African American man, use the symbolism of a noose to make false accusations? How could someone look at the hatred of suffering associated with that symbol and see an opportunity to manipulate that symbol to further his own public profile?"

Johnson spends his days dealing with savage crime in Chicago, so he doesn't know the very simple answer as to why Smollett, or anyone, would fake a hate crime for personal advancement.

Smollett did nothing more than put into practice what the social justice movement teaches its followers. Because he is both black and gay, he recognized that his status on the intersectionality hierarchy was high enough that he could convincingly claim to have been victimized by a specific kind of aggressor: white men—who supported Trump, no less.

On January 29, 2019, Smollett told police that he had been attacked around 2 a.m. that day by two white males "who yelled racial and homophobic slurs and wrapped a rope around his neck," according to the *New York Times*.[47]

Smollett claimed that he had been walking back to his Chicago apartment from a Subway restaurant when the two men approached him and called him "that faggot *Empire* nigger."[48] He said they splashed a bleach-like substance on his body, punched and kicked him, and that when it was over, he noticed that a rope had been placed around his neck.

---

47 Sopan Deb, "Jussie Smollett, Star of 'Empire,' Attacked in What Police Call a Possible Hate Crime," *New York Times*, Jan. 29, 2019: https://www. nytimes.com/2019/01/29/arts/television/empire-jussie-smollett-attacked. html?module=inline.

48 "'Empire' Star Jussie Smollett Victim of Homophobic Attack By MAGA Supporters," TMZ.com, Jan. 29, 2019: https://web.archive. org/web/20190129170202/https://www.tmz.com/2019/01/29/ empire-star-jussie-smollett-attacked-hospitalized-homophobic-hate-crime/.

This all happened, according to Smollett's lie, while his cell phone lay nearby on the ground with his manager, Brandon Z. Moore, listening on the line.

After the "attack," Smollett went to his apartment and waited for police—with the rope still around his neck, where it remained until the police arrived.[49] After they got to the apartment, police suggested that Smollett go to the hospital, so he went.[50] During a follow-up interview later in the morning at the hospital, Smollett told police that his assailants had said, "This is MAGA country," a reference to Trump's 2016 campaign slogan, "Make America Great Again."[51]

Smollett also said he had recently received a call on his cell phone, in which the person on the other end said, "Hey, you little faggot," before hanging up.

The story was ridiculous, and the problems with it were glaring. Were there really Trump supporters…in Chicago? Were they just out milling about, looking for someone to assault…at 2:00 a.m.? Were there really Trump supporters in general who knew who Jussie Smollett was and could readily identify him…in the dead hours of the night? Why had Smollett left a rope tied around his neck for what could have been hours before police got to his apartment?

The national media bought Smollett's story from the beginning—they had been predicting all along that Trump's supporters would do something like this. But Chicago news outlets knew there was something wrong and immediately began scrutinizing Smollett's claim.

49 Deb, "Jussie Smollett Attacked": https://www.nytimes.com/2019/01/29/arts/television/empire-jussie-smollett-attacked.html?module=inline.

50 Deb, "Jussie Smollett Attacked": https://www.nytimes.com/2019/01/29/arts/television/empire-jussie-smollett-attacked.html?module=inline.

51 Mary Mitchell, "Smollett beating investigation bombshell gives fresh fodder to Trump supporters," *Chicago Sun-Times*, Feb. 17, 2019: https://chicago.suntimes.com/columnists/smollett-beating-investigation-bombshell-gives-fresh-fodder-to-trump-supporters/.

Local police at the same time were publishing regular updates on Smollett's lack of cooperation with their investigation. They said in a public statement that although Smollett claimed to have been on the phone with his manager at the time of the attack, both he and the manager had refused to turn over their phones so that their timeline of events could be corroborated by authorities.[52] Smollett did eventually provide police with phone records, but police said they were so limited and redacted that they were effectively useless.[53]

Smollett's lie was deteriorating faster than Ilhan Omar's memory about her first marriage and yet he still agreed to a nationally televised interview with ABC's Robin Roberts that aired just sixteen days after his initial police report. In the interview, a teary-eyed, runny-nosed Smollett recounted his fake attack, again alleging that a masked man saw him on the street, told him, "This is MAGA country, nigger," and punched him in the face.

"So I punched his ass back," lied gay gangster Smollett.[54] (During a live music performance a few days before, Smollett had microwaved his story for the audience and declared himself "the gay Tupac."[55]) He said that he and the attacker continued to fight and that a second person began kicking him in the back.

Of his skeptics, he said, "It feels like if I had said [the attacker] was a Muslim or a Mexican or someone black, I feel like the doubters would have supported me a lot, much more—a lot more. And that says a lot

52 Neetu Chandak, "Chicago police say 'Empire' actor refuses to turn over phone records during alleged 'MAGA' attack,'" DailyCaller.com, Jan. 31, 2019: https://dailycaller.com/2019/01/31/maga-attack-jussie-smollett-phone/.

53 William Lee, "Jussie Smollett reiterates his cooperation, day after police say they need more phone records from night of attack," *Chicago Tribune*, Feb. 12, 2019: https://www.chicagotribune.com/news/local/breaking/ct-met-smollett-update-20190211-story.html.

54 ABC's *Good Morning America*, Feb. 14, 2019.

55 Associated Press, Feb. 3, 2019: https://www.theguardian.com/music/2019/feb/03/im-the-gay-tupac-jussie-smollett.

about the place that we are in our country right now." His comments were strikingly similar to the lyrics of a 2017 song by Smollett about Trump and bigotry. In the song's music video, Muslims and other minorities are persecuted by whites and Trump supporters.[56]

Who was he kidding? If Smollett had identified his attackers as Muslim or Mexican, media coverage would have been limited to some local papers and TV affiliates. If it got any national attention at all, it would have been relegated to a blurb in the newspapers and a brief read by the anchor on the networks. An even more likely scenario is that national news organizations wouldn't have identified any alleged attackers by their race at all if they had been anything other than white. There's little news value in a B-list TV actor assaulted by minorities in Chicago, and it wouldn't have fit the privileged victim narrative.

In what may have been his most delusional moment of the ABC interview, Smollett offered that a likely reason he would be the target of a hate crime is because he's a daring and formidable foe of Donald Trump.

Ha ha ha ha.

"I come really, really hard against [Trump]," he said with an impressively straight face. "I come really, really hard against his administration and I don't hold my tongue." Literally nobody outside of *Empire* watchers had ever heard of Smollett, let alone what he had to say about national affairs. His belief that whatever ignorant political ramblings he posted on Twitter might make him a target for a hate crime certainly indicates at least some level of mental or emotional instability. After that remark, he could have pleaded guilty to the hoax for reasons of mental retardation, and any charges would have immediately and justifiably been dismissed.

---

56 Jussie Smollett, "F.U.W.," March 15, 2017: https://www.youtube.com/watch?v=O2WjyxR79Bc.

The day after the ABC interview aired, Chicago police confirmed that they had detained two men of interest. But they weren't the MAGA maniacs Smollett had described. They were two black men, brothers, taken into custody after landing in Chicago on a flight back from Nigeria.[57]

In other words, the suspects weren't white. They were Wakandan!

One of the brothers had even previously been cast in a minor role on *Empire*.

After nearly two full days of being held in custody and hours of interrogation by police, the brothers were released without being charged.

Less than a week later, police named Smollett as a suspect in the case, calling on him to surrender himself to Chicago authorities for filing a false police report.[58]

At his press conference on February 21, Chicago police superintendent Eddie Johnson divulged even more devastating details about the hoax. He said that when Smollett had been seen by police at the hospital after his initial claim, he had scrapes and bruises from the alleged brawl he endured. But Johnson said they were only surface wounds and that they were likely self-inflicted by Smollett. Johnson said that after several hours of questioning, the two brothers confessed that the whole thing was a setup. And he said that Smollett's lie about the hate crime came after the actor had previously failed to get adequate media attention for a racist and threatening letter he claimed to have received in the mail. The letter, appearing about a week before the hoax assault, said

---

57   "The Latest: Chicago police release men held in Smollett case," Associated Press, Feb. 15, 2019: https://apnews.com/35dc59643bbc42408b27b8d7118 13192?utm_source=Twitter&utm_medium=AP&utm_campaign=SocialFlow.

58   Miles Bryan, "Chicago Police Say Actor Jussie Smollett Is Now A Suspect For Filing False Report," NPR.org, Feb. 20, 2019: https://www.npr.org/2019/02/ 20/696467705/chicago-police-say-actor-jussie-smollett-is-now-a-suspect-for-filing-false-repor.

in magazine-cutout letters, "You will d[ie] black fag." The message was accompanied by a drawing of a hanged man.[59]

The letter was another concoction of Smollett's sick, 1990s-TV-drama-like imagination. He had sent it to himself.

Smollett compensated the brothers for their participation in his pretense, paying them $3,500, with a promise of another five hundred dollars upon their return from Nigeria, according to Johnson. Police reports also show that the brothers said they were given one hundred dollars by Smollett to purchase the masks and the one red hat that they used, as well as the rope that was tied around the actor's neck. The brothers also said that they had left the clothes they wore during the staged attack back in Nigeria. Asked about a hot sauce bottle that was found at the scene of the incident, they said that they had filled it with bleach and doused Smollett during the "attack."

Other, minor details: The police reports say that Smollett used the brothers to obtain cocaine and ecstasy, and that the siblings ran a personal fitness training business called Team Abel. The brothers said that they ideally wanted fifty dollars per hour per client. They said, however, that they might work for as low as twenty dollars per hour and that at the time of the police report, they were training eleven clients for free. According to my own math, after living expenses and rent in Chicago, that means the two Nigerian brothers would have been netting about 50 Cent. And by that I mean the rapper, 50 Cent, when he was $33 million in debt. Chicago police were either dealing with two complete idiots or two fraudsters who were making money by other, less legitimate means.[60]

---

59 Sam, "Exclusive: 'Empire' Star Jussie Smollett Hospitalized After Homophobic Hate Attack," ThatGrapeJuice.net, Jan. 29, 2019: https://thatgrapejuice.net/entertainment/2019/01/jussie-smollett-hospitalized-homophobic-hate-attack/.
60 Chicago Police Department. "Case Supplementary Report JC133190." May 23, 2019: https://crexternal.blob.core.usgovcloudapi.net/smolett/smollett-Batch3.pdf.

Smollett's motive in faking the attack, Johnson said, was his dissatisfaction with his salary. *New York* magazine later figured that Smollett's pay per episode of *Empire* was around $125,000.[61]

A salary increase, however, was certainly not the extent of Smollett's ambitions. He was more likely interested in more business opportunities, national fame, and higher status. Once upon a time, when a normal person wanted more money, or any of those things, he would have to work overtime to get it. That's no longer an attractive option now that social justice is involved. Privileged victims know that the reward comes a lot faster and is far greater when they claim to have been oppressed, aggrieved, and victimized.

Before the hate crime hoax, only *Empire* viewers had heard of Smollett. But immediately afterward, his name was in the *New York Times*, the *Washington Post*, and *USA Today*, and on every national TV news program.

He took a shortcut to the top using the social justice formula for the oppressed: virtuous minority + attack by bigoted whites (Trump supporters) = $$$.

He wasn't happy with his career and he knew that playing into the social justice scheme was the quickest way to change that. TMZ reported that his main focus had recently been his music recordings. "He was upset his first album didn't do well," TMZ said, "and was stressed out over the debuts of his new songs and music videos."[62]

Smollett wasn't a troubled actor. He was a greedy liar cashing in as a privileged victim.

What happened next can be described as nothing less than a late-term abortion of justice. On March 26, 2019, the state attorney dropped all of the charges and had the case records sealed. Smollett was

---

61   Josef Adalian, "Jussie Smollett Made 'Zero Rumblings' About His *Empire* Pay: Sources," Vulture.com, Feb. 21, 2019: https://www.vulture.com/2019/02/jussie-smollett-empire-salary.html.

62   "'Empire' execs don't believe 'attack' staged over salary issues," TMZ.com, Feb. 26, 2019: https://www.tmz.com/2019/02/26/jussie-smollett-empire-money-contract-staged-attack/.

cleared of everything. And Smollett even continued claiming that his attack had been real. There was no admission of guilt.

The office of Cook County, Illinois, state attorney Kim Foxx said that it had let go of the charges "after reviewing all of the facts and circumstances of the case, including Mr. Smollett's volunteer service in the community and agreement to forfeit his [ten-thousand-dollar] bond to the City of Chicago."[63] (TMZ found out that Smollett's "community service" amounted to two days with Jesse Jackson.)[64]

Seeing the breaking news that the charges against Smollett were dropped would have been laughable if it weren't so depressing, though it was particularly funny when CNN's Brian Stelter threw his hands up to say we "may never really know what happened on the street that night in Chicago."[65]

Sorry folks, but it's a wash! We may never know!

A report in the *Chicago Sun-Times* should have more or less served as notice that Smollett's case would get the shaft.[66] Two weeks before the charges were cleared, the *Sun-Times* reported, Foxx had phone conversations with one of Smollett's relatives about the investigation. Thereafter, Foxx, for unknown reasons, told the relative that she intended to ask police superintendent Eddie Johnson to turn the investigation over to the FBI.

"OMG this would be a huge victory," Smollett's relative replied.

---

63 Megan Crepeau, Madeline Buckley, and Jason Meisner, "In latest plot twist, Cook County prosecutors abruptly drop all charges against Jussie Smollett," *Chicago Tribune*, March 26, 2019: https://www.chicagotribune.com/news/local/breaking/ct-met-jussie-smollett-charges-dropped-20190326-story.html.

64 "Jussie Smollett put in 2 days community service Rainbow PUSH Coalition," TMZ.com, March 26, 2019: https://www.tmz.com/2019/03/26/jussie-smollett-community-service-rainbow-push-jesse-jackson-charges-dropped/.

65 *Inside Politics*, CNN, March 26, 2019.

66 Andy Grimm, "Records: Former Michelle Obama aide, Smollett relative reached out to Kim Foxx," *Chicago Sun-Times*, March 13, 2019: https://chicago.suntimes.com/news/records-former-michelle-obama-aide-smollett-relative-reached-out-to-kim-foxx/.

Foxx recused herself from the investigation on February 13, the same day as her last conversation with the relative, according to the *Sun-Times*.

Foxx had intervened in the investigation on behalf of Smollett's relative, and it looks like she recused herself because she knew that in the hands of her deputy, Joseph Magats, the case would end in the charges being dropped. That's one possibility but, like CNN's Brian Stelter said, we may never really know!

The case wasn't confusing; it wasn't a mystery; and, contrary to the distraction put forth by a lot of liberals, it contained no lessons whatsoever about the prevalence of *real* hate crimes. But after the charges were dismissed, social justice believers racked their brains for a way to explain what had just happened. They landed on anything but the obvious: The prosecutor's office was corrupt, and Smollett was yet another example of grievance, especially fake grievance, functioning as the new privilege.

Police were 100 percent certain that they had busted Smollett, and a grand jury agreed with the police, slapping Smollett with more than a dozen felony charges that could have earned him decades in prison.

In an instant, it all went up in smoke.

Smollett's legal team made a mockery of the outcome by continuing to talk about it in the media. On NBC's *Today*, his lawyer Tina Glandian suggested with a straight face that it was possible that Smollett had misidentified the race of one of his attackers because the guy may have been in whiteface.

"Obviously, you can disguise that," Glandian said, referring to the black-as-pavement skin tone of the Nigerian brothers. "You can put makeup on.... You know, I was looking up the brothers [online], and one of the first videos that showed up, actually, was one of the brothers in whiteface, doing a Joker monologue with white makeup on, so it's not implausible."[67]

---

67 *Today*, NBC, March 28, 2019.

Yes, dear reader, go look that one up for yourself using the footnote here and tell me whether it's possible that you might confuse the black man in the video for a white Trump supporter because he was wearing white face paint.[68]

Not all hope was lost. A Chicago judge in late May ruled that the court records in the Smollett case should be unsealed and made public. They revealed only more corruption. The *New York Times* reported that after Smollett was officially charged in late February, police detectives met with a prosecutor from Foxx's office. The attorney expressed to the detectives that "she felt the case would be settled with Smollett paying the city of Chicago $10,000 in restitution and doing community service," according to detective notes that were released in the unsealed court documents. In short, Foxx had determined early that the whole case should be swept away.[69]

On June 20, 2019, a Cook County judge ordered the instatement of a special prosecutor to investigate the "unprecedented irregularities" in the case. Depending on what turned up from the probe, it could have meant nullifying the original decision by state prosecutors to drop the charges.[70]

The Smollett saga was everything you could expect with a privileged victim. Smollett attempted to fake a hate crime for financial gain, and even after he was exposed, he faced minimal consequence.

---

68 Jennifer Smith, "'They could have worn white face': Jussie Smollett lawyer offers bizarre explanation as to why the Empire actor told police his Nigerian assailants were white - and points to old video of one of them wearing make-up to play the Joker as potential proof," *Daily Mail*, March 28, 2019: https://www.dailymail.co.uk/news/article-6860095/Jussie-Smolletts-lawyer-says-thought-brothers-white-wearing-make-up.html.

69 Julia Jacobs, "Documents Suggest Prosecutors Quickly Changed Mind on Jussie Smollett Case," *New York Times*, May 30, 2019: https://www.nytimes.com/2019/05/30/arts/television/jussie-smollett-attack-case.html.

70 Megan Crepeau, "Judge orders special prosecutor be appointed to look into Jussie Smollett controversy," *Chicago Tribune*, June 21, 2019: https://www.chicagotribune.com/news/criminal-justice/ct-jussie-smollett-special-prosecutor-20190621-jkpbw7sm4jcw3mm5ompfk7htxe-story.html.

Fake hate crimes are shockingly common.

Wilfred Reilly, a political science professor at Kentucky State University and author of *Hate Crime Hoax: How the Left Is Selling a Fake Race War*, has compiled hundreds of examples of fake hate crimes. He wrote in *USA Today* that Smollett's fabricated story had always been suspect, not just because it was on its face dumb, but because "there is very little brutally violent racism" in America.

FBI data for 2017, the most recent year for which the information is available, backs up that assertion. Of homicides with a black offender, less than 20 percent that year involved a white victim. Of homicides with a white offender, less than 10 percent involved a black victim.[71]

As Reilly noted, violent crimes between people of different races represent "a very small part of total crimes."

But the facts on race and violence don't matter under social justice. What matters is the extent to which an individual can claim to have been aggrieved and oppressed based on their race, gender, and sexuality. That explains the initial outpouring of solidarity, encouragement, and support for Smollett by Hollywood, high-profile Democrats, and the national media immediately following his claim about having been attacked.

The always ignorant Representative Alexandria Ocasio-Cortez (Democrat of New York), tweeted that the incident "was a racist and homophobic attack. If you don't like what is happening to our country, then work to change it. It is no one's job to water down or sugar-coat the rise of hate crimes."[72]

CNN host Brooke Baldwin described the alleged assault as "absolutely despicable," adding that "hopefully the police run this down really quickly."[73]

---

71 FBI, Uniform Crime Report, 2017: https://ucr.fbi.gov/crime-in-the-u.s/2017/crime-in-the-u.s.-2017/tables/expanded-homicide-data-table-6.xls.
72 Alexandria Ocasio-Cortez, Twitter.com, Jan. 29, 2019; https://twitter.com/AOC/status/1090491674575454208.
73 "CNN Newsroom," CNN, Jan. 29, 2019: http://transcripts.cnn.com/TRANSCRIPTS/1901/29/cnr.05.html.

Actress Emma Watson tweeted that she was "[d]isgusted by the ugly prejudice and bigotry behind this violence. Sending love to @ JussieSmollett & to anyone that has been hurt by the hatred of those who fear difference."[74]

Mariah Carey posted a photo and video of her and Smollett hugging, with the caption "Jussie, I'm so heartbroken over what happened to you. You are one of the most talented, beautiful, kind hearted and courageous people I know. I stand with you and I love you."[75]

America's culture fascists in the news media and Hollywood have contributed to a system that rewards Smollett's appalling conduct. They reinforce the message that the more of a victim you are, the better— and how much more of a victim can you be than a gay black man beat up by Trump supporters? Smollett would have truly won the social justice lottery of grievance if his story had been true. He had nothing to lose and everything to gain by creating a hoax centered on race and sexuality.

Smollett's case is the apex of an extended history of hate crime hoaxes. It is today's Tawana Brawley, today's Duke lacrosse players, today's O. J. Simpson.

Wait, scratch that last one. But I swear there are more!

⌘　⌘　⌘

Smollett's story isn't even original or in any way different from nearly dozens of claims made before his. White Trump supporters' committing crimes against minorities is a fairy tale told time and time again.

A day after the 2016 presidential election, a female Muslim student at San Diego State University claimed to police that she had been

---

74 Emma Watson, Twitter.com, Jan. 30, 2019: https://twitter.com/emmawatson/status/1090568342170025985.

75 Mariah Carey, Instagram, Feb. 2, 2019: https://www.instagram.com/p/BtZq8X0nU7r/.

assaulted and robbed by two men who "made comments about President-Elect Trump and the Muslim community."[76] The student also said that her car had been stolen, apparently as part of the attack. Two months later, police dropped the investigation because the "victim" no longer wanted to cooperate. And her car hadn't been stolen after all. She told police she had simply forgotten where she parked it. (It's, without a doubt, totally unrelated that the student was a member of the Muslim Student Association, which had been planning an upcoming protest of Trump's election.)[77]

The exact same day as that fake attack, another Muslim woman at the University of Louisiana at Lafayette claimed that two white men had assaulted her, robbed her, and snatched a hijab from her head. She described one of them as wearing a white Trump hat. A day later, investigators said she confessed to having fabricated the entire incident.[78]

On December 1, 2016, eighteen-year-old Yasmin Seweid told New York City police that three drunken white guys had taunted her about Trump's election victory and tried to pull a hijab from her head on the subway as other passengers watched without intervening. "It made me really sad after when I thought about it," she told the *New York Daily News*. "People were looking at me and looking at what was happening and no one said a thing. They just looked away." She

76 San Diego State University Police Department, Facebook.com, Nov. 9, 2016: https://www.facebook.com/165977713436348/photos/a.183329528367833.44318.165977713436348/1335305786503529/?type=3&theater.

77 R. Stickney, "SDSU Police: No Suspect in Attack on Muslim Student," NBCSandiego.com, Jan. 10, 2017: https://www.nbcsandiego.com/news/local/SDSU-Police-Attack-on-Muslim-Student-Unfounded-410296485.html.

78 Derek Hawkins and Fred Barbash, "Louisiana student 'fabricated' story of hijab attack, police say," *Washington Post*, Nov. 10, 2016: https://www.washingtonpost.com/news/morning-mix/wp/2016/11/10/women-in-hijabs-on-2-campuses-say-they-were-attacked-by-men-invoking-donald-trump/?utm_term=.84e2512d8aa4.

said the men called her a terrorist and told her to "get the hell out of the country."[79]

A month later, she confessed that none of it was real. "Nothing happened, and there was no victim," New York police said. The *Daily News* thereafter reported that Seweid had made up the story "because she didn't want to get in trouble for breaking her curfew after being out late drinking with friends."[80]

You can take solace in one thing, though. Seweid's parents, disappointed by her hoax, reportedly punished her by making her shave off her hair.

If Smollett's case was at all a surprise, it should only be in that anyone took so seriously a lie that had been told so many times before. It's like if Barack Obama told you today, "If you like your plan, you can keep your plan." The only person who might be reasonably expected to say, "Wow, that's great!" is Michelle. The rest of us should know not to trust him.

Yet the fictions, falsehoods, and fabrications about politically-driven hate crimes continue uninterrupted and with great assist from the news media.

In November 2016, immediately after Trump's election, the *Indianapolis Star* reported that Saint David's Episcopal Church of Bean Blossom, Indiana, had been vandalized with graffiti on its walls.[81] In

79 Laura Dimon, Ross Keith, Rocco Parascandola, and Graham Rayman, "Drunk men screaming Trump's name try to rip off Muslim student's hijab as straphangers stand idly by on East Side subway, cops say," *New York Daily News*, Dec. 3, 2016: https://www.nydailynews.com/new-york/nyc-crime/drunk-men-screaming-trump-attack-muslim-straphanger-article-1.2896163.

80 Rocco Parascandola and Leonard Greene, "Muslim college student made up Trump supporter subway attack story to avoid punishment for missing curfew," *New York Daily News*, Dec. 15, 2016: https://www.nydailynews.com/new-york/muslim-woman-reported-trump-supporter-attack-made-story-article-1.2910944.

81 Kara Berg, "Indiana church vandalized with slurs," *Indianapolis Star*, Nov. 13, 2016: https://www.indystar.com/story/news/2016/11/13/indiana-church-vandalized-slurs/93772448/.

black spray paint were a swastika, "Heil Trump," and "Fag church," an apparent reference to the church's reputation within the community for welcoming gays.[82]

Six months later, twenty-six-year-old gay man George Nathaniel Stang, an organist at Saint David's, admitted to police that he was the perpetrator. He had sprayed the graffiti because he was "disappointed in and fearful of the outcome of the national election."[83]

On November 3, 2018, a synagogue in Brooklyn, New York, was defaced with graffiti spelling out "Die Jew Rats," "End it Now," and "Jew Better Be Ready." The incident understandably shook the community, given that it happened just one week after a mass shooting at a Pittsburgh synagogue that left eleven people dead (a tragedy that was also falsely blamed on Trump). Democratic New York governor Andrew Cuomo denounced the attack on the Brooklyn synagogue. "The disgusting rhetoric and heinous violence in this nation has reached a fever pitch and is ripping at the fabric of America," he said.[84] State-level lawmaker Jim Gaughran wrote on Twitter that the apparent hate crime highlighted "the need for a change in our current political climate. Hate, bigotry, and fear-mongering have become all too common in today's society and that needs to change."[85]

Police two days later found the suspect, a thirty-year-old blonde, blue-eyed, white male who confessed that he had been inspired to

82 St. David's Episcopal Church—Beanblosson, IN, Facebook.com, Nov. 13, 2016: https://www.facebook.com/permalink.php?story_fbid=60753758276235 9&id=319153721600748.

83 "Police: Brown County church organist admitted to November vandalism," WTHR.com, May 3, 2017: https://www.wthr.com/article/ police-brown-county-church-organist-admitted-to-november-vandalism.

84 CNN, "Brooklyn man faces four hate crime charges after synagogue defaced with anti-Semitic messages," WTOP.com, Nov. 4, 2018: https://wtop. com/national/2018/11/brooklyn-man-faces-four-hate-crime-charges-after- synagogue-defaced-with-anti-semitic-messages/.

85 Jim Gaughran, Twitter.com, Nov. 2, 2018: https://twitter.com/ Gaughran4Senate/status/1058536317494149121.

act by President Trump. Wait, no that's not right. My mistake! In reality, after reviewing surveillance video that clearly showed the perpetrator, police detained twenty-six-year-old James Polite, a black gay male who, as fate would have it, was highly active in local Democratic politics.[86]

Polite was the exact opposite of the type of person we're told to expect this kind of thing from. He had worked as an intern in the office of Democrat Christine Quinn, the very loud lesbian who in 2013 lost her bid for city mayor and who had served as New York City Council speaker. In a delicious twist to the plot, Polite's area of responsibility as an intern in Quinn's office included...oversight of local hate crimes.

More than a year before the graffiti incident, the *New York Times* had profiled Polite as a down-on-his-luck black orphan saved by government programs. The article said Polite interned with Quinn and for several years had worked on "initiatives to combat hate crime, sexual assault and domestic violence."[87]

A city initiative sponsored by the *Times* itself even helped Polite find a set of caretakers who would functionally act as his parents, who it turned out were Jewish.

Still, Polite's Facebook activity showed an extensive history of anti-Semitic remarks and a preoccupation with race that you can find only in a privileged victim. He posted photos of himself wearing lipstick, along with messages like, "A dream with eyes wide open. civil

86   CNN, "Brooklyn man faces four hate crime charges after synagogue defaced with anti-Semitic messages," WTOP.com, Nov. 4, 2018: https://wtop.com/national/2018/11/brooklyn-man-faces-four-hate-crime-charges-after-synagogue-defaced-with-anti-semitic-messages/.

87   Emily Palmer, "After Years in Foster Care, Intern 'Adopted' by City Hall Catches a Break," *New York Times*, Dec. 14, 2017: https://www.nytimes.com/2017/12/14/nyregion/after-years-in-foster-care-intern-adopted-by-city-hall-catches-a-break.html.

war is here. Nobody gotta die. Mexico, latin America, carribean vs. Jew nigger pigs. One person touch me this whole shit a smoking."[88]

Andrew Cuomo, for some reason, never spoke again about this particular case of "fever pitch" hate in America.

A week before the 2016 election, a 110-year-old black community church in Greenville, Mississippi, was set ablaze and had the words "Vote Trump" spray-painted on the outside of one of its walls.

Several weeks later, Andrew McClinton turned himself into police and he was charged with vandalism and arson. McClinton is black and he was a member of the church.[89]

Nassau Community College in New York from October through December 2016 saw its campus defaced with graffiti, including swastikas, "KKK," and "Heil Hitler."

The incident drew national attention in the aftermath of the 2016 election, and yet the perpetrator wasn't a white Trump supporter. He was identified by police as ethnic Indian twenty-year-old Jasskirat Saini, who acting police commissioner Thomas Krumpter said had been motivated by a belief that "he was being harassed by members of the Jewish community" in his own neighborhood.[90]

In September 2018, nineteen-year-old Adwoa Lewis of Long Island, New York, claimed that she had been driving home late one night when she somehow was "confronted" by four teenagers who harassed her, yelling "Trump 2016" and telling her that she "didn't belong here," according to NBC 4 New York. She said that the morning after, she awoke to find one of her tires slashed and a note on her car that said, "Go Home."

---

88 Luke Rosiak, "NYC synagogue vandalism suspect is former city hall anti-hate crime intern," DailyCaller.com, Nov. 3, 2018: https://dailycaller.com/2018/11/03/nyc-synagogue-vandalism-suspect/.

89 Christopher Mele, "Member Charged in Arson of Black Church With 'Vote Trump' Scrawled on Side," *New York Times*, Dec. 21, 2016: https://www.nytimes.com/2016/12/21/us/mississippi-church-fire.html.

90 Deon J. Hampton, "Student drew swastikas on Nassau college buildings, police say," *Newsday*, Dec. 20, 2016: https://www.newsday.com/long-island/nassau/cops-student-drew-swastikas-on-nassau-college-buildings-1.12785584.

Two weeks later, she told police that her encounter with the teenagers had never happened. She'd made it up.[91]

November 2018 was practically Racist Hoax Month on college campuses.

Protests by black students broke out at Goucher College in Maryland after a building was defaced on two separate occasions with a swastika and graffiti reading, "I'm gonna kill all niggers." There were also scribblings of room numbers of several black students who lived on campus.[92] More than one hundred black students led a "blackout" protest calling attention to the display. "We are demonstrating today to ask Goucher to be accountable," junior student JaVaunte Neumann told the *Baltimore Sun*. "I've seen white supremacy be tolerated. Now, students are angry. White supremacists are getting pretty bold now with Donald Trump as president. We are at the point where we can't wait for the administration or Baltimore County Police."

A few days later, following an investigation led by the FBI and Goucher school officials, police arrested black male Fynn Ajani Arthur. He confessed to the graffiti, citing his "built up anger with no way to vent it."[93]

Even with the graffiti revealed as a hoax, Goucher students refused to give it up. They continued to insist that racism on campus was real and prevalent. They created safe spaces, initiated a buddy system for black students to walk in pairs, and issued a list of demands from the

91 "Woman Who Said She Found Hateful Note on Car After Teens Yelled 'Trump 2016!' Made Up Story: Police," NBCNewYork.com, Sep. 15, 2018: https://www.nbcnewyork.com/news/local/Woman-Who-Found-Hateful-Note-on-Car-After-Teens-Yelled-Trump-2016-Made-Up-Story-Police-493375511.html.

92 Catherine Rentz, "African-American Goucher College students respond to racist graffiti, threat with 'Black Out,'" *Baltimore Sun*, Nov. 16, 2018: https://www.baltimoresun.com/news/maryland/education/higher-ed/bs-md-goucher-racism-black-out-20181116-story.html.

93 Jenny Fulginiti, "Arrest made as more racist graffiti surfaces on Goucher College campus," WBALTV.com, Nov. 30, 2018: https://www.wbaltv.com/article/arrest-made-as-more-racist-graffiti-surfaces-on-goucher-college-campus/25359091.

faculty, including the hiring of more black staff and a requirement that first-year students complete a "cultural competency" course.[94]

That's how social justice works. *No crime? No problem! Now here's a list of our demands…*

The same month as the Goucher hoax, Drake University in Iowa saw a rash of racist notes sent to the dorm rooms of multiple students. One of the notes received by a black student said, "We've decided that we no longer want [you] on our campus. Which means you need to leave or else."[95]

Almost all of the notes were traced back to Kissie Ram, a petite girl with glasses who looks less like Hitler Youth and more like a cross between actress Mindy Kaling and Velma from *Scooby-Doo*. Of the five racist notes found on campus, four were deemed hoaxes, and I'll make the leap to assume that, while the latest reports didn't get to the bottom of the fifth, that one was most certainly a hoax, too.[96] Ram was charged with and pleaded guilty to sending at least one of the notes.[97]

Just as the Goucher hoax did nothing to tamp down the social justice flames on that campus, the result was the same at Drake.

---

94   Lillian Reed, "Goucher College student arrested in two racist graffiti incidents," *Baltimore Sun*, Nov. 30, 2018: https://www.baltimoresun.com/news/maryland/baltimore-county/bs-md-goucher-hate-incident-20181129-story.html.

95   Linh Ta, "Confirmed racist threat at Drake University tells student to leave 'or else,'" *Des Moines Register*, Nov. 9, 2018: https://www.desmoinesregister.com/story/news/crime-and-courts/2018/11/09/racist-threat-drake-university-student-tells-student-leave-else-thisisdrake-microaggressions/1943046002/.

96   Kathy A. Bolten, "Drake University officials: Four of the five racist notes found on campus were hoaxes," *Des Moines Register*, Nov. 30, 2018: https://www.desmoinesregister.com/story/news/crime-and-courts/2018/11/30/drake-university-student-fakes-alleged-racist-note-racism-campus-des-moines/2162705002/.

97   "Former Drake University student pleads guilty in fake racist notes investigation," *Des Moines Register*, Jan. 16, 2019: https://www.desmoinesregister.com/story/news/crime-and-courts/2019/01/16/drake-university-des-moines-iowa-ia-college-racist-racism-notes-crime-court-fake-hoax-kissie-ram/2596084002/.

The racist notes were all a hoax and yet, student Morgan Coleman told a local NBC affiliate that the letters nonetheless showed "that white supremacy is a huge problem and we have to actively work to combat it." She said that students remained "very afraid…regardless of who sent whatever note."[98]

Privileged victims are insatiable, and will always have a new demand. If you meet the one, there's another one, and then a third.

Just before the midterm elections in November 2018, Kansas State student Brodrick Burse posted a photo on Twitter that purported to show a note on his apartment door warning passersby, "Beware N****** Live Here!!! Knock at Your Own Risk," according to the *Wichita Eagle*.[99] "[I]t's 2018 and this was posted on my apartment door," Burse wrote shortly after on Twitter. "[T]his is still happening here at [Kansas State] so if isn't as evident as it already was everyone needs to get out and vote I refuse to let this blatant racism stop me from moving onward and upward."

Police later found that he had put the note up himself. "Upon questioning, the person who reported the incident admitted to creating and posting the note to their own door," police said, according to WHOTV's report.[100]

Vowing to move "onward and upward" in the face of fabricated racism is the social justice way. It's how the privileged victim advances.

In April 2017, a racist note was found on the windshield of Samantha Wells, a student at Saint Olaf College, a liberal arts school

98 Laura Barczewski, "Drake Students React to Findings in Racist Letters Investigation," WHOTV.com, Nov. 30, 2018: https://whotv.com/2018/11/30/drake-students-react-to-findings-in-racist-letters-investigation/.

99 Jason Tidd, "For second time in two years, racist slur at Kansas State was a hoax, police say," *Wichita Eagle*, Nov. 8, 2018: https://www.kansas.com/news/local/education/article221373355.html.

100 Dan Hendrickson, "Drake University says One Alleged Victim is Responsible for Four Racist Notes Left on Campus," WHOTV.com, Nov. 30, 2018: https://whotv.com/2018/11/30/police-say-drake-student-lied-about-one-racist-note-found-on-campus-charges-pending/.

in Northfield, Minnesota. "I am so glad that you are leaving soon," the note said. "One less nigger that this school has to deal with. You have spoken up too much. You will change nothing. Shut up or I will shut you up."

Protests ensued, classes were canceled, safe spaces were needed.

Days later, school president David Anderson told everyone on the campus in an email that authorities had found a suspect and that "[t]he reason…this was not a genuine threat is that we learned from the author's confession that the note was fabricated." The author had written the note as "a strategy to draw attention to concerns about the campus climate."[101]

But that grand reveal didn't kill the issue. It served instead as a catalyst for a *bigger discussion.*

Precious Ismail, a student at the school and the spokeswoman for the campus diversity group Collective for Change on the Hill, told the Minneapolis *Star Tribune,* "Our movement wasn't about one individual. Our movement was about a pattern of institutional racism."[102]

Social justice acolytes are never *not* victims, even when the crimes against them are faked.

The day after the election in 2016, someone in South Philadelphia spray-painted three cars and one house with messages that said, "Trump Rules" and "Trump Rules Black Bitch."[103] Weeks later, a review

---

101   Peter Holley and Lindsey Bever, "A racist note sparked protests at a Minnesota college. The school now says the message was fake," *Washington Post,* May 10, 2017: https://www.washingtonpost.com/news/grade-point/wp/2017/05/10/a-racist-note-sparked-protests-at-a-minnesota-college-the-school-now-says-the-message-was-fake/?utm_term=.e3df8cd4ba36.

102   Jennifer Brooks and Paul Walsh, "St. Olaf: Report of racist note on black student's windshield was 'fabricated'," *Star Tribune,* May 11, 2017: http://www.startribune.com/st-olaf-report-of-racist-note-on-black-student-s-windshield-was-fabricated/421912763/.

103   Michael Tanenbaum, "VIDEO: Suspect wanted for racist Trump vandalism in South Philly," PhillyVoice.com, Nov. 9, 2016: https://www.phillyvoice.com/more-racist-donald-trump-vandalism-found-south-philly/.

of surveillance video led to the arrest of fifty-eight-year-old William Tucker for vandalism. He's black.[104]

That same day, twenty-one-year-old Halley Bass in Ann Arbor, Michigan, said a middle-aged white man had attacked her in public while she was out walking. She said it must have been prompted by her wearing a pin opposing Brexit, the movement supporting the United Kingdom's withdrawal from the European Union. "[He] must have seen the pin and picked on me," she told police, claiming that the man had scratched her across the face. "That's my best guess. No other reason why he would be targeting me."

She said she was wearing the pin "to sort of, like, to show a solidarity with immigrants who feel threatened by Brexit. Um…but now it's…for people who feel threatened by president elect—Trump's his name."

Surveillance footage showed no evidence of Bass' being where she said she had been, nor of any attack. Two months later, she admitted that she had in fact cut herself because she was depressed.[105]

In February 2017, a series of bomb threats were made against Jewish community centers, schools, and the Anti-Defamation League. Journalists ran wild with assumptions that it was part of a wave of anti-Semitism born in the aftermath of Trump's election—you know, the president whose favorite child is Jewish and whose son-in-law is also a Jew.

A journalist at the popular liberal website Vox wrote, "Hostility toward Jews is growing—both among 'anti-globalist' ideologues and among young people who simply think that anti-Semitism is funny."

---

104   Elisa Lala, "New Jersey man arrested, charged in racist pro-Trump vandalism incidents in South Philly," PhillyVoice. com, Dec. 1, 2016: https://www.phillyvoice.com/ new-jersey-man-arrested-racist-trump-vandalism-south-philly/.

105   John Counts, "Ann Arbor woman pleads guilty to making up hate crime," MLive.com, March 7, 2017: https://www.mlive.com/news/ ann-arbor/2017/03/ann_arbor_woman_pleads_guilty_1.html.

She said both groups "believe that, on some level, President Trump is on their side."[106]

Reporter Eleanor Goldberg of *HuffPost* said that Trump's rhetoric had "emboldened anti-Semites and racists."[107]

It was a "wave of bigotry" that was "fueled, at least in part, by Trump's divisive leadership that has emboldened bigots to express themselves openly."[108]

Admittedly, that would be a lot of hatred for Trump to have drummed up against God's chosen people.

And yet, just a little more than a week went by before Juan Thompson, a thirty-one-year-old former journalist, was arrested in connection with the bomb threats. Thompson, by the way, is black, and he made the threats "as part of a sustained campaign to harass and intimidate" a girlfriend who had broken up with him.[109]

Incidentally, Thompson had been the center of controversy exactly one year before when he was exposed as a serial fabricator for the news website the Intercept.[110] It's with a dash of irony, then, that

---

106 Dara Lind, "Call it by its name: anti-Semitism," Vox.com, Feb. 21, 2017: https://www.vox.com/policy-and-politics/2017/2/21/14685608/ trump-anti-semitism-condemn.

107 Becket Adams, "The Jewish community centers arrest is a reminder that pundits should shut up and wait," *Washington Examiner*, March 3, 2017: https://www.washingtonexaminer.com/the-jewish-community-centers-arrest-is-a-reminder-that-pundits-should-shut-up-and-wait.

108 Dahleen Glanton, "On anti-Semitic acts and how Trump can send a strong message to bigots," *Chicago Tribune*, Feb. 23, 2017: https://www.chicagotribune.com/news/columnists/glanton/ct-trump-jews-glanton-20170222-story.html.

109 Aaron Katersky, Josh Margolin, Mike Levine, and Emily Shapiro, "Man accused of making threats against Jewish community centers arrested in St. Louis," ABC News, March 3, 2017: http://abcnews.go.com/ US/man-accused-making-threats-jewish-community-centers-arrested/ story?id=45884069.

110 Becket Adams, "Reporter with Dylann Roof 'scoop' exposed as serial fabricator," *Washington Examiner*, Feb. 2, 2016: https://www.washingtonexaminer.com/ reporter-with-dylann-roof-scoop-exposed-as-serial-fabricator.

before Thompson was arrested in 2017, the Intercept wrote of the bomb threats that Trump's "allies are targeting Jews." An editor's note was subsequently added to the story to clarify that it was in fact not a Trump ally but one of the website's former employees who had perpetuated the anti-Semitic scare.[111]

Oops!

Three months after his arrest, Thompson pleaded guilty to charges related to his anti-Jew bomb threats, and he apologized in court.[112] He was sentenced to five years in prison.[113]

How does this keep happening? Because social justice never sleeps. Privileged victims never tire.

Again, just after the election of President Trump in 2016, a Muslim student at the University of Michigan claimed to police that a man had approached her threatening to set her on fire if she wouldn't remove her hijab.

"Our nation's leaders, and particularly President-elect Donald Trump, need to speak out forcefully against the wave of anti-Muslim incidents sweeping the country after Tuesday's election," said Dawud Walid, executive director of the Michigan chapter of the Council on American-Islamic Relations.[114]

---

111   Robert Mackey, "Trump Suggests Anti-Semitic Acts Might Be Faked to Make His Movement 'Look Bad,'" TheIntercept.com, Feb. 28, 2017: https://theintercept.com/2017/02/28/trump-suggests-anti-semitic-acts-might-faked-make-movement-look-bad/.

112   "'I deeply apologize': Ex-journalist pleads guilty in Jewish bomb threats case," CBS News, June 13, 2017: https://www.cbsnews.com/news/juan-thompson-pleads-guilty-ex-journalist-jcc-bomb-threats/.

113   Doyle Murphy, "Juan Thompson Sentenced to 5 Years for Cyber Stalking, Jewish Bomb Threats," *Riverfront Times*, Dec. 20, 2017: https://www.riverfronttimes.com/newsblog/2017/12/20/juan-thompson-sentenced-to-5-years-for-cyber-stalking-jewish-bomb-threats.

114   Jennifer Dixon, "Hijab-wearing U-M student threatened with being set on fire," *Detroit Free Press*, Nov. 12, 2016: https://www.freep.com/story/news/local/2016/11/12/hijab-wearing-u-m-student-threatened-being-set-fire/93726806/.

A little more than a month after the initial report, police identified "numerous inconsistencies" in the supposed victim's complaint and "determined the incident in question did not occur."[115]

A Muslim lied about having been threatened with being set ablaze by a Trump supporter. *Just another day in America!*

On November 9, 2016, the day after the election, Bowling Green State University student Eleesha Long told police that she had been walking down a street when "three boys began to throw rocks" at her. She identified all three as white and wearing "Trump shirts."

Long posted about the alleged incident on Facebook but didn't tell police. It was only after her father saw the post and alerted authorities that an investigation took place. Long was taken to the police station, where she gave a statement but was inconsistent in her story; she "changed her story about what happened, where it happened, and when it happened," according to local police lieutenant Dan Mancuso.[116] Upon viewing her Facebook post and phone history, police determined that "she was not in the location that of when [sic] she said it occurred." Long's motive apparently had been that she was frustrated with people in her personal life, friends and family, who had supported Trump.

Two months after her claim, Long pleaded no contest to two misdemeanors and was ordered to pay a two-hundred-dollar fine.[117]

A day after Trump's election victory in 2016, a twenty-five-year-old Canadian moviemaker named Chris Ball was in Santa Monica,

---

115 Kat Stafford, "Cops: U-M student lied about man threatening to burn hijab," *Detroit Free Press*, Dec. 21, 2016: https://www.freep.com/story/news/local/michigan/2016/12/21/cops-u-m-student-lied-man-threatening-burn-hjiab/95704464/.

116 Brigette Burnett, 13ABC.com, "BG police say student lied about politically driven attack," Nov. 17, 2016: https://www.13abc.com/content/news/BG-police-say-student-lied-about-politically-driven-attack-401814426.html.

117 "Fabricating an assault nets woman $200 fine," *Toledo Blade*, Jan. 31, 2017: https://www.toledoblade.com/local/courts/2017/01/31/Fabricating-an-assault-nets-woman-200-fine/stories/20170130255.

California, when a friend of his posted a photo on social media showing Ball with what appeared to be streams of blood running all over his face and neck.

"To celebrate Trump's win last night, some Trump supporters decided to smash a beer bottle into my close friend's head last night for being gay, sending him to the ER," wrote Ball's friend Noah Kentis on Facebook. "And it's not Trump that I fear, it's his supporters that have already resorted to violence, just because of the energy they feed off of him."[118]

The poor guy supposedly had been taken to the hospital, and yet the Santa Monica police department said no hospital within the city had a record of Ball having been treated. Authorities asked Ball to come to them for an investigation, but he never did.[119]

To rebut accusations that he had faked his injuries, Ball released what he said were medical records from having checked in as a patient at West Hills Hospital, a care center nearly an hour away from Santa Monica. That would mean Ball was attacked and brutally beaten, then taken to a car and inexplicably driven an hour away from the incident in order to receive care.[120]

No police report was ever filed, and laws prohibit West Hills from releasing any patient information. Stated more bluntly, there's no publicly available evidence to back up any of Ball's account of what he says happened to him.

Heading into spring 2017, a small store in Charlotte, North Carolina, run by South Asian immigrants, had its window smashed and

---

118   Jake Kivanc, "Calgary Man Who Says He Was Attacked by Trump Supporters for Being Gay Accused of Hoax," Vice.com, Nov. 11, 2016: https://www. vice.com/en_ca/article/wdbpqm/calgary-man-who-says-he-was-attacked-by-trump-supporters-for-being-gay-accused-of-hoax.

119   Santa Monica Police Department, Facebook.com, Nov. 10, 2016: https:// www.facebook.com/santamonicapd/posts/1248837835137297.

120   "Calgary man shows medical record as proof of election night assault (HOAX)," Metro News, Free Republic, Nov. 11, 2016: http://www. freerepublic.com/focus/f-news/3492990/posts.

a burning object was tossed at its front door with a note that said, "Our newly elected president Donald Trump is our nation builder for White America. You all know that, we want our country back on the right track. We need to get rid of Muslims, Indians and all immigrants." The note, according to police, also threatened to "torture" the store's owner.[121]

Surveillance tape led police to arrest thirty-two-year-old Curtis Flournoy. He's black.[122]

It's weird how easy these scenarios are to replicate. It's almost like our culture has been jiggered to see this kind of thing play out over and over.

And yet, where's all that "right-wing violence" we've been warned about? The phrase has no meaning, but the media breathlessly cite "studies" that supposedly show "right-wing domestic violence" as being the most pervasive kind of ideologically driven violence.

There's never any hysteria in the media about "extreme left-wing violence" despite overwhelming evidence of it. After the 2008 election of Barack Obama, a black Democrat, we were told to be on high alert for violence from the right. Eight years later, after the 2016 election of Donald Trump, a white Republican, we were told to be on high alert for yet more violence from the right. Funny how that works.

The weekend after Trump's election victory, what appeared to be blood was poured up and down the main hall of a campus building at Williams College in Massachusetts. The phrase "AMKKK KILL" was written on one of the walls.

University President Adam Falk said in a statement afterward, "In the current post-election climate, we have a heightened awareness for any actions or expressions that may be bias incidents."

---

121 Mark Price and LaVendrick Smith, "Arsonist's threat to 'torture' immigrants a hate crime, say Charlotte police," *Charlotte Observer*, April 7, 2017: https://www.charlotteobserver.com/news/local/article143296274.html.

122 Mark Price, "Internet conspiracies roil after hate crime by 'White America' leads to black suspect," *Charlotte Observer*, April 11, 2017: https://www.charlotteobserver.com/news/local/article143696479.html.

Falk's statement might capture a fair sentiment if the "bias incidents" weren't invariably expected to come from the right. But as always, the Williams College incident was caused by anything *but* the right.

Two days after the defacement of the Williams College building, Falk issued another statement to inform the student body that the incident wasn't what it had appeared. A couple of students had confessed that they were responsible and that they "had committed the vandalism to bring attention to the effects of the presidential election on many within our community."[123] Just gonna go out on a limb and assume that it wasn't a Trump supporter defacing school property with "KKK" and "KILL" to send a message about an election that their own candidate had won. Those were definitely Hillary Clinton people.

At North Park University a week after the 2016 election, student Taylor Volk, a bisexual woman, claimed to have received emails and notes attached to her door "containing harassing, threatening language and mentions of President-elect Donald Trump." One note reportedly said, "Back to hell," and "#Trump."[124] On her Facebook profile, Volk wrote that the harassment was part of "a countrywide epidemic."[125]

The incident was never reported to police, and days later, university president David Parkyn said Volk's claims had all been made up. "Sadly, we discovered that the incident and related messages were fabricated,"

---

123 "An Update on the Vandalism in Griffin Hall," Office of the President of Williams College, Nov. 14, 2016: https://president.williams.edu/writings/an-update-on-the-vandalism-in-griffin-hall/.

124 Richard Ray, "Hateful 'Trump' Notes Allegedly Aimed at Student Were Fabricated, University Says," NBCChicago.com, Nov. 22, 2016: https://www.nbcchicago.com/news/local/north-park-fabricated-notes-402556366.html.

125 Dick Johnson and Richard Ray, "'I Just Want Them to Stop': Chicago Student Says Threatening 'Trump' Note Taped to Her Door," NBCChicago.com, Nov. 15, 2016: https://www.nbcchicago.com/news/local/north-park-harassment-trump-note-401408916.html.

he wrote. "The individual responsible for the incident is not continuing as a student at North Park."[126]

Again just after the 2016 election, a whiteboard hanging in the hall of an Elon University residential building had the message, "Bye Bye Latinos Hasta La Vista" written across it. There was, understandably, an uproar on campus. Almost immediately after it was reported, campus authorities found that it was a hoax perpetuated by… a Latino.[127]

With Trump-related hate crimes, the formula is always the same. *Hasta la vista* becomes *El engaño era bueno*. The scam was good.

Days after Trump's election, Ashley Boyer, a black woman in Delaware, said on Facebook that she had been attacked by Trump supporters while she was pumping gas in her car.

"Just experienced one of the WORST THINGS in my entire life!!!" she wrote. She said that four men pulled up next to her and "proceed[ed] to talk about the election and how they're glad they won't have to deal with niggers much longer." She said one of the men walked over to her to say, "How scared are you, you black bitch! I should just kill you right now…you're a waste of air!"

Boyer said that she was directly called a "nigger" by her alleged harassers and that one of the men threatened to shoot her.[128] She also claimed to have filed charges, though police in the immediate area said they had no record of any from her. She never responded to media requests related to her story.

After her story caught the attention of authorities and other news outlets, Boyer's posts magically disappeared from Facebook.

---

126   "Campus message from North Park University President David L. Parkyn," North Park University, Nov. 22, 2016: https://www.northpark.edu/ stories/campus-message-north-park-university-president-david-l-parkyn/.

127   Bryan Anderson, "Note reading 'Bye Bye Latinos Hasta La Vista' found in Kivette Hall," Elon News Network, Nov. 10, 2016: http://www.elonnewsnetwork.com/ article/2016/11/note-found-whiteboard-kivette-bye-bye-latinos.

128   Brian Hickey, "Police: No official report of ugly racial incident at Delaware gas station," PhillyVoice.com, Nov. 10, 2016: https://www.phillyvoice.com/ police-no-official-report-ugly-racial-incident-del-gas-station/.

Not to belabor the point but, once again, the day after the 2016 election, Kathy Mirah Tu, an Asian student at the University of Minnesota, claimed in a lengthy Facebook post that she had been verbally harassed and physically accosted by a white male.

She said that while she was walking across a very public bridge, the man yelled at her to "go back to Asia." She said she ignored him but that he stopped her and told her that she was only a student at the school "because of affirmative action." She gave no indication as to how he would have known she was a student at the university.

Tu said that she again tried to walk away, but the guy grabbed her by the arm and said, "I don't understand why you are walking away from me when I am trying to have a conversation with you." She said that he told her, "I know more than you."

Finally getting to the climax of her exhausting post, Tu said that she'd had enough of the guy's "ignorance and white privilege," so she told him that he "literally [had] exactly one minute" to release her.

Continuing with the social justice samurai-like plot, Tu said that her aggressor told her, "You can't beat me anyways look [sic] at how small and shrimpy you are."

(One can only imagine this dialogue taking place while the villain of the story laughs with a sinister sneer and our hero stands in defiance just before a fight scene breaks out atop a forest of bamboo.)

Tu said she then employed her "self defense skills" and "punched him straight up in the throat." She said that police came, handcuffed her, and checked her background without listening to her side of the story.

Tu's Facebook tale went viral, garnering seventeen thousand shares and thirty thousand comments.[129]

---

129   Jessie Bekker, "On social media, police say they did not respond to University student's alleged campus assault," *Minnesota Daily*, Nov. 10, 2016: https://www.mndaily.com/article/2016/11/umpd-not-involved-in-hand-cuffed-university-student.

But there never was an altercation between Tu and a white male (Trump supporter) after the election. Though she claimed to have been arrested, local police had no record of the incident. Campus police said they never responded to any report at the location that Tu pinpointed. They were interested in talking to her, but she abruptly ended her communication with them.

Still, the lie that minorities are perpetually targeted for harassment and violence by a privileged class never dies.

On November 18, 2016, the *Boston Herald* reported what it called "the latest case of a faked hate crime."[130]

The phenomenon of faked hate crimes is so prolific that a major city newspaper would actually have to begin its report by qualifying it as, "the latest case."

The *Herald* report said that a man had claimed to have gotten off a public bus late one night and been approached by two white men, who said something about lynching and told him that it was "Trump country now." After interviewing the "victim," police revealed that the story was a lie. "The alleged victim admitted that he had made up the entire story" in order to "raise awareness about things that are going on around the country," police said.

In early 2017, the *New York Times* fed the hysteria over America having fallen under a cloud of hate following Trump's election by publishing a series of reports on vandalism and threats to Jewish cemeteries, community centers, and synagogues.

Beginning in January and through February, synagogues and Jewish community centers saw a spate of bomb threats delivered by phone. The *Times* described the calls as coming from someone with a "rambling"

---

130 Brian Dowling, "Man admits to faking hate crime in Malden," *Boston Herald*, Nov. 18, 2016: https://www.bostonherald.com/2016/11/18/man-admits-to-faking-hate-crime-in-malden/.

and "high-pitched" voice, who would warn of mass violence and state that a bomb had been set onsite.[131]

Adding to the panic, in late February, nearly two hundred gravestones in a Jewish cemetery in Missouri were knocked over, resulting in thirty thousand dollars' worth of damages.[132]

The *Times* wrapped the threats and the vandalism together in one article with the headline "Threats and Vandalism Leave American Jews on Edge in Trump Era." The somber report said that the combination of incidents had "stoked fears that a virulent anti-Semitism has increasingly taken hold in the early days of the Trump administration."[133]

But none of them had anything to do with Trump. The man making the bomb threats was an Israeli—in fact, he was in Israel when authorities arrested him in late March 2017. He was convicted a year later in his home country for making hundreds of threatening calls to people and places in the U.S., New Zealand, and Australia.[134]

DNA evidence at the Missouri cemetery led police not to an anti-Semite inspired by Trump, but to Alzado Harris, a black man who was high, drunk, and angry with a friend when he, by his own admission, pushed over the gravestones.

---

131   Alan Blinder, Serge F. Kovaleski, and Adam Goldman, "Threats and Vandalism Leave American Jews on Edge in Trump Era," *New York Times*, Feb. 28, 2017: https://www.nytimes.com/2017/02/28/us/jewish-community-center-donald-trump.html?action=click&module=RelatedCoverage&pgtype=Article&region=-Footer.

132   Joe Millitzer and Erika Tallan, "Man admits to Jewish cemetery vandalism in University City," Fox2Now.com, April 25, 2018: https://fox2now.com/2018/04/25/man-admits-to-jewish-cemetery-vandalism-in-university-city/.

133   Alan Blinder, Serge F. Kovaleski, and Adam Goldman, "Threats and Vandalism Leave American Jews on Edge in Trump Era," *New York Times*, Feb. 28, 2017: https://www.nytimes.com/2017/02/28/us/jewish-community-center-donald-trump.html?action=click&module=RelatedCoverage&pgtype=Article&region=Footer.

134   Niraj Chokshi, "Israeli Judge Convicts Man on Charges of Threatening U.S. Jewish Groups," *New York Times*, June 28, 2018: https://www.nytimes.com/2018/06/28/world/middleeast/israel-convict-jewish-threats.html.

A friend had dropped Harris off at the cemetery. Intoxicated and irate, he jumped the fence into the graveyard and began pushing over the tombstones. Police would eventually say there was "no evidence to indicate the incident was racially, ethnically or religiously motivated."[135]

To be sure, there were actual victims in the cemetery vandalism and the threatening phone calls. The Jewish people involved were *real* victims. But interest from the news media—the *New York Times* in particular—was in pursuing a social justice narrative: the privileged (Trump and his white supporters) oppressing the aggrieved. There was no privilege to blame here. It was the fault of an intoxicated black guy.

Here's one more just for fun: On the last day of January 2017, a Muslim student at Beloit College in Wisconsin alerted police that the door to his dormitory and the wall next to it in the hall had been spray-painted with "a bias symbol and phrases related to his religion and ethnicity." During questioning, the Muslim student admitted he had painted his own door and that he had done it because he wanted attention.[136]

This is acceptable today because it's what social justice calls for and it's the message that culture fascists in Hollywood, the national media, Washington, and academia reinforce. Privileged victims learned well from them all that getting ahead is a matter of grievance, oppression, and victimhood. Whether the form of victimization is real or not is beside the point. What matters is the outcome.

---

135 Christine Byers, "Man was drunk, mad at friend when he toppled headstones at Jewish cemetery in U. City, police say," *St. Louis Dispatch*, April 25, 2018: https://www.stltoday.com/news/local/crime-and-courts/florissant-man-charged-in-vandalism-at-jewish-cemetery-in-university/article_dd4cd8ae-8088-516c-9c70-7aa7435fe082.html.

136 Logan Wroge, "Beloit College student arrested for falsely reporting bias incident, police say," *Wisconsin State Journal*, Feb. 1, 2017: https://madison.com/wsj/news/local/crime-and-courts/beloit-college-student-arrested-for-falsely-reporting-bias-incident-police/article_52bafd90-dff8-56be-b3ea-2b6d1dfea5ac.html.

CHAPTER 5

SEE NO EVIL, HEAR NO EVIL, SPEAK NO EVIL— UNLESS YOU'RE IN THE MEDIA

"Just remember: what you're seeing and what you're reading is not what's happening."—President Donald Trump, July 24, 2018

Wherever there's conflict or even mass terror, you can depend on the news media to leap into action and sniff out the link to "privilege." The link is rarely found, but that won't stop reporters from making one up when it's not found.

During the Obama years, the media's immediate go-to villain in any mass shooting was the National Rifle Association, and coverage at least loosely involved a debate around guns and money in politics. Under President Trump, there's no debate about who is the villain and who is the victim. No, where there's violence or contention, it is invariably assumed to be rooted in bigotry stirred up by Trump and his supporters. They, in all of their working class glory, are portrayed by America's culture fascists as the emblem of privilege.

A responsible news media might at least wait twenty-four hours before blaming a mass shooting, or even just a heated argument, on Trump and his millions of supporters. But we don't have a responsible news media. We have the American news media and we have the social justice cult.

They go through the same formula time and time again. No matter what controversy or day of the week, the national media remain ever certain that there's a vast swath of white supremacists (usually Trump supporters) and anti-Semites (usually Trump supporters) menacing the innocent.

It happens all of the time and the outcome is always the same, most notably in the appalling tale of the kids of Covington Catholic High, an all-boys private school in Kentucky. The Covington students were maligned in the most shocking way by liberal social media mobs, Democratic lawmakers, celebrities, and journalists, all of them having eagerly pushed a lie about the Covington kids because it had looked bad for Trump and his supporters—the "privileged."

On January 19, 2019, a video surfaced online showing a group of the Covington kids in Washington, D.C., for the annual antiabortion March for Life protest. They wore MAGA hats and appeared to taunt an elderly American Indian in front of the Lincoln Memorial. One student, a white boy named Nick Sandmann, was seen standing just inches from the face of Nathan Phillips, an Indian of the Omaha people. Phillips was attending the Indigenous Peoples March protest held that same day.

While Phillips banged a traditional Indian drum, Sandmann stared at him with what was viewed by the press who saw the short video as a self-satisfied smirk. The scene, with the other students circling both Sandmann and Phillips, was framed by the media as a group of self-entitled, private-school teens intimidating an elderly Indian.

The video quickly went viral on social media, garnering thousands of views within minutes. Opinionated dorks on Twitter weighed in, and writeups of the video popped up on every political news website.

"Teens in Make America Great Again hats taunted a Native American elder at the Lincoln Memorial," CNN reported at the time.[137]

A BuzzFeed article said, "Several viral videos show the young men, nearly all of whom are white and wearing pro-Trump gear, chanting at and mocking the man on the steps of the Lincoln Memorial."[138]

Ruth Graham at the liberal website *Slate* noted "the physical contrast between the young white punk and the Native elder, and between the teen's cruelty and Phillips' calm."[139]

Laura Wagner at the liberal sports and culture website Deadspin captured the privileged-victim sentiment neatly, writing that, "If you wanted to compress the history of relations between the powerful and the powerless in America, or the dynamics of the current moment, into a single image, you couldn't do much better than to present a white teen in a MAGA hat, surrounded by a screaming horde of his peers, smirking into the face of an old Native American man."[140]

Jessica Valenti, a feminist author who's been published in the *New York Times*, tweeted that the "defining image of this political era will be that smug white MAGA teen disrespecting a Native elder and veteran."[141] Perhaps feeling particularly hormonal, Valenti tweeted moments

137 David Williams, "Teens in Make America Great Again hats taunted a Native American elder at the Lincoln Memorial," CNN, Jan. 19, 2019: https://web.archive.org/web/20190120014635/https://www.cnn.com/2019/01/19/us/teens-mock-native-elder-trnd/index.html.

138 Julia Reinstein, "The MAGA Hat–Wearing Teens Who Taunted A Native American Elder Could Be Expelled," BuzzFeed, Jan 19, 2019: https://web.archive.org/web/20190120010213/https://www.buzzfeednews.com/article/juliareinstein/teens-taunted-native-american-elder-indigenous-peoples-march.

139 Ruth Graham, "The MAGA Teenager Who Harassed a Native American Veteran Is Still Unnamed, but We've Seen His Face Before," *Slate*, Jan. 19, 2019: https://slate.com/news-and-politics/2019/01/maga-teenager-native-american-veteran-harassment-smile.html.

140 Laura Wagner, "Don't Doubt What You Saw With Your Own Eyes," Deadspin, Jan. 21, 2019: https://theconcourse.deadspin.com/dont-doubt-what-you-saw-with-your-own-eyes-1831931203.

141 Jessica Valenti, Twitter.com, Jan. 19, 2019: https://twitter.com/JessicaValenti/status/1086761623103176704.

later that she had not "stopped thinking about that MAGA kid all day" because "so many of us have been on the receiving end of the face he was making: a smug, untouchable, entitled 'fuck you'."[142] May a deeply internalized smirk be the worst thing that happens to poor Valenti.

Yet, in a third tweet, Valenti wrote, "And let's please not forget that this group of teens who crowded around to mock & harass Nathan Phillips were there for the March for Life: There is an inextricable link between control over women's bodies, white supremacy & young white male entitlement."[143] (All three tweets by Valenti were subsequently deleted.)

Making the Covington kids look like even bigger assholes than before, news reports described Phillips, the drum banger, as a Vietnam War veteran.

After that, Democrats, journalists, and liberal celebrities reacted with haste to further condemn the Covington kids.

Representative Deb Haaland, Democrat of New Mexico, tweeted, "This Veteran put his life on the line for our country. The students' display of blatant hate, disrespect, and intolerance is a signal of how common decency has decayed under this administration. Heartbreaking."[144]

Liberal activist Alyssa Milano tweeted that the red MAGA hat "is the new white hood." She added that, "Without white boys being able to empathize with other people, humanity will continue to destroy itself."[145]

BuzzFeed reporter Anne Helen Petersen said that Sandmann's face bore "the look of white patriarchy."[146]

---

142   Jessica Valenti, Twitter.com, Jan. 19, 2019: https://twitter.com/jessicavalenti/
        status/1086762000384962560.

143   Jessica Valenti, Twitter.com, Jan. 19, 2019: https://twitter.com/JessicaValenti/
        status/1086766198128291841.

144   Deb Haaland, Twitter.com, Jan. 19, 2019: https://twitter.com/
        RepDebHaaland/status/1086662398071566337.

145   Alyssa Milano, Twitter.com, Jan. 20, 2019: https://twitter.com/Alyssa_Milano/
        status/1087021713651421184.

146   Anne Helen Petersen, Twitter.com, Jan. 20, 2019: https://twitter.com/
        annehelen/status/1087140834946953216.

CNN's Ana Navarro, a Republican who hates Trump and still weeps about Jeb Bush's defeat in 2016, cut to the chase. Rather than consider whether she might have missed any nuance in the situation, she called the high-school minors racist.[147]

Spokespeople for American Indians also came out to censure the Covington kids. Chase Iron Eyes, an attorney representing the Lakota People's Law Project, said the incident qualified as an assault. The students, he said, "were very loud and very aggressive, very vocal, and they were disrupting."[148]

The trail of tears never ends.

Overwhelming criticism led the school and the Diocese of Covington to reprimand the students in a public statement. "We condemn the actions of the Covington Catholic High School Students toward Nathan Phillips specifically, and Native Americans in general," the joint statement said. "This behavior is opposed to the Church's teachings on the dignity and respect of the human person. The matter is being investigated and we will take appropriate action, up to and including expulsion."[149]

That didn't satisfy Kathy Griffin, the perpetually out-of-work comedienne, who demanded the individual identities and locations of each of the kids in the video. She called the statement from the diocese "pathetic" and called on the students' school to publicly name "these fuckers." "I want NAMES. Shame them," she wrote on Twitter.[150]

---

147 Tweet by Ana Navarro, published in article by Ashe Schow, Daily Wire, Jan. 21, 2019: https://www.dailywire.com/news/42441/blue-checkmarks-delete-tweets-defaming-covington-ashe-schow.

148 "S.E. Cupp Unfiltered," CNN, Jan. 19, 2019: https://www.mediaite.com/tv/indigenous-peoples-march-spox-speaks-out-after-teens-mob-native-elder-trump-is-giving-license-to-this-behavior/.

149 Allison Elyse Gualtieri, "School, diocese condemn behavior of teens who harassed Native American veteran," *Washington Examiner*, Jan. 19, 2019: https://www.washingtonexaminer.com/news/school-diocese-condemn-behavior-of-teens-who-harassed-native-american-veteran.

150 Kathy Griffin, Twitter.com, Jan. 20, 2019: https://twitter.com/kathygriffin/status/1086927762634399744.

Unfortunately for everyone who so eagerly weighed in, a longer clip of the incident disproved the quickly established narrative. It wasn't white high school kids facing down a peaceful, elderly American Indian after all. It was, in fact, Phillips who was inflaming the situation after a group of Black Hebrew Israelites began hurling insults at everyone on the spot.

The Black Hebrew Israelites are known throughout Washington for verbally harassing virtually anyone who passes them by. They're a black fringe group with a mission not worth explaining, but their key qualities are anti-Semitism, homophobia, and chauvinism.

In other words, the Black Hebrew Israelites are everything social justice acolytes would hate but refuse to acknowledge. They can't recognize it because this specific group is made up of black people. Case in point, a January 2019 *New York Times* profile, in earnest, described the Black Hebrew Israelites this way: "They shout, use blunt and sometimes offensive language, and gamely engage in arguments aimed at drawing listeners near." It further summed up their ideology as "uncomfortable doctrine."[151] Wow, that sounds fairly harmless. It's a free country after all!

And yet, here are some things the Black Hebrew Israelites shouted at the Covington high school kids:

- "Bring your cracker ass up here. Dirty ass crackers, your day coming."

- "You crackers are some slithery ass bastards. You better keep your distance."

- "Look at these dirty-ass crackers. You're a bunch of future school-shooters. You crackers are crazy."

---

151   John Eligon, "Hebrew Israelites See Divine Intervention in Lincoln Memorial Confrontation," *New York Times*, Jan. 23, 2019: https://www.nytimes.com/2019/01/23/us/black-hebrew-israelites-covington-catholic.html.

- "Your president is a homosexual."
- "It says on the back of the dollar bill that 'In God We Trust,' and you give faggots rights."
- And this is what the Black Hebrew Israelites said to the American Indians:
- "It's always your women coming up with their loud mouth… thinking they can come and distract things with their loud-ass mouth, because they're not used to dealing with real men."
- "You ain't no child of God. You are the Indian. You are a blue-eyed demon. That's the last Mohican."
- "You're still worshipping totem poles."
- "A damn buffalo ain't gonna save you."
- "You're a bunch of Uncle Tomahawks."

At the *New York Times*, this is apparently what one does when "gamely engaging" in "uncomfortable doctrine" with random passersby.

People who live in Washington know that the Black Hebrew Israelites are weird and should only be ignored. But for anyone visiting the city, it's a jarring experience to take a stroll down the sidewalk, only to be confronted by someone yelling, "Faggot."

The Covington kids began chanting their school's fight song to drown out the hate—excuse me, "uncomfortable doctrine"—flung at them by the Black Hebrew Israelites. That's when Phillips approached them to obnoxiously pound on his drum and chant in their faces. I don't know about you, but that's exactly what I do when trying to lower the temperature in a heated situation.

"There was a disturbance there on the Lincoln Monument grounds," Phillips told CNN afterward in describing the scene. "We were finishing up with Indigenous Peoples March and rally and there were some folks there that were expressing their rights there, freedom of speech…. Then there was this young group of young students that came there and were offended by [the Black Hebrew Israelites'] speech, and it escalated into an ugly situation that I found myself in the middle of. Yeah, I found myself in the middle of it, sort of woke up to it."[152]

By "found myself in the middle of it," and "sort of woke up to it," Phillips presumably meant he deliberately marched into a crowd of teenagers while hammering away on a drum, as clearly seen on video. Phillips "found" himself "in the middle of it," the same way Larry Craig found himself in a wide stance in an airport men's room.

Phillips also said that the students had been "looking for trouble."

Either he lied about his version of events, or he suffers from serious narcolepsy to have woken up in the middle of a crowd chanting and heaving away at a drumskin.

Phillips is not, as had been widely reported, a "war veteran." He served in the Marines, and God bless him for that, but did not see combat. The *New York Times*, *Washington Post*, and CNN all retracted their initial descriptions of him as a Vietnam War veteran, which put the national news organizations in great danger of earning reputations as Indian givers.

When the truth about Phillips and the Black Hebrew Israelites came out, the media, Hollywood, and the Twitter mob didn't recant and go away. They either deleted their social media comments attacking the Covington kids as if they had never happened, came up with a different reason to hate the high schoolers, or explained that, well, there's still a lot of Trump-related racism even if the kids weren't guilty of it themselves. The aftermath provided a spectacular window into how the national media operate: *Hey, look! These people got some attention, and even if it's for nothing, let's pick their lives apart!*

---

152 Sara Sidner, "Native American elder Nathan Phillips, in his own words," CNN, Jan. 21, 2019: https://www.cnn.com/2019/01/21/us/nathan-phillips-maga-teens-interview/index.html.

The *New York Daily News* dug up an old photograph of Covington Catholic High students in "blackface" at a basketball game.[153] It turned out that the photo had been taken at what is commonly known as a "blackout" game, at which students are encouraged to wear top-to-bottom black.[154]

NBC dug deep and found a gay college kid to complain about a supposedly toxic culture at Covington Catholic High. "Gay valedictorian banned from speaking at Covington graduation 'not surprised' by D.C. controversy," read the story's headline. But the kid, Christian Bales, didn't even go to Covington Catholic High. He went to Holy Cross High, a school that was nearly two hours away. NBC was able to link him to Covington only because both schools are overseen by the same diocese.[155] That's not a particularly strong connection, but that's okay. So long as it reinforced the narrative about privilege in the Covington story.

The network also aired a one-on-one interview with Nick Sandmann, but that wasn't any better. Savannah Guthrie conducted the sit-down and, even after the world could see that the Covington kids weren't at fault in the original incident, here were some of the questions she had for Sandmann:

---

153 "SEE IT: Covington Catholic High students in blackface at past basketball game," *New York Daily News*, Jan. 21, 2019: https://www.nydailynews.com/news/national/ny-sports-covington-nathan-phillips-nick-sandmann-20190121-story.html.

154 Becket Adams, "New York Daily News searches desperately for real dirt on Covington students, accuses them of 'blackface,'" *Washington Examiner*, Jan. 22, 2019: https://www.washingtonexaminer.com/opinion/new-york-daily-news-searches-desperately-for-real-dirt-on-covington-students-accuses-them-of-blackface.

155 Ben Kesslen, "Gay valedictorian banned from speaking at Covington graduation 'not surprised' by D.C. controversy," NBC News, Jan. 22, 2019: https://www.nbcnews.com/feature/nbc-out/gay-valedictorian-banned-speaking-covington-graduation-not-surprised-d-c-n961446.

- "Do you feel from this experience that you owe anybody an apology?"

- "Do you see your own faults?"

- "Do you think if you weren't wearing that [Make America Great Again] hat, this might not have happened or it might have been different?"

- "There's something aggressive about standing there, standing your ground."[156]

- "Do you regret killing your girlfriend and hiding her body in the school cafeteria freezer?"

Okay, she didn't actually ask that last one, but the sentiment is the same. Over and over again, Guthrie suggested that Sandmann, a teenager, should feel guilty for a situation he hadn't instigated, couldn't have controlled, and for which he should never have been held accountable.

For the journalists who conceded that the Covington story wasn't at all as originally portrayed, it was striking to watch them become suddenly so thoughtful, with a renewed view of the world and human nature in all its complexities. It's the same thing they do when they immediately assume any act of violence must be linked to President Trump or the right, only to find out that the perpetrator was either mentally ill or, worse, a Democrat. Journalists believe that if they can't blame their intended target, there must at least be an equal amount of shame for everyone.

It was the media and the Twitter mob, an exclusively liberal phenomenon, that pushed the false narrative that a bunch of white, privileged kids were attempting to intimidate a defenseless minority. Yet *New York Times* columnist Frank Bruni somehow found equal

---

156 *Today*, NBC, Jan. 22, 2019: https://www.today.com/news/nick-sandmann-encounter-native-american-elder-nathan-phillips-i-respect-t147217.

fault in conservatives who drew attention to those who had perpetuated the lie. "Some conservatives are gleeful about how this went down," wrote Bruni. "But isn't their vengeful joy its own rushed celebration, its own self-serving simplification of a complex sequence of events?"[157]

Why, no, Frank, it was neither "rushed" nor "self-serving" for anyone to identify the inaccuracy of the mob's portrayal of events—and especially not after the media pushed the fake story for nearly two full days, besmirching the reputations of the Covington kids. Not only was it not "rushed" for honest people to get the truth out, but it couldn't come fast enough. Had the lie persisted for any longer, who knows what could have happened to any of the students identified in the video? Within twenty-four hours after the initial clip circled online, Sandmann had become the media's poster child for white male privilege and Kathy Griffin was calling on the mob to name and shame the students. Even if conservatives were "gleeful" about the truth coming out, that's better than how liberals reacted to the original lie. They weren't gleeful. They wanted to see Sandmann punched in the face—literally. Reza Aslan, a formerly respected religion critic, was one of the media people who weighed in on Twitter, describing Sandmann's face as "punchable."[158]

Jonathan Capehart at the *Washington Post* offered what should have been labeled a parody, but he was serious. If his aim was to prove that big-city liberals live in a bubble, incapable of understanding the life experiences of anyone outside of New York and Washington, he succeeded in epic fashion. Capehart wrote that the students and their chaperones, all of whom live in Kentucky, should have known better

---

157 Frank Bruni, "Covington and the pundit apocalypse," *New York Times*, Jan. 22, 2019: https://www.nytimes.com/2019/01/22/opinion/covington-teenagers-twitter.html.

158 Reza Aslan, Twitter.com, Jan. 19, 2019: https://twitter.com/rezaaslan/status/1086806539552284672.

than to cross paths with the Black Hebrew Israelites. According to victim-blamer Capehart, it was the visiting students' fault that they were verbally harassed by an onslaught of hatred from the Black Hebrew Israelites. "If the ranting and raving Black Hebrew Israelites are the kind of folks who necessitate my crossing the street or altering my path before I make it into their line of sight, why would the Covington kids and their minders think it's okay to engage crazy, hateful people raising hell in a national park?" he wrote, well after it was clear that the Covington controversy was the exact opposite of what it had initially appeared. "They should have ignored the Black Hebrew Israelites the way most everyone else does."[159]

Recall that the incident with the Covington kids took place on the grounds of the Lincoln Memorial. Nearly every single tourist who comes to Washington visits that site, and yet Capehart was insisting that doing so was tantamount to asking for trouble.

The Lincoln Memorial is one of the most recognizable landmarks in America. It's a place you can reasonably expect tourists to visit. Why would anyone outside of Washington expect to be confronted at the monument by a little-known black nationalist cult?

Capehart couldn't acknowledge reality, so instead he made up an absurd excuse to continue blaming the real victims. That's how social justice operates. If the facts are inconvenient, make up a new reason to shake down the "privileged."

Had Nick Sandmann been black, his life would have without question been a lot easier than it was after the video that day went viral. The whole thing would have never been a national controversy. We would have never heard about it, because it wouldn't have fit what

---

159 Jonathan Capehart, "Nothing justifies what the Covington students did," *Washington Post*, Jan. 22, 2019: https://www.washingtonpost.com/opinions/ 2019/01/23/nothing-justifies-what-covington-students-did/?utm_term=. 09998737f2d8.

social justice teaches—white males (especially Trump supporters) are the current root of all oppression. Liberals in the news media eagerly embrace and weaponize that idea with every new story that has even the smallest connection to race, gender, or sexuality. If no connection exists, they make one up.

The Covington case was essentially the same thing the media did in 2017 with James Hodgkinson after he shot up a field where Republicans had been practicing baseball. Had Hodgkinson been a Republican, the media would ensure that the blame rested squarely on the shoulders of white men, conservatives, and Trump supporters. Hodgkinson was white but he wasn't a Republican and he wasn't a Trump supporter. He was a Democrat who supported Bernie Sanders and hated Trump. When those details trickled out, well, "both sides" were made to bear some responsibility for that violent episode.

On June 14, 2017, Hodgkinson pulled up to a field in northern Virginia where some Republican congressmen and their staffers were practicing for the annual congressional baseball game. He asked GOP representatives Ron DeSantis and Jeff Duncan as they left the field early whether it was Republicans or Democrats that were there practicing.

"He was just a normal guy," recalled Duncan. "He says, 'Excuse me sir, can you tell me whether these are Democrats or Republicans practicing?' I said, 'This is a Republican team', he said 'OK,' [and went] back toward home plate."[160]

Thereafter, Hodgkinson, a man in his late sixties, picked up a semi-automatic rifle and entered the field, where he fired round after round. He critically wounded Representative Steve Scalise of Louisiana and injured U.S. Capitol police officer Crystal Griner, as well as congressional aide Zack Barth. Matt Mika, a lobbyist, was also shot.

160 Gabrielle Levy, "Lawmakers Say They're Sure They Spoke to Gunman," *U.S. News and World Report*, June 14, 2017: https://www.usnews.com/news/national-news/articles/2017-06-14/duncan-desantis-we-spoke-to-scalise-shooter-james-hodgkinson.

Griner was shot in the ankle, Barth in the leg, and Mika in the chest.[161]

A bullet went into Scalise's pelvis and through several organs and bones, requiring intensive surgery.[162] He survived and now walks with a cane.

The motivation is clear. Hodgkinson hated Republicans and Trump in particular. He belonged to the Facebook groups Terminate the Republican Party and The Road To Hell Is Paved With Republicans. One note on his Facebook profile said, "It's Time to Destroy Trump & Co."[163]

"I know he wasn't happy with the way things were going, the election results and stuff," Hodgkinson's brother said after the shooting.[164]

A volunteer for the Bernie Sanders 2016 presidential campaign remembered having worked on the campaign with Hodgkinson in Iowa.[165]

The proof that Hodgkinson was a liberal Democrat was irrefutable. But why should that have stopped the media from evenly dealing out the blame for us all to shoulder?

---

161 Rachel Bade, Theodoric Meyer, John Lauinger, and Kyle Cheney, "Who were the people injured at Wednesday's baseball practice shooting?" Politico, June 14, 2017: https://www.politico.com/story/2017/06/14/victims-congress-baseball-shooting-239564.

162 Melissa Chan, "Steve Scalise Was Shot at a Congressional Baseball Practice. Here's What You Need to Know," *Time*, June 14, 2017: http://time.com/4817818/steve-scalise-alexandria-shooting/.

163 "Congressional Shooter Recently Wrote, 'It's Time To Destroy Trump & Co,'" TheSmokingGun.com, June 14, 2017: http://www.thesmokinggun.com/buster/james-t-hodgkinson/congressional-baseball-shooter-729035.

164 Nicholas Fandos, "Virginia Shooting Suspect Was Distraught Over Trump's Election, Brother Says," *New York Times*, June 14, 2017: https://www.nytimes.com/2017/06/14/us/politics/virginia-shooting-suspect-james-hodgkinson.html?action=Click&contentCollection=BreakingNews&contentID=65436420&pgtype=article&smid=tw-nytimes&smtyp=cur&_r=1.

165 Robert Costa, "Acquaintance describes campaigning for Bernie Sanders with shooting suspect," *Washington Post*, June 14, 2017.

A bemused editorial in the *Washington Post* asked, "Who knows what mixture of madness and circumstance causes someone to pick up a gun and go on a rampage?"[166]

Hodgkinson hated Trump and had specifically targeted Republicans to shoot while they were practicing baseball. But "who knows" what that whole thing was about?! It's apparently still a mystery for the *Post*'s editorial board.

In the face of all evidence that Hodgkinson was a left-winger who supported Sanders for the 2016 Democratic nomination, and that he was motivated to go on a shooting rampage by his own political frustrations, *New York Times* political reporter Glenn Thrush looked for Trump to claim responsibility.

"Any debate about civility in politics begins with Trump," Thrush tweeted at the time of the shooting. "No one has degraded discourse more, while embracing the fringe."[167]

Whatever "fringe" Trump appeals to, no one in it has ever picked up a rifle intending to gun down multiple members of Congress. That was a Bernie bro.

In an effort to split the difference between the GOP and Democrats, the *New York Times* chalked up the crazed shooting to some vague idea of "vicious American politics." Well, that's very bipartisan sounding. But then the *Times* made sure to repeat the claim that "the link to political incitement was clear" between 2008 GOP vice presidential candidate Sarah Palin and the 2011 shooting of Democratic representative Gabrielle Giffords. You see, when a Republican can be blamed, "the link to political incitement" is "clear." But when the fault

---

166   Editorial Board, "The shooting at a GOP baseball practice was an assault on democracy," *Washington Post*, June 14, 2017: https://www.washingtonpost.com/opinions/the-shooting-at-a-gop-baseball-practice-was-an-assault-on-democracy/2017/06/14/06587d9a-5131-11e7-91eb-9611861a988f_story.html.

167   Glenn Thrush, Twitter.com, June 15, 2017: https://twitter.com/glennthrush/status/875333573984866304?lang=en.

lies squarely with Democrats, well, that's simply a matter of "vicious American politics" with no clear party association.

As for that line about the shooting of Gabrielle Giffords, however, readers with fresher memories reminded the *Times* that the "clear" link between Palin and the incident was established to have been a lie nearly ten years ago. The paper later removed that part from its editorial, and added a note at the bottom admitting that there actually was "no such link."[168]

All evidence indicated that Hodgkinson was a partisan Democrat who acted out because of a political grudge over the 2016 election. But a willfully clueless Scott Pelley of *CBS Evening News* ended his program a day after the shooting by decrying nonspecific "leaders and political commentators" for having "led us into an abyss of violent rhetoric." He then somberly declared that it was "time for all of us—presidents, politicians, reporters, citizens, all of us—to pause to think again."[169]

Democrats and their friends in the media have anticipated Trump-inspired violence ever since he launched his first campaign in 2015. And yet, when a liberal activist opens fire on a group of Republicans practicing baseball, we're all supposed to take responsibility for the "abyss of violent rhetoric."

No, no, no, no, no. One person was responsible for the shooting, and he was a Democrat. It was not "time for all of us to pause and think again" just because the facts were inconvenient for liberals. Liberals were right about predicting political violence. What they got wrong was which side it would come from.

And yet, the belief that any day there would be mass blood shed by a Trump-inspired (white) terrorist lived on.

---

168   Editorial board, "America's lethal politics," *New York Times*, June 14, 2017: https://www.nytimes.com/2017/06/14/opinion/steve-scalise-congress-shot-alexandria-virginia.html.

169   Scott Pelley, *Evening News*, CBS, June 15, 2017.

On June 28, 2018, Jarrod Ramos, a man in his late thirties, used a shotgun to blast open the glass doors of the *Capital Gazette* newspaper offices in Annapolis, Maryland. He barricaded the back door to prevent anyone inside from fleeing and then opened fire in the newsroom, killing five people.[170]

Liberals immediately and predictably blamed the shooting on Trump, not because he had ever called for violence against any news media outlet but because, unlike every other Republican, he dared to respond to the overwhelmingly unfair reporting regarding the 2016 campaign and his administration.

The news media honestly believe it was the beginning of the end of democracy for Trump to call them "fake news" and "enemy of the people."

The monster.

This is in contrast to the things said about Trump on cable news on a minute-by-minute basis: "racist," "sexist," "Nazi," "bigot," "white supremacist," "pig"—and that's just when Ana Navarro is on the air.

The news cycle is basically a twenty-four-hour roast of the president and all of his supporters, but we're supposed to believe that the president's sophomoric "fake news" tease is an irreparable debasement of the national dialogue. This is how journalists in Washington and New York think the First Amendment works: It protects their right to say absolutely anything, but some people—even a president they hate and who they believe is illegitimate—should never feel entitled to exercise that same right.

Lauren Duca, a genuine dope who wrote columns for *Teen Vogue* and who somehow landed a job teaching journalism at New York University, tweeted that the *Capital Gazette* shooting "cannot reasonably be separated from the President's mission to villainize the press as 'the enemy of the American people.'"[171]

170 Timothy Williams and Amy Harmon, "Maryland Shooting Suspect Had Long-Running Dispute With Newspaper," *New York Times*, June 29, 2018: https://www.nytimes.com/2018/06/29/us/jarrod-ramos-annapolis-shooting.html.

171 Lauren Duca, Twitter.com, June 28, 2018: https://twitter.com/laurenduca/status/1012429565111791616.

Andrew Feinberg writes for the obscurest of online blogs but nonetheless has a pass for the White House press briefing room. "You caused this, Mr. President," he tweeted the day of the shooting.[172] (Question: Why does any lunatic bother jumping the White House fence to get on the premises when, as demonstrated by Feinberg, they're allowed in the front door with a press pass?)

David Simon, creator of HBO's *The Wire* series, which takes place in Baltimore, also blamed Trump for the *Gazette* shooting and summoned his renowned writing skills to call the president a "vile, fascist son of a bitch."[173]

Rob Cox, an editor at Reuters, tweeted, "This is what happens when @realDonaldTrump calls journalists the enemy of the people. Blood is on your hands, Mr. President."[174]

Within hours of the shooting, it was made clear that, once again, the incident wasn't even remotely linked to Trump or the White House or anything the president had said about the media.

Ramos hadn't been inspired to act against the "fake news," which should have been evident from his choice to target a small local newsroom rather than, say, the *New York Times* or the *Washington Post*. His motive was a long-simmering grudge against the *Capital Gazette* dating back to 2011. The paper had covered a harassment suit brought against Ramos by a former high school classmate. Ramos had been sending her threatening emails and even called her employers on the phone to tell them to fire her.[175]

---

172 Andrew Feinberg, Twitter.com, June 28, 2018: https://twitter.com/ andrewfeinberg/status/1012438187510296576?lang=en.

173 David Simon, Twitter.com, June 28, 2018: https://twitter.com/aodespair/status /1012441981920915464?lang=en.

174 Mandy Mayfield, "Reuters editor apologizes for calling out Trump for anti-press rhetoric after Annapolis newsroom shooting," *Washington Examiner*, June 29, 2018: https://www.washingtonexaminer.com/news/ reuters-editor-apologizes-trump-anti-press-rhetoric-capital-gazette-shooting.

175 Timothy Williams and Amy Harmon, "Maryland Shooting Suspect Had Long-Running Dispute With Newspaper," *New York Times*, June 29, 2018: https:// www.nytimes.com/2018/06/29/us/jarrod-ramos-annapolis-shooting.html.

Ramos pleaded guilty to the harassment charge, and after his case was reported in the *Gazette*, he sued the paper in 2012, alleging that he had been defamed. The claim was dismissed. He appealed the decision, and another court upheld the dismissal.

Unsuccessful in the courts, Ramos turned his harassment toward the newspaper, calling its offices and sending more threatening letters. He also taunted the paper's employees and publisher by name on social media. He sent antagonistic notes to Maryland's Court of Special Appeals, one to a Baltimore judge, and one to a lawyer who had previously represented the *Gazette*. The letter sent to the lawyer was dated June 28, the day of the shooting, and Ramos said in it that he was heading to the paper's newsroom "with the objective of killing every person present."[176]

There was not a whiff of evidence that would connect Trump or anything he had said to the shooting. Yet more than a month later, the *Columbia Journalism Review*, a magazine about the journalism industry, continued spreading the myth. "[W]ith the memory of June's shooting at the *Capital Gazette* in Annapolis fresh in everyone's mind," an article in the magazine said, "the rising tide of hatred toward the press at Trump rallies has taken on a new dimension."[177]

Journalists and the rest of the grievance industry keep up the lie that Trump and his backers are responsible for widespread violence even when all evidence is to the contrary. It's the best way to reinforce the notion that the "privileged" are deserving of only resentment and scorn.

On the morning of October 27, 2018, Robert Bowers, a heavyset forty-eight-year-old, burst through the doors of the Tree of Life

---

176   Ian Duncan and Talia Richman, "Capital Gazette suspect allegedly mailed threatening letters before Thursday's shooting," *Baltimore Sun*, July 2, 2018: https://www.baltimoresun.com/news/maryland/crime/bs-md-ramos-letters-20180702-story.html.

177   Pete Vernon, "A climate of hate toward the press at Trump rallies," *Columbia Journalism Review*, Aug. 2, 2018: https://www.cjr.org/the_media_today/trump-acosta-rally.php.

synagogue in Pittsburgh with an assault rifle. He pumped out round after round on the congregants, who had been worshipping in peace.

When police arrived, Bowers engaged them in a shootout at the door of the synagogue before retreating and barricading himself in a room on the building's third floor. The police chased him and he eventually surrendered, but only after he had killed eleven congregants and wounded several more.[178]

The bodies had only just cooled when the media leaped into action, blaming—who else?—Trump.

Washington Post columnist Eugene Robinson, the paper's worst writer, wrote two days later in response to the synagogue massacre that "'Both sides' are not responsible for the horrific political terrorism we have seen this past week." He continued, "Only the right is to blame—starting with President Trump and his complicit enablers in the Republican Party."[179]

This is what Robinson and so many of his media colleagues get paid to do: react with the worst take possible (even if it's a deliberate lie) and hope it pans out or that people forget about it once the facts prove them wrong.

The facts in this case would naturally prove Robinson wrong. Bowers was not registered with any political party, according to the Associated Press.[180] He spent his days on a social media platform called Gab airing out his festering hatred for Jews and the people who don't his share

---

178 Campbell Robertson, Christopher Mele, and Sabrina Tavernise, "11 Killed in Synagogue Massacre; Suspect Charged With 29 Counts," *New York Times*, Oct. 27, 2018: https://www.nytimes.com/2018/10/27/us/active-shooter-pittsburgh-synagogue-shooting.html.

179 Eugene Robinson, "Don't tell me that 'both sides' need to do better," *Washington Post*, Oct. 29, 2018: https://www.washingtonpost.com/opinions/dont-tell-me-that-both-sides-need-to-do-better/2018/10/29/78eb0d8e-dbb2-11e8-b732-3c72cbf131f2_story.html?noredirect=on&utm_term=.101a78498f39.

180 Michael Biesecker, Michael Kunzelman, and Michael Balsamo, "Suspect in synagogue slayings spewed online hate for Jews," Associated Press, Oct. 27, 2018: https://www.apnews.com/b1c50ba4f0964df89a266e490aea6961.

his antipathy. Among Bowers' ramblings on Gab were his feelings that Trump is "surrounded by kikes," that he's "a globalist, not a nationalist," and that "[t]here is no #MAGA as long as there is a kike infestation."

He explicitly said in one posting that he never supported the president.[181] "For the record, I did not vote for him, nor have I owned, worn or even touched a maga hat," Bowers wrote on Gab.

He wasn't a Trump supporter. In fact, he hated the president. He wasn't even a Republican.

But wait, Bowers *did* hate immigrants. And that's all the press needed to make the Trump connection.

Because Bowers had griped on Gab about the "caravans" of thousands of Central American migrants making their way to the U.S., Robinson and others in the media latched on and blamed Trump, who had also been warning about the caravan during rallies leading up to the 2018 midterms.

Robinson wrote in his column that "Bowers was fixated on the so-called caravan of Central American migrants, which Trump and the Republicans have cynically exploited to drive turnout in the mid-term election."

CNN anchor Alisyn Camerota insisted that "You can draw a direct line from all of the vitriol and hate rhetoric about the caravan that's some 2,000 miles away from our border and the gunman in Pittsburgh, who referenced that, and somehow turned it into an attack on Jews."[182]

No need to rewind that bit on DVR to make sure you heard what Camerota said. You heard right. She said that there was a "direct line"

---

181 Saeed Ahmed and Paul P. Murphy, "Here's what we know so far about Robert Bowers, the Pittsburgh synagogue shooting suspect," CNN.com, Oct. 28, 2018: https://www.cnn.com/2018/10/27/us/synagogue-attack-suspect-robert-bowers-profile/index.html.

182 Katelyn Caralle, "CNN host: 'Direct line' between Trump rhetoric on immigration and synagogue massacre," *Washington Examiner*, Oct. 29, 2018: https://www.washingtonexaminer.com/news/cnn-host-direct-line-between-trump-rhetoric-on-immigration-and-synagogue-massacre.

between Trump's "hate rhetoric" about the caravan of Central Americans and the gunman, who "turned it into an attack on Jews." This is like if I were to blow up a Muslim mosque and then someone traced the attack to my intense distaste for Spanish food. It's stupid.

The Atlantic's Adam Serwer asserted that the "apparent spark" for the shooting was the caravan story, "inflamed by a U.S. president seeking to help his party win a midterm election." He wrote with certitude that "no political gesture, no public statement, and no alteration in rhetoric or behavior…will change this fact."[183]

Telepathist Joe Scarborough read into Trump's mind and said on his MSNBC show that the president's having held a campaign rally the same day as the shooting, in spite of the tragedy, "was done intentionally to send a message to white nationalists: 'This doesn't bug me that much.'"[184]

Washington Post opinion editor Ruth Marcus wrote that even though there wasn't "cause and effect" linking Trump directly to Bowers' shooting rampage, he at least bore a "moral culpability for creating this overheated climate of fear."[185]

Ah, yes. It is Trump creating an "overheated climate of fear" for pointing out the obscene numbers of migrants from poverty-stricken, gang-ridden countries marching their way to the U.S. border. *That's* what caused this all.

We might also start blaming weathermen for warning of oncoming category-five hurricanes.

Dealing with the media is a never-ending chore of refuting things made up out of nowhere. But here it goes: Bowers really was preoccupied with the caravan, but not because he had a sound criticism of

---

183 Adam Serwer, "Trump's Caravan Hysteria Led to This," *The Atlantic*, Oct. 28, 2018: https://www.theatlantic.com/amp/article/574213/.

184 Joe Scarborough, *Morning Joe*, MSNBC, Oct. 29, 2018.

185 Ruth Marcus, "Trump has stoked the fears of the Bowerses among us," *Washington Post*, Oct. 28, 2018: https://www.washingtonpost.com/opinions/trump-has-stoked-the-fears-of-the-bowerses-among-us/2018/10/28/2d4cc088-daf0-11e8-b3f0-62607289efee_story.html?utm_term=.1ec8fc92436e.

America's borderless immigration policy. He had no apparent thoughts on immigration at all. His fixation on the caravan was inspired by a bizarre conspiracy theory about it having been coordinated and funded by rich and powerful Jews.

That brings us back to the thing with Jews, the people whom Bowers believed Trump was too enmeshed with. For Bowers, everything was about Jews.

He was convinced that the caravan was a product of HIAS, the Hebrew Immigrant Aid Society, which provides aid to refugees. "HIAS likes to bring invaders in that kill our people," he said in a Gab post shortly before the killing spree. "I can't sit by and watch my people get slaughtered. Screw your optics, I'm going in."[186]

Incidentally, Trump has never spoken a single word about HIAS. But only the news media could listen to Trump ring the alarm over immigrants coming from shithole countries and find its true connection to a Pittsburgh synagogue shooting carried out by a crazed anti-Semite. Even when they acknowledge that there's no evidence to support their paranoid suspicions, journalists can still find a reason to blame Trump.

A day after the shooting, the always hysterical Julia Ioffe wrote that Trump's supporters "were at pains to point out that Robert D. Bowers…was in fact anti-Trump." She reasoned, however, that "Trump has had enough to say about the Jews that his supporters may easily make certain pernicious inferences."[187]

Her evidence? That Trump had once joked about not wanting money from the Republican Jewish Coalition—he had campaigned on

---

186   Katie Zezima and Wesley Lowery, "Suspected synagogue shooter appears to have railed against Jews, refugees online," *Washington Post*, Oct. 27, 2018: https://www.washingtonpost.com/national/suspected-synagogue-shooter-appears-to-have-railed-against-jews-refugees-online/2018/10/27/e99dd282-da18-11e8-a10f-b51546b10756_story.html?utm_term=.68979aacda98.

187   Julia Ioffe, "How much responsibility does Trump bear for the synagogue shooting in Pittsburgh?," *Washington Post*, Oct. 28, 2018: https://www.washingtonpost.com/outlook/2018/10/28/how-much-responsibility-does-trump-bear-synagogue-shooting-pittsburgh/?fbclid=IwAR0X8JF8vd8Y6EF1KuYL-gBHaPFwy61W9wG6esMidfFE0jCDgifDOXKTcDM&utm_term=.8d5fb12057e7.

not taking special interest money from anyone—and that she had once been on the receiving end of a bunch of anti-Semitic tweets.

Zzzz…anyone with even a modest public profile is subjected to harassment online. That Ioffe is Jewish makes no difference to me or anyone else who has experienced the same level of harassment. It comes with the territory.

With the media, it's always a game of heads, they win; tails, we lose. They cry rape and when there's no evidence of assault, they explain that, well, there *might* have been one if we had just waited a little longer.

Even four months later, when all the facts established that the synagogue shooter was not a Trump supporter and had not been inspired by the president in any way, Joe Scarborough was still linking the attack to the White House. "Who was the synagogue shooter inspired by?" Scarborough yelled at one of his mild-mannered guests in late February. "Who was the synagogue shooter inspired by, talking about the caravan?"[188]

To repeat, Bowers was not some immigration restrictionist harboring dreams to resurrect the confederacy. His grudge against the caravan was rooted in a fringe conspiracy about omniscient Jews hoping to overrun America with foreigners. (If Bowers weren't a deranged, mentally ill person, he might have recognized that no conspiracy is needed. The Democratic Party and the media advocate for this very thing in plain sight.)

For the media, anything can be true if they repeatedly lie about it. For a brief moment, the media also pushed the idea that a white supremacist apprehended in Maryland for plotting a mass terror attack was another Trump-inspired racist.

Coast Guard officer Christopher Hasson, age forty-nine, was arrested in February 2019 for plotting to kill several high-profile Democrats, journalists, and cable news personalities.

Read news reports about the arrest and you will certainly get the impression that he was, at least in some peripheral sense, a Trump

---

188   Joe Scarborough, *Morning Joe*, MSNBC, Feb. 21, 2019.

supporter.[189] But read the actual full court filing instead (which the media count on no one doing) and you get the truth. There was, once again, no evidence submitted by prosecutors to demonstrate that Hasson was a Trump fan.

Joe Scarborough was allegedly one of the people Hasson targeted. The court filing says that on December 27, 2018, Hasson searched the internet for information about Scarborough after reading a news story quoting Scarborough as having called Trump "the worst ever." Hasson then added Scarborough to a spreadsheet of names that included other Democrats and media personalities.[190]

Trump's name came up exactly twice in the court filing. Among the things Hasson searched the internet for on January 17, 2019 included "what if trump illegally impeached" and "civil war if trump impeached." Those details made it into news reports on Hasson's arrest by the *New York Times*, the *Washington Post*, NBC News, and others. Still, the motivation for Hasson's unrealized roughshod plan for "complete destruction," as he wrote in his own emails, wasn't Trump. The court document shows that the motivation was a preoccupation with race and a nihilistic view that had no clear attachment to partisan politics at all, outside of an unspecified antipathy for "liberalist/globalist ideology."

To put it plainly, Hasson was crazy. Sometimes, it really is as simple as that.

According to prosecutors, Hasson wrote in an email drafted June 2, 2017, "I am dreaming of a way to kill almost every last person on the earth." That's quite an aspiration, but he was at least lucid enough to acknowledge that to come close, he would need "the unwitting help

---

189   Diana Stancy Correll, "Prosecutors say Coast Guard officer was plotting mass murder in service of a 'white homeland,'" *Washington Examiner*, Feb. 20, 2019: https://www.washingtonexaminer.com/news/prosecutors-say-coast-guard-officer-was-plotting-mass-murder-in-service-of-a-white-homeland.

190   United States of America v. Christopher Paul Hasson, Motion for Detention Pending Trial, Feb. 19, 2019: https://drive.google.com/file/d/1wl1WR4NJ95llQmNo7bmfVg6pvrq-cgzX/view

of another power/country." He faulted "liberalist/globalist ideology" for "destroying traditional peoples esp[ecially] white" ones. His preferred method for what he called "complete destruction" was a mass plague of disease or a poison.

Later in the email, he wrote to himself, "Read and get education have to move to friendly area and start to organize. Get leadership within the community, sheriff, city manager, mayor, lawyer?" (It's unclear whether his campaign for mayor or his career as a lawyer would begin before or after the extermination of the human race.)

He also wrote that he wanted to "start small" by learning "basic chemistry."

A little later, you get to the part of the email that makes sense of his interest in the potential impeachment of Trump or, otherwise, some civil war that might result from something that happens during Trump's presidency. "Look up tactics used during Ukrainian civil war," Hasson wrote. "During unrest target both sides to increase tension. In other words provoke [government]/police to over react which should help to escalate violence. [Black Lives Matter] protests or other left crap would be ideal to incite to violence."

Hasson didn't care about Trump's presidency or his political agenda. He cared about using Trump as a means to his end. He was looking for a catalyst that would spark his fanaticized chaos. He saw potential for mayhem in the impeachment of Trump, should it be driven by partisan Democrats. Hasson believed such an event would spark his twisted dream, which apparently included the violent death of everyone, becoming town sheriff, and then eventually learning the periodic table.

The court filing says that in September 2017, Hasson wrote to an unnamed "known American neo-Nazi leader" to say, "We need a white homeland." But that wish wasn't inspired by Trump either. It was the 2011 terrorist attacks in Norway carried out by far-right activist Anders Behring Breivik. Prosecutors said that "from early 2017 through the date of his arrest [February 15], the defendant routinely perused portions of the Breivik manifesto that instruct a prospective assailant to amass appropriate firearms, food, disguises, and survival supplies."

Guess what animated Breivik to detonate a bomb at a summer camp in Norway, blowing up eight people? Hint: It's not Trump. The fact that the terror attack happened in 2011, four years before Trump's official campaign for president, should be a clue.

Nowhere outside of Hasson's two internet searches for Trump and "impeachment," and Trump and "civil war" is the president mentioned at all. Not once. There was the search for info on Scarborough after the host criticized Trump, but that indicates only that Hasson used criticism of Trump as a way of gauging who fit his hazy idea of "liberalist/globalist" ideology.

Hasson said nothing about fake news, nothing about making America great again. He said nothing coherent about immigrants, Muslims, or Jews. He only harbored hatred for nonwhites and a dim hope that someday he might kill a lot of "liberalist/globalists." He also had aspirations to run for city council and to get a better grasp of chemical science.

That doesn't sound like a true-believing Trump supporter. It sounds like a mental wreck. And that's exactly what all evidence suggests that Hasson is. Hasson is yet another item on the long list of "Trump-inspired hatred" that never was.

⌘　⌘　⌘

The supposed "surge in right-wing extremist violence" or "rise of white supremacist violence" are yet more media fabrications.

Whenever there's a terrorist attack committed by a Muslim fanatic, the media invariably attribute the carnage to a "lone wolf." But the second an attack is found to have been perpetrated by a white male, it's assumed to be yet more evidence of "right-wing extremism on the rise."

On June 17, 2019, twenty-two-year-old U.S. Army veteran Brian Isaack Clyde fired shots outside a federal courthouse building in Dallas.

He was seen wearing a mask and dressed in military-style clothing, with additional ammunition stocked in a waist belt.[191] Police were able to shoot Clyde dead before anyone else was injured.

Some early reports on the gunman's social media activity more or less painted the picture of a geeky introvert, a young guy who enjoyed anime, was a fan (perhaps in irony) of internet conspiracy theorist Alex Jones, and who may have posted memes that featured the swastika. In short, he was an isolated kid who probably played a lot of video games.[192]

There was, of course, an immediate effort to portray the incident as more "right-wing violence."

The day after the shooting, Jake Tapper on CNN opened a segment questioning whether it "represents a growing threat in the U.S. of extremist right-wing violence." Though he admitted that an investigation was still underway, Tapper said that "what officials are finding" about the gunman "is pretty disturbing, including [social media posts] with Nazi imagery."

That "Nazi imagery" was actually a graphic Clyde published on Facebook depicting a warped political compass, the meaning of which was indecipherable, and a swastika next to "Libertarian national socialist green party."

A political compass is a matrix that aims to measure an individual's degree of liberal or authoritarian tendencies. There are online tests you can take that purport to show whether you're more libertarian or authoritarian on the economy or society or both and your results are placed somewhere on the matrix with the compass.

---

191   Martin Kaste, "Heavily Armed Gunman Shot Dead Outside Federal Courthouse In Dallas," NPR.org, June 18, 2019: https://www.npr.org/2019/06/18/733568066/dallas-police-fatally-shoot-heavily-armed-gunman-outside-federal-courthouse-buil.

192   Jasmine Aguilera, "Gunman Killed in Shootout After Opening Fire on Dallas Federal Courthouse," Time.com, June 17, 2019: https://time.com/5608396/gunman-shot-controlled-explosion-dallas-courthouse/.

The "Nazi" graphic Clyde posted on his Facebook page appears to have originated in April 2019 on a Reddit forum called "Political Compass Memes."[193] For context on how seriously a person can take this section of Reddit, other popular memes on the forum include a *King of the Hill* political compass, which uses images from the *King of the Hill* cartoon; a cursed-images political compass, which features a photo of a man dressed as a Teletubby; and a political compass of Eminem albums, which ranks the rapper's albums by level of economic and social authoritarianism.

Almost everything on the "Political Compass Memes" Reddit forum is posted as an inside joke for internet dorks, or is shared with a heightened sense of irony. No one who doesn't spend three-fourths of their day on the internet has heard of the "Libertarian National Socialist Green Party." It sounds like a joke. And that's probably intentional, because it more than likely *is* a joke. Run a search for it on Google, and you will find no concrete description for the Libertarian National Socialist Green Party, but you'll find plenty of people guessing what it is or assuming that it's, yes, a joke. Clyde shared the graphic on his Facebook page with the caption, "I have found the solution to all of our nation's political problems," which was also more than likely written in sarcasm. He posted a lot of memes on Facebook, including one with the wry caption, "When you see your girl talking to someone else but he only has 7 scars on his wrists."[194] The joke there is that a man could prove his superior virility by displaying how depressed he is.

Clyde also posted videos of himself on Facebook talking nonsense. In one, he looks down at the camera and says, "You dare underestimate

193   "Libertarian National Socialist Green Party," Reddit.com, April 9, 2019: https://www.reddit.com/r/PoliticalCompassMemes/comments/bbb0d4/ libertarian_national_socialist_green_party/.

194   Stephen Young, "Dallas Courthouse Shooting Suspect's Facebook Paints Picture of Weeks Prior to Shooting," DallasObserver. com, June 17, 2019: https://www.dallasobserver.com/news/ dallas-suspected-shooter-brian-isaack-clyde-facebook-page-11689472.

my power?" before gulping down a cup of some red liquid and then burping. That's the end of the video.

Yes, it's all weird. But, again, sometimes insanity is the bottom line. Not every violent act is six degrees separated from Trump.

But because the media don't care about context so long as they can sell the "right-wing violence" narrative, CNN's Dianne Gallagher called the Dallas shooting an example of "another young, white, American man" who had "launched an attack on the innocent." She said that Clyde spread hate on social media, citing the dumb political compass meme. She also said that Clyde's Facebook page contained Confederate flag memes.

The meme that Gallagher was referring to was a picture of two Shiba Inu dogs (often used in humorous memes), one with a Confederate flag-patterned cap superimposed on its head, the other looking sad as both stand in front of a truck that also has a Confederate flag painted on it. The meme's caption says, "Why did you spend my college funds on your truck dad?" The humor rests on the notion that a trashy parent would use his or her child's college savings to decorate a car with the Confederate flag. Guess where that meme was published? On a Reddit forum, more than a month before the Dallas shooting.[195]

Those images may not make you bounce with laughter, but they're not evidence that Clyde was looking for a second Holocaust. Clyde had a weird sense of humor and was, more likely than not, mentally unstable.

Nonetheless, Gallagher on CNN tied the Dallas shooting to a study by the Anti-Defamation League (ADL) purporting to show that "nearly all the extremist murders in 2018 were committed by right-wing radicals."

The ADL does one of these little reports every year and consistently obscures crucial information, like all the specific examples of the violence that it uses as evidence to back up its conclusion. But even in

---

195 "Le waste of money has arrived," Reddit.com, May 6, 2019: https://www.
reddit.com/r/dogelore/comments/blb6ao/le_waste_of_money_has_arrived/.

the few concrete examples that the ADL does provide, you get ones like this from the same report that was cited by Gallagher: "Richard Starry shot and killed four relatives at a local nursing center and at his home in an apparent act of domestic violence before killing himself. According to local media, Starry had been a member of a white supremacist group while in prison." Or like this: "James Mathis, a member of the Georgia-based white supremacist prison gang Ghostface Gangsters, and his wife, Amanda Oakes, allegedly killed their six-month-old son and put his body in a freezer in a hotel room."[196]

So, when white people kill their own family members, even their own babies, that's what the Anti-Defamation League means when it talks about right-wing violence.

These are examples of white people killing other *white* people. That's not the same as, say, a Muslim shooting up an Orlando nightclub out of loyalty to the Islamic State terrorist group, or a Muslim driving a truck down a busy New York sidewalk, mowing down dozens of pedestrians, for the same cause. The ADL's "white supremacists" aren't rampaging through the country, indiscriminately targeting blacks, Hispanics, or Jews. They're killing other whites, and oftentimes for reasons that have nothing to do with race.

On top of that, as described in the chapter on hate-crime hoaxes, FBI data shows that interracial homicide is exceedingly rare.[197]

Simply looking at the select violent crimes committed by members of ideological or racial supremacy groups tells only half the story of the ADL's report. The group even admits that despite a higher number of "incidents" in the "white supremacy" category, the ones perpetrated by Islamic extremists have a far higher body count.

---

196 Mark Pitcavage, *Murder and Extremism in the United States in 2018*, ADL Center on Extremism, 2019: https://www.adl.org/media/12480/download.

197 Amy Sherman, "An updated look at statistics on black-on-black murders," PolitiFact.com, May 21, 2015: https://www.politifact.com/florida/article/2015/may/21/updated-look-statistics-black-black-murders/.

"Compared to right-wing extremists," says the report, "domestic Islamist extremists in the U.S. have been involved in far fewer lethal incidents—but a number of those attacks have been high-casualty events, including most notably the Pulse nightclub attack in Orlando, Florida, in 2016, which left 49 dead."

What a difference that makes.

Anytime there's a white person involved, the media invariably trot out some half-baked statistic to demonstrate that the number of domestic terror attacks by "right-wing extremists" or "white suprem-acists" far surpasses anything committed by Muslims or some other "oppressed" group. The stats are always a joke.

Another one of the media's favorite studies is the 2017 report by the Government Accountability Office (GAO) on "countering violent extremism." The report lists a number of violent incidents between 2001 and 2016 that the GAO believes were motivated by either "far-right extremists" or "radical-Islamist extremists." The supposed far right includes "white supremacists," "anti-government" people, and "right-wing extremists," coming in at a total of sixty-two incidents with 106 victims. The "radical-Islamist extremists," by contrast, who are literally just Muslims and no one else, accounted for twenty-three inci-dents with a total of 119 victims.

Using light arithmetic, that's less than two victims per "far-right" attack versus at least five victims per Muslim attack. Put another way, Muslim extremists had a third of the "incidents" that the "far-right" had during that time period, but they claimed more victims.

Included in the radical-Islamist extremist category of the GAO study are some well-remembered episodes of mass terror, like the Orlando nightclub shooting by Omar Mateen in June 2016, resulting in the death of nearly fifty people; the San Bernardino, California, shooting spree in December 2015 by Syed Farook and Tashfeen Malik, which ended with fourteen deaths; and the Boston Marathon bombing in 2013 perpetrated by the Tsarnaev brothers, which the study says killed three, without acknowledging all the limbs and muscle tissue lost by nearly three hundred more.[198] Though the study looked as far back as 2001, not included in the GAO report is 9/11, since it looked at data starting only after September 12, 2001, not taking into account three thousand Americans who lost their lives in that episode. That's convenient.[199]

Details in the report of "right-wing violence" are far less comprehensive or even comprehensible. One entry in the report says that in Mesquite, Texas, in 2001, a "White Supremacist member of Aryan Brotherhood killed a man." Okay, but what was the victim's race? The odds are that he was also white, given the extremely low number of interracial homicides and the noted tendency of these extremist violence trackers to count nearly every crime involving a white person as another incident of "right-wing extremism." Other entries lack the same information. Another one tells of a "White supremacist [who] shot and killed 9 at his community college." That one is a reference to twenty-six-year-old Chris Harper-Mercer, who shot up Umpqua Community College in Roseburg, Oregon, but he wasn't targeting minorities. Witnesses say he was targeting a specific religion, asking his victims if they were Christians before pulling the trigger on those who said yes.[200]

The GAO obviously padded the numbers for "right-wing violence" just like the ADL did for "white supremacist" violence. They're not the only ones to do these kinds of pseudo studies.

A *Washington Post* headline in November 2018 blared that "right-wing violence is on the rise" in America. The story asserted that "violence by white supremacists and other far-right attackers has been

---

198 "Boston Marathon Terror Attack Fast Facts," CNN.com, June 3, 2013: https://www.cnn.com/2013/06/03/us/boston-marathon-terror-attack-fast-facts/index.html.

199 GAO, *Countering Violent Extremism*, April 2017, 34: https://www.gao.gov/assets/690/683984.pdf.

200 Helen Davidson, "Oregon college shooting: 'He asked are you Christian? Then he shot and killed them,'" Guardian.com, Oct. 2, 2015: https://www.theguardian.com/us-news/2015/oct/02/oregon-college-shooting-he-asked-are-you-christian-then-he-shot-and-killed-them.

on the rise since Barack Obama's presidency—and has surged since President Trump took office."[201]

The *Post* relied on data compiled by the Global Terrorism Database (GTD), which is hosted by the University of Maryland.

To give you an idea of how loosely the GTD defines "right-wing," it includes Stephen Paddock, the perpetrator of the 2017 Las Vegas mass shooting that killed nearly sixty people. Though U.S. authorities never concluded that Paddock had a motive—any motive at all—the GTD went ahead and labeled him "an anti-government extremist."[202]

This is like what the Anti-Defamation League does with its regular push notifications of some new "study" that purports to show a spike in anti-Semitic crime or "incidents," which can refer to anything from a heated argument to random graffiti depicting Trump as a Nazi (which would more likely be an insult directed at the president and not at the entire Jewish population).

In February 2018, the ADL produced a new "report" claiming a nearly 60 percent increase in anti-Semitic incidents across America. The study's parameters are so broad as to include "schoolyard bullying" and "one-off expressions of harassment." So, were the bullying and the harassment from or inspired by the left or the right? What exactly are "expressions of harassment" and how might they be different from standard harassment? What's more, specifically with regard to "assaults," the number of them was halved between 2016 and 2017. So, there was a sharp increase in "incidents," however that's defined. But at the same time, there was a vast *decrease* in actual physical violence.[203]

---

201 Wesley Lowery, Kimberly Kindy, and Andrew Ba Tran, "In the United States, right-wing violence is on the rise," *Washington Post*, Nov. 25, 2018: https://www.washingtonpost.com/national/in-the-united-states-right-wing-violence-is-on-the-rise/2018/11/25/61f7f24a-deb4-11e8-85df-7a6b4d25cfbb_story.html?utm_term=.39000cafe4a9.

202 "Global Terrorism in 2016," Global Terrorism Database, July 2018: https://www.start.umd.edu/pubs/START_GTD_Overview2017_July2018.pdf.

203 "2017 Audit of Anti-Semitic Incidents," Anti-Defamation League, Feb. 27, 2018: https://www.adl.org/resources/reports/2017-audit-of-anti-semitic-incidents#themes-and-trends-

You might call that progress.

Included as examples of anti-Semitism in that ADL report are the headstones that were turned over in the Missouri cemetery, even though, as noted in the chapter of this book about hate-crime hoaxes, the guy who did it was determined by police to have simply been drunk and angry at a friend, and not motivated by hostility toward Jews.

When the facts are obscured, it's easy to instigate a panic over white supremacy and right-wing extremism.

Liberal news outlets like BuzzFeed and the Daily Beast do it all the time by combing through message boards in remote corners of the web to find a racist joke or a sardonic "conspiracy theory." When one is found, they get to work on another article about right-wing extremism and white nationalism creeping into the mainstream.

If you never read the Daily Beast or BuzzFeed, you have no idea who the Proud Boys are. You have never heard of QAnon. And you may think 4chan is a local news station. But about once per week, the Daily Beast or BuzzFeed or some other liberal website finds a reason to write about any of these things in their perpetual campaign to convince normal people that so long as Trump is president, we live in darkness.

None of these groups pose a threat to anyone who isn't still clinically depressed about the 2016 election. The Proud Boys is a self-help group for disaffected men. QAnon is a gag internet story about how the "deep state" has attempted to assassinate President Trump, and how Hillary Clinton and former president Barack Obama are on the cusp of being thrown in prison. And 4chan is a general-interest online message board with particular popularity among high school- and college-age males due to its high volume of anime and video game-related content.

The Daily Beast has shown a downright unhealthy obsession with the Proud Boys story, even covering how the group's members masturbate.[204] BuzzFeed has an entire section for stories related to 4chan.

---

204 Will Sommer, "New Proud Boy Rules: Less Fighting, Less Wanking," Daily Beast, Nov. 27, 2018: https://www.thedailybeast.com/new-proud-boy-rules-less-fighting-less-wanking.

On and on it goes. It's one more tool for the social justice crowd to keep the "privileged" in check.

⌘ ⌘ ⌘

The one episode of Trump-related violence that the media can point to is the lunatic Hispanic pipe bomber, Cesar Sayoc, age fifty-seven. And that case doesn't even involve actual violence.

In October 2018, Sayoc sent several dud explosives to Democrats and journalists who had been critical of Trump.

There were no casualties, and the guy, again, was more unhinged than he was pro-Trump. On his work résumé, Sayoc claimed to have been a pro soccer player who one day hoped to be a veterinarian, as well as a master of finances capable of resurrecting dying businesses. You can look at photos of Sayoc's Etch A Sketch-like hair and know immediately that none of what he purports to be is true. He, in fact, worked as a dancer at some point but also lived out of his van.[205]

Ronald Lowy, a lawyer who knows Sayoc and his family, said in news reports that Sayoc frequently made claims that weren't true. "He lives in a little bit of a fantasy world," Lowy told the *Naples Daily News*. "He says he's a Seminole Indian, which he's not. He has no Indian blood. He's 50 percent Filipino and 50 percent American Italian." Lowy described Sayoc as "immature," "low I.Q.," and "emotionally stunted."

When police found Sayoc after the slew of fizzled mail bombs, they described him as "a guy who was upset that his electricity was turned off."

It's not even clear that the bombs were put together in any serious way or that they were intended to go off at all. In court, Sayoc said

---

205   Sara Marino and Ryan Mills, "Family saw early signs of mental problems in mail bomber suspect Cesar Sayoc, but no help," *Naples Daily News*, Oct. 27, 2018: https://www.naplesnews.com/story/news/local/florida/2018/10/27/cesar-sayoc-early-signs-mental-health-problems-mail-bomber-suspect/1789945002/.

he intended them to only look like bombs and that they were meant merely to "intimidate and scare" the recipients.[206] "What started out as hoax, decoys, devices, were not ever meant to work…hurt or harm anyone," Sayoc wrote in a letter to the judge.[207]

In another letter to the judge, he said he abused "heavy amounts of steroids"; he claimed he was "malested [sic] by Brother Raymond" when he attended Catholic school; he claimed he was both Jewish and Catholic; he said his mother was suicidal and that he himself often had the same tendencies; he thanked God for "self help tapes" produced by Donald Trump, Zig Ziglar, and Tony Robbins; and he claimed to have played pro-level soccer and that he could have "delivered" a national title in the sport.

Sayoc did say in that letter that he donated one hundred dollars to Trump's campaign and that he received tickets to a Trump rally in Florida. But he said he didn't know Trump "the political guy." He knew Trump only as "the playboy" and for his "big properties." Sayoc said he attended the Florida rally, where he "met people from all walks of life, creed, color, etc." He said it was "fun" and "like a newfound drug." And then he went back to remembering Trump's self-help tapes and his own alleged molestation in Catholic school.

The letter finally concluded with a plea that the judge in his case be lenient because Sayoc wanted to "start a non-profit organization for loneliness."[208]

This is it. This is the one psychotic whom Democrats and the media can point to as having caused a panic that is at least tangentially related to Trump. It resulted in no victims and, from what we can tell, Sayoc knew basically nothing about politics.

---

206 Erica Orden and Nicole Chavez, "Mail bomb suspect Cesar Sayoc pleads guilty," CNN.com, March 21, 2019: https://www.cnn.com/2019/03/21/us/cesar-sayoc-guilty-plea/index.html.

207 Cesar Sayoc, court letter, April 2, 2019: https://www.documentcloud.org/documents/5792184-Order.html.

208 Cesar Sayoc, court letter, April 25, 2019: https://www.usatoday.com/documents/5975837-Letter/.

Every other violent incident that the media and Democrats pounce on to prove the myth that the president and his supporters are blood-thirsty animals turns up empty.

From the Covington Catholic High kids to the demented neo-Nazi of Maryland, a narrative about the toxicity of "privilege" is hammered home. The story is always the same, and it's always a lie. When the lie is exposed, don't look for an apology.

This is how the culture fascists in the media reinforce privileged victims. They spread terror and malign the innocent. That's considered fair under social justice. It's what the oppressed and aggrieved *deserve*.

If it can happen to a group of high school teenagers who support Trump and who were guilty of nothing more than being in the right place at, in fact, the right time, it can happen to anyone. That's the message and the social justice movement wants everyone to receive it.

CHAPTER 6

¡*PARA* PRIVILEGED VICTIMS, *MARQUE DOS*!

For average Americans, immigration as a political issue is about two things: one, the extent to which they're willing to share their country's limited wealth with foreigners rather than with people who are already here; and two, the extent to which they're willing to see their livelihoods, neighborhoods, and communities change with an influx of new people who come from different backgrounds and lower standards of living.

For the national media, Hollywood liberals, and Democrats, immigration is about one thing: how to reduce the "privileged" and elevate the oppressed.

If you were a Martian hovering over the United States in a spacecraft, you'd see a country of vast but limited wealth, and a never-ending stream of people from poorer, less advanced countries pushing their way in from just below Texas. You'd say in Martian, "In order to protect that rich country from all the others, they will need to erect some kind of barrier—a wall, and probably several of them." As an extraterrestrial, you would have just made sense of the immigration debate in a way that liberals, Hollywood, and the national news media never will.

For them, it's not so much an honest policy disagreement as it is a struggle between the privileged and the aggrieved. But this is one area in which the American public at large isn't immediately ready to submit to the social justice movement. When Americans are asked if they want to give away their personal space and wealth to a steady stream of people from a less developed foreign country, the answer is a clear no.

Not only do Americans feel that we're not required to help whoever shows up at the border—though we're happy to, when we can—we also recognize that under a sane immigration policy, we would have the right as a nation to decide how many people, if any, should be allowed in, where they should come from, and how they should conduct themselves upon arrival.

This isn't any different from discriminating against who gets to enter your home. Most people are willing to allow in well-behaved friends, family, and guests who respect the household, just as most people would slam the door on violent criminals, drug dealers, and freeloaders. Also, Jehovah's Witnesses.

It's common sense, but the culture fascists don't operate under common sense. They operate under social justice.

During a meeting with congressional leaders in January 2018, President Trump reportedly asked, "Why are we having all these people from shithole countries come here?"[209] He was referring to Haiti and other dumps where crime rates and poverty are high, skills are low, and disease is rampant. In short, shithole countries.

Congress had been negotiating a deal on immigration policy, and Democrats wanted to extend protections for immigrants who had temporary immigration status for having fled disaster-stricken areas like Haiti. The "shithole countries" line, which the president has denied ever took place, predictably worked the media into a frothy mess.

---

209   Josh Dawsey, "Trump derides protections for immigrants from 'shithole' countries," *Washington Post*, Jan. 12, 2018: https://www.washingtonpost.com/politics/trump-attacks-protections-for-immigrants-from-shithole-countries-in-oval-office-meeting/2018/01/11/bfc0725c-f711-11e7-91af-31ac729add94_story.html?utm_term=.79c8744eba95.

CNN's Anderson Cooper went on air to say how awful Trump was for calling Haiti a shithole. Cooper then continued to describe Haiti as, well, a shithole. "[I]'ve never met a Haitian who isn't strong," Cooper said as he choked back tears. "You have to be to survive in a place where the government has often abandoned its people, where opportunities are few, and where Mother Nature has punished the people far more than anyone should ever be punished."[210]

With that rave review of Haiti—its negligent government, its dearth of economic opportunities—can you tell me why, again, Americans should be eager to import any number of people from that place?

Maybe Trump said "shithole countries" and maybe he didn't. Regardless, that some countries really are shitholes is a truth as transparent as any mimosa poured by Lindsay Lohan.

Later on Don Lemon's show, the always hysterical Rick Wilson, an anti-Trump Republican, completely mischaracterized what Trump reportedly said.

"Your idea that these peoples should be bounded out of here because they happen to come from the 'shithole' country is absurdly un-American," he said.[211]

No one said anything about anyone being "bounded out of here." According to the *Post* report, Trump had only questioned why an immigration bill should function as more welfare for other countries with massive crime and high poverty. The average American doesn't swing the door open to anyone who knocks and claims to need to use the phone. Why should our country?

Wilson could have stopped at misrepresenting Trump's perfectly logical point, but he went on to out himself as likely racist.

"Are you cool with [white immigrants] coming here to take highly skilled and educated jobs from Americans?" he said on the show. "Is that what you're saying, or is it just that brown people who are willing

---

210 Anderson Cooper, *Anderson Cooper 360*, CNN, Jan. 11, 2018.
211 Rick Wilson, *CNN Tonight*, CNN, Jan. 11, 2018.

to go and work in restaurant kitchens and hotels or on Trump golf courses are unacceptable to you?"

Someone please tell Wilson that "brown" immigrants aren't relegated to a life preparing his food. Some surely have higher aspirations. They may dream to someday talk on TV as an outmoded political consultant, for example.

Democrats and even some Republicans, like Wilson, think it's acceptable to stereotype "brown" immigrants as uneducated swamp creatures who can do only slave-like service work. And yet it was Trump whom *HuffPost* reporter Ashley Feinberg called a racist.[212] Don Lemon also called him a racist.[213] Liberal *New York Times* columnist David Leonhardt called him—what else?—a racist.[214]

Trump is a racist for questioning immigration policy the same way a zombie apocalypse survivor is a misogynist for opening his bunker to a healthy six-foot-two male while locking out a sniffling woman with a bite mark on her neck. Maybe the woman was simply attacked by a scared dog and she really isn't about to transform into a grotesque demon. Is that a risk anyone should be willing to take? I wouldn't and that doesn't mean I have a general hatred for the opposite sex.

But that's how any sane American should view the United States. It's an emergency shelter. It doesn't have unlimited space, and what resources we have inside are also finite. We can't afford to be indiscriminate, otherwise we'll all die. But so long as we still have some space, perhaps we should get a little selective about who we allow in.

That certain countries are less ideal than others is not a controversial concept. American celebrities dare set foot in Haiti, Honduras, Guatemala, or anywhere in Africa only so long as they can get a photo of themselves with starving children. None stay there because no one

212 Ashley Feinberg, Twitter.com, Jan. 11, 2018: https://twitter.com/ashleyfeinberg/status/951573433334321154.
213 Don Lemon, "CNN Tonight," CNN, Jan. 11, 2018.
214 David Leonhardt, "Just say it: Trump is a racist," *New York Times*, Jan. 12, 2018: https://www.nytimes.com/2018/01/12/opinion/trump-racist.html.

willfully spends free time in a cesspool of gang violence, poverty, and government corruption, least of all liberal celebrities. Before the 2016 election, several of them said they would leave the U.S. if Trump were elected. Among them were: Chelsea Handler, who would go to Spain; Lena Dunham, to Vancouver; Barbra Streisand, to Australia or Canada; Snoop Dogg, to Canada; former cohost of ABC's *The View* Raven-Symoné Pearman, to Canada; Amy Schumer, to Spain; and Samuel L. Jackson, to South Africa.

Wow, that's strange! Not a single one of them identified his or her final destination as the slums of El Salvador, or the stunning vistas of Somalia. *Because nobody wants to go there.* Why, then, should Americans be expected to invariably say yes when people from those places want to come here, bringing all of their problems with them? All of the celebrities named above, by the way, still live in the U.S., if that tells you anything at all about how miserable their lives are under Trump.

In December 2017, a Muslim immigrant set off a bomb in a New York subway station in an attempt to kill unknown numbers of innocent people. You probably don't remember that, because the media buried it under their coverage of what they deemed to be far more important: a Senate election that they hoped would serve as a rebuke of Trump.

The day after Republican U.S. Senate candidate Roy Moore's defeat in Alabama—he was accused of chasing underage girls around a local mall—the *New York Times* immediately ran four op-eds and an editorial on the electoral race, which was covered in the paper's news pages as a national story. After the terrorist attack, by comparison, the paper ran just one editorial about it, and its news coverage of the incident was relegated to the "New York region" pages.

A heavy snowstorm in the Northeast is invariably front-page national news, but a terrorist attack in the country's biggest city? *Nah, that's a local story.*

Hurricane Sandy in 2012 hit New Jersey, the unloved stepchild to New York, and yet the *Times* ran multiple stories in its national news section on the storm and its aftermath.[215, 216] But every news story the *Times* published on Akayed Ullah, the twenty-seven-year-old Bangladeshi national who strapped a bomb to his chest and detonated it in a crowded Times Square subway station, was relegated to the regional pages.

The pipe bomb Ullah had strapped to his chest fizzled, failing to properly detonate, injuring only Ullah, who told authorities thereafter that he had been inspired to act by the Islamic State. In November 2018, he was convicted of federal terrorism charges. That, too, was placed in the *Times*' regional section.[217]

Ullah's ticket into the U.S. came in the form of a green card, which he received not because he had something substantial to offer—he drove for a car service, which anyone with legs, arms, and at least one eye can do—but because he had a mother whose sister was a U.S. citizen. That's the way the vast majority of immigrants come to the U.S., while other foreigners, including highly skilled workers who want a better life, wait their turn and hope for the best.

In standard English, to get an advantage by way of family connections is called nepotism or unfair preferential treatment. In American English, however, we simply call it chain migration.

After Ullah's failed attack, President Trump renewed calls for Congress to end the chain-migration scam and move the U.S. immigration process to a merit-based system. Citizenship and Immigration Services director L. Francis Cissna made the case for it during a

215 James Barron, "After the Devastation, a Daunting Recovery," *New York Times*, Oct. 30, 2012: https://www.nytimes.com/2012/10/31/us/hurricane-sandy-barrels-region-leaving-battered-path.html.

216 James Barron, "Sharp Warnings as Hurricane Churns In," *New York Times*, Oct. 28, 2012: https://www.nytimes.com/2012/10/29/us/east-coast-braces-for-severe-storm-surge.html

217 Benjamin Weiser and Emily Palmer, "Akayed Ullah Guilty of ISIS-Inspired Bombing Near Times Square," *New York Times*, Nov. 6, 2018: https://www.nytimes.com/2018/11/06/nyregion/port-authority-bombing-verdict.html.

press conference, telling reporters that under the current system, the standards to chain-migrate or to win a green card through the random lottery are so low that virtually anyone—like, say, a Muslim Uber driver who might eventually want to blow up a subway station—can abuse it.[218]

Yahoo! News reporter Hunter Walker thought he was making a smart point when he suggested to Cissna at the press conference that "immigrants actually commit fewer crimes than native-born Americans."

That tired claim is what we in the biz call "bullshit." There are no truly reliable statistics on the crime rates of immigrants, especially when it comes to illegal aliens, in large part because government agencies don't categorize crimes by immigration status, but also because immigrants so often do not report when they're victimized. And when they're victims of a crime, it's usually perpetuated by someone of their same ethnicity—that is, someone they know.

A 2018 *New York Times* article said that from 2016 to 2017, Houston police saw a 16 percent drop in domestic violence reports, likely because immigrant victims feared that they themselves or someone close to them might be deported.[219] The rate at which Latinos reported rape to police had also dropped 40 percent from the previous year.[220]

"Undocumented immigrants and even lawful immigrants are afraid to report crime," Houston police chief Art Acevedo told the paper.

Los Angeles, San Diego, and Denver, cities with high Hispanic populations, saw similar declines in reports of crime to the police, according to the *Times*.

---

218   L. Francis Cissna, White House press briefing, Dec. 12, 2017.

219   Cora Engelbrech, "Fewer Immigrants Are Reporting Domestic Abuse. Police Blame Fear of Deportation," *New York Times*, June 3, 2018: https://www.nytimes.com/2018/06/03/us/immigrants-houston-domestic-violence.html.

220   Jennifer Medina, "Too Scared to Report Sexual Abuse. The Fear: Deportation," *New York Times*, April 30, 2017: https://www.nytimes.com/2017/04/30/us/immigrants-deportation-sexual-abuse.html.

You can say that this is President Trump's fault, since it was his first year in office, but anyone would be kidding themselves to believe that before Trump, illegal aliens and even legal immigrants didn't have the same fears. They did, even if it may have intensified with Trump.

Any study aiming to prove that immigrants commit crimes at a lower rate than native-born Americans would also need to be adjusted for the number of illegals apprehended by border authorities. U.S. Customs and Border Protection from fiscal years 2016 to 2018 apprehended nearly thirty thousand aliens who had prior criminal convictions.[221] That includes domestic violence, burglary, fraud, drunk driving, homicide, drug dealing, and sexual offenses. Immigrants like those are caught and then deported, and so any additional crimes they would have almost certainly committed after entering the country can't be factored into any study.

Then there's the rate of recidivism for convicted criminals once they're released from prison. It's about 50 percent within a year of being released from prison for both native-born and immigrant Hispanics, including illegals. But if the immigrant is deported upon completing his prison sentence, there's no way to know what other crime he would have had a 50 percent chance of committing had he been released back into America, and thus that isn't factored into any study, either.[222]

Every U.S. Border Patrol agent will tell you that rapists, child molesters, sex offenders, drug dealers, and gang members routinely cross the border into the U.S. And even if statistics could prove that immigrants, whether illegal or not, commit crimes at a lower rate than native-born citizens (they can't), so what? Any one immigrant shouldn't

---

221 "Criminal Alien Statistics Fiscal Year 2019," U.S. Customs and Border Protection, May 6, 2019: https://www.cbp.gov/newsroom/stats/cbp-enforcement-statistics/criminal-alien-statistics.

222 Mariel Alper, Matthew R. Durose, and Joshua Markman, *2018 Update on Prisoner Recidivism: A 9-Year Follow-up Period (2005-2014),* Department of Justice, Office of Justice Programs, Bureau of Justice Statistics, May 2018: https://www.bjs.gov/content/pub/pdf/18upr9yfup0514.pdf.

be committing *any crimes at all*. That's especially true for ones who were let in legally because they had a random uncle who was here to serve as their sponsor. We already have to deal with our own native-born criminals. Why should we open the gates to the rest of the world's, too?

It's not written anywhere that the most prosperous country must function as the planet's welfare system, and yet that's the notion that the culture fascists reinforce every day. The only reason average Americans haven't risen up against it in a violent fury is because they're by and large well-meaning, nonconfrontational people, and they hate being called racist.

Everyone in America knows that the second you say, "Hold on, I'd like to check these people out before we turn them loose on our cities," the media will be there to call you racist.

Representative Alexandria Ocasio-Cortez, Democrat of New York, has likened the migrant detention facilities on the border to Nazi concentration camps.[223]

Senator Kamala Harris, Democrat of California, suggested in a congressional hearing that there are "parallels" in "the power and the discretion" of Immigration and Customs Enforcement (ICE) under President Trump and that of the Ku Klux Klan.[224]

When the Trump administration sought to add a question regarding U.S. citizenship to the 2020 Census, House Speaker Nancy Pelosi said it was an attempt to "make America white again."[225]

---

223 Tim Pearce, "'I don't use those words lightly': AOC compares US southern border to the Holocaust," *Washington Examiner*, June 18, 2019: https://www. washingtonexaminer.com/news/i-dont-use-those-words-lightly-aoc-compares-us-southern-border-to-the-holocaust.

224 Anna Giaritelli, "Kamala Harris draws parallel between ICE and the KKK," *Washington Examiner*, Nov. 15, 2018: https://www.washingtonexaminer.com/news/kamala-harris-draws-parallel-between-ice-and-kkk.

225 Ellie Bufkin, "Nancy Pelosi says Trump wants to 'make America white again' with citizenship question," *Washington Examiner*, July 9, 2019: https://www. washingtonexaminer.com/news/nancy-pelosi-says-trump-want-to-make-america-white-again-with-citizenship-question.

There is no variation in the pattern. If you're an American who believes that immigration should be a matter of picking and choosing the people who get to enter our collective home, the Democratic Party will be there to call you racist.

In Summer 2017, the White House backed a bill by Senators David Perdue, Republican of Georgia, and Tom Cotton, Republican of Arkansas, that aimed to sharply reduce all immigration and put a priority on admitting foreigners who know English and have higher levels of education.

During a press briefing on the bill, deluxe anchorman imitator Jim Acosta declared that the proposal "does not sound like it's in keeping with American tradition when it comes to immigration." He took great exception to a bill that would make entry into the U.S. more of a privilege for those with something to contribute and less of an entitlement for every sick and poor person who hops across the Texas border.

White House senior policy adviser Stephen Miller explained to Acosta that "the history of immigration, it's actually ebbed and flowed," a statement based on the fact that the U.S. hasn't always admitted the same number of immigrants. In 1970, about ten million people in the U.S. were foreign-born. A decade later, four million had been added. After another decade, an additional six million. In 2000, ten million more had been added. This is all according to U.S. Census data, and those are not consistent numbers of immigrants.[226]

This shouldn't be up for debate. There's no reason that the U.S. absolutely must continue adding a million immigrants to the country every year. And the proposal to move toward a merit-based system while the country takes time to absorb new generations of foreigners is only common sense. It follows the same logic that says one plus one is two; if it's raining, the ground is wet; and when Cory Booker gives a speech, it's cringey.

---

226 U.S. Census Bureau, Census of Population, 1850 to 2000, and the American Community Survey, 2010: https://www.census.gov/newsroom/pdf/cspan_fb_slides.pdf.

Still, the media never tire of reframing the immigration debate as a matter of racism, xenophobia, and bigotry.

During a speech in Poland in July 2017, Trump said the U.S. "will always welcome new citizens who share our values and love our people" but that "our borders will always be closed to terrorism and extremism of any kind."

Liberal *Washington Post* columnist Eugene Robinson described the speech as a "thirst for a clash of civilizations." He then asked his readers to "imagine Italy without tomato sauce, a gift from the New World."[227]

A more apt comparison would be to imagine the Twin Towers still standing, but Robinson fretted over his meatballs. It should tell you something that food was the one thing Robinson thought of when justifying mass importation of other cultures. It wasn't the work ethic of Spain, or the traditions of Somalia, or the religious customs of Afghanistan; it was the sauce.

History books should refer to 2018 as the year of immigration hysteria. Like with Trump's reported "shithole countries" remark, every angle of the immigration issue was set up as a battle between the privileged (average Americans who don't want their country turned into a jungle) and the oppressed (brown foreigners who we're told merely want a better life for their children). Any aspect of the issue that didn't fit neatly into that framework was either lied about or ignored altogether.

Remember the two pairs of black parents who were invited by President Trump to the 2018 State of the Union in order to show the tragedy wrought by our current immigration system? I didn't think so. Their appearance was mostly ignored by the press.

In his address, Trump told the heartbreaking story of how the young daughter of Robert Mickens and Elizabeth Alvarado, and another of

---

227 Eugene Robinson, "Trump's dangerous thirst for a clash of civilizations," *Washington Post*, July 6, 2017: https://www.washingtonpost.com/opinions/trumps-dangerous-thirst-for-a-clash-of-civilizations/2017/07/06/fb5398ea-6282-11e7-a4f7-af34fc1d9d39_story.html?utm_term=.c5b8bc7d4496.

Evelyn Rodriguez and Freddy Cuevas, were both viciously murdered by illegal-immigrant gang members.

"Their two teenage daughters, Kayla Cuevas and Nisa Mickens, were close friends on Long Island," Trump said. "But in September 2016, on the eve of Nisa's sixteenth birthday—such a happy time it should have been—neither of them came home. These two precious girls were brutally murdered while walking together in their hometown."

On September 13, 2016, Mickens' body was found on the side of a road near an elementary school. The next day, Cuevas' body was recovered from a wooded area a few blocks away. The two had been walking together when several members of MS-13, a gang made up largely of immigrants from the squalor of Central America, jumped them while wielding machetes and baseball bats. The girls, who had been friends since childhood, were gashed and bludgeoned to death, reportedly over an altercation that started on social media.

New York's *Newsday* reported in 2017 that the machete is MS-13's "weapon of choice" and is "used to mutilate and dismember victims during attacks that sometimes are recorded."[228]

So ravaged is Suffolk County by MS-13 that New York and the federal government are pouring tens of millions of dollars into the area for the sole purpose of combating the gang's aggressive presence.[229]

Though the Democratic Party and the news media insist that every single immigrant coming into the country is a future nun or Nobel Prize winner, members of MS-13 crawl their way across the border all

---

228   Joye Brown, "Kayla Cuevas' mom tells how MS-13 gang recruits at school," *Newsday*, June 24, 2017: https://www.newsday.com/long-island/columnists/joye-brown/kayla-cuevas-mom-tells-how-ms-13-gang-recruits-at-school-1.13761633.

229   "Governor Cuomo Announces $20 Million to Combat MS-13 Gang Violence on Long Island," Governor.Ny.Gov, Oct. 29, 2018: https://www.governor.ny.gov/news/governor-cuomo-announces-20-million-combat-ms-13-gang-violence-long-island.

the time. Take any time period at random and it's always the same. In February 2019 alone, agents at the Rio Grande Valley border in Texas alerted the public of the following:

- "Rio Grande City agents working near Roma, Texas, arrested a Salvadoran man after he entered the United States illegally. Record checks revealed he is a Mara Salvatrucha (MS-13) gang member with an extensive criminal history in the state of New York." (February 28.)

- "Rio Grande Valley Sector agents arrested a Mexican man near Edinburg, Texas. Record checks revealed the man is a member of the Mara Salvatrucha (MS-13) gang." (February 26.)

- "[A]gents patrolling the local ranchlands near Sarita, Texas, arrested eight illegal aliens. During processing, agents noticed one of the subjects displayed several tattoos affiliated with the Mara Salvatrucha (MS-13) gang." (February 22.)

- "Rio Grande Valley agents arrested an MS-13 and a Sureño gang member in separate incidents." (February 19.)

- "Weslaco agents working in Hidalgo, Texas, apprehended a Salvadoran man after he entered the United States illegally. During processing, record checks revealed the man is a member of the Mara Salvatrucha (MS-13) gang." (February 14.)

- "[A]gents from the Rio Grande City station arrested five illegal aliens. While being processed, record checks for a Salvadoran man revealed he is a MS-13 gang member." (February 19.)

- "[A]gents working near Progreso, Texas, arrested 16 illegal aliens after making their illegal entry into the United States. Record checks for a Honduran male revealed he is a member of the MS-13 gang with criminal history." (February 7.)[230]

---

230 Eddie Scarry, "MS-13 has taken over El Salvador and now it's everywhere in the US," *Washington Examiner*, March 4, 2019: https://www.washingtonexaminer. com/opinion/ms-13-has-taken-over-el-salvador-and-now-its-everywhere-in-the-us.

This is in addition to the child molesters, drug dealers, and human traffickers apprehended around the clock at the border—and, more importantly, the ones *not* caught because agents are tied up acting as caretakers and babysitters for the hundreds of thousands of families turning up to claim asylum. We'll never know how many violent MS-13 criminals are slipping into the U.S., where they go on to infest and ravage American schools and neighborhoods.

The *Washington Post* reported in March 2019 that El Salvador's police force has begun fleeing the country because MS-13 has taken over. "With salaries of $300 to $400 per month, the low-level police officers who make up the majority of the force often have no choice but to live in neighborhoods vulnerable to gangs," the report said. "And so, in the vast majority of the cases, police officers are killed when they are home from work or are on leave."[231]

The decay is no longer confined to Central America. It has spread throughout the U.S., thanks to our decades-long open-border policies.

In June 2018, the *Post* reported on an MS-13 stronghold, an entire Maryland middle school. "Gang-related fights are now a near-daily occurrence at Wirt, where a small group of suspected MS-13 members at the overwhelmingly Hispanic school in Prince George's County throw gang signs, sell drugs, draw gang graffiti and aggressively recruit students recently arrived from Central America," the report said.[232]

---

231   Kevin Sieff, "It's so dangerous to police MS-13 in El Salvador that officers are fleeing the country," *Washington Post*, March 3, 2019: https://www.washingtonpost.com/world/the_americas/its-so-dangerous-to-police-ms-13-in-el-salvador-that-officers-are-fleeing-the-country/2019/03/03/e897dbaa-2287-11e9-b5b4-1d18dfb7b084_story.html?utm_term=.1bcb6c8a2d1e.

232   Michael E. Miller, "'A ticking time bomb': MS-13 threatens a middle school, warn teachers, parents, students," *Washington Post*, June 11, 2018: https://www.washingtonpost.com/local/a-ticking-time-bomb-ms-13-threatens-a-middle-school-warn-teachers-parents-students/2018/06/11/7cfc7036-5a00-11e8-858f-12becb4d6067_story.html?utm_term=.587707098d99.

"Teachers feel threatened but aren't backed up. Students feel threatened but aren't protected," one of the school's teachers said. "The school is a ticking time bomb."

And from a report by the *Post* in December 2017: "As the gang has grown in strength in recent years, so has its sway over communities across the country. From Boston to Northern Virginia to Houston, a string of grisly MS-13 murders has highlighted its resurgence."[233] Innocent people who find themselves in the grips of MS-13-controlled neighborhoods complain of gangbangers, frequent robberies, drug dealing, and extortion. A woman who unknowingly moved into an MS-13-ravaged neighborhood in Maryland told the *Post* that one MS-13 leader threatened her and demanded she pay sixty dollars "rent" to him each week.[234]

This is the culture, and these are the people dumped into the U.S. by way of our current immigration system, so much as you can call it a "system." And it's all encouraged by the culture fascists who care about only one thing: the reorganization of America.

After Trump's 2018 State of the Union address, NBC's *Meet the Press* moderator Chuck Todd immediately complained that the president "didn't lead with a conciliatory tone on immigration." (If they had been asked, Evelyn Rodriguez, Freddy Cuevas, Elizabeth Alvarado, and Robert Mickens, presumably would have said that they were personally more upset that the illegals who killed their daughters failed to "lead with a conciliatory tone" when they took machetes to the girls' bodies.)[235]

233 Michael E. Miller, "'People here live in fear': MS-13 menaces a community seven miles from the White House," *Washington Post*, Dec. 20, 2017: https://www.washingtonpost.com/local/people-here-live-in-fear-ms-13-menaces-a-community-seven-miles-from-the-white-house/2017/12/20/6cebf318-d956-11e7-b859-fb0995360725_story.html?utm_term=.31ccfe10604a.

234 Michael Miller, "'People here live in fear,'" *Washington Post*.

235 Chuck Todd, NBC special State of the Union coverage, January 30, 2018.

The *New York Times* editorial board said Trump had "injected only poison and confusion" into the immigration debate.[236]

Lest there remain any doubt that the national press work in concert, the *Washington Post* sang the exact same tune, writing in an editorial that Trump had "injected more ethno-nationalist venom into a debate he already has done much to poison." As though the brutal murders of Nisa Mickens and Kayla Cuevas were a freak accident that only happens once in a millennium, the *Post* said that Trump "chose in the most inflammatory way possible to associate immigrants with a horrific crime committed by a vicious gang."[237]

Here's the "poison" Trump injected into the immigration debate, per the speech's transcript: "Tonight, I am extending an open hand to work with members of both parties, Democrats and Republicans, to protect our citizens of every background, color, religion, and creed. My duty, and the sacred duty of every elected official in this chamber, is to defend Americans, to protect their safety, their families, their communities, and their right to the American Dream. Because Americans are dreamers too."

He said reform of the immigration laws should include legal protections and a path to citizenship for the nearly two million so-called Dreamers, illegal immigrants brought to the country as children; an end to chain migration, wherein immigrant citizens can sponsor an endless trail of relatives coming to the U.S.; and an end to the visa lottery, which doles out green cards to foreigners at random.

The system should ideally favor immigrants with high potential for assimilation and contribution. It would then hopefully preempt horrific cases like that of Cuevas and Mickens. This shouldn't be difficult.

---

236 Editorial board, "What Trump Doesn't Get About the State of the Union," *New York Times*, Jan. 30, 2018: https://www.nytimes.com/2018/01/30/opinion/editorials/donald-trump-sotu-boasting.html?.

237 Editorial board, "Trump could have embraced an immigration deal. Instead, he poisoned the debate," *Washington Post*, Jan. 31, 2018: https://www.washingtonpost.com/opinions/trump-could-have-embraced-an-immigration-deal-instead-he-poisoned-the-debate/2018/01/31/3126ef62-06c5-11e8-b48c-b07fea957bd5_story.html?utm_term=.7aa0befd43a2.

It's worth noting, by the way, that Cuevas, Mickens, and their parents are black only because of the media's unrelenting accusation that any immigration policy outside of "complete open borders" is *rrrraaaccciiiissssttttt*!

Trump spent the better part of 2018 being called a racist because he suggested limiting immigration from "shithole countries." But right there at the State of the Union address were four black parents who saw their children snatched from them forever by illegal immigrant criminals. That fact interested virtually no one in the national media.

Of course not. It doesn't fit the scheme wherein the privileged (white) are pitted against the oppressed, aggrieved, and victimized (racial minorities).

That narrative is forever on repeat.

When Trump in May 2018 rightfully described the murderous MS-13 gang members as "animals," the media couldn't have bent themselves more out of shape than if every reporter in the country had scoliosis.

During a meeting at the White House with officials from California, Trump commended the state's law enforcement, but accurately acknowledged that their police force has its hands tied when it comes to ridding California communities of illegal immigrants, and gang members in particular. He noted that so-called sanctuary cities in the state prevent police from cooperating with federal authorities on immigration.

"We're suing on that, and we're working hard, and I think it will all come together, because people want it to come together," the president said. "It's so ridiculous. The concept that we're even talking about it is ridiculous. We'll take care of it, Margaret. We'll win."

He was talking to Margaret Mims, the sheriff for Fresno County.

"Thank you," she replied. "There could be an MS-13 member I know about [but] if they don't reach a certain threshold, I cannot tell ICE about it."

America's biggest cities are dealing with this same problem. Where illegal immigrants are concentrated, local governments mandate that their police force and judges do everything possible to prevent deportation of aliens unlawfully residing in the U.S.

"You wouldn't believe how bad these people are," Trump said at the White House meeting. "These aren't people. These are animals. And we're taking them out of the country at a level and at a rate that's never happened before."

The only thing erroneous with that declaration is that the rate at which the Trump administration was deporting illegals actually had happened before. The number of deportations was, in fact, higher under former president Obama. In 2014, the Obama administration deported nearly 415,000 illegal immigrants.[238] Trump's administration, in contrast, had deported less than 160,000 in 2018. Granted, the Obama administration broadly defined "deportation," so that anyone immediately caught crossing illegally into the U.S. and sent back to Mexico was considered a "deportation" rather than a standard detention and removal, but the press didn't quibble over those details. It was Trump's reference to "animals" that lit their fuses.

"President Trump used extraordinarily harsh rhetoric to renew his call for stronger immigration laws Wednesday, calling undocumented immigrants 'animals' and venting frustration at Mexican officials who he said 'do nothing' to help the United States," read the first line of *USA Today*'s report on the meeting.[239]

The opening of a *New York Times* story said that Trump "lashed out at undocumented immigrants during a White House meeting on Wednesday, warning in front of news cameras that dangerous people

---

238   Ana Gonzalez-Barrera and Jens Manuel Krogstad, "U.S. immigrant deportations declined in 2014, but remain near record high," Pew Research Center, Aug. 31, 2016: https://www.pewresearch.org/fact-tank/2016/08/31/u-s-immigrant-deportations-declined-in-2014-but-remain-near-record-high/.
239   Gregory Korte and Alan Gomez, "Trump ramps up rhetoric on undocumented immigrants: 'These aren't people. These are animals,'" *USA Today*, May 16, 2018: https://www.usatoday.com/story/news/politics/2018/05/16/trump-immigrants-animals-mexico-democrats-sanctuary-cities/617252002/.

were clamoring to breach the country's borders and branding such people 'animals.'"[240]

Eugene Scott, a political blogger for the *Washington Post*, wrote that Trump had "pointedly referred to undocumented immigrants as 'animals' in a statement his critics say betrays a gross misunderstanding of the plight of people who came to the United States illegally, and beyond that, little sympathy for them."[241]

Senator Chuck Schumer, Democrat of New York, tweeted in response to Trump, "When all of our great-great-grandparents came to America they weren't 'animals,' and these people aren't either."[242]

Representative Eric Swalwell, Democrat of California, called on the officials who were present for Trump's remarks to "denounce" him.[243]

Representative Nancy Pelosi, also of California, wondered in earnest whether Trump understood that no one is an animal, because, she said, "we are all God's children."[244]

CNBC correspondent and *New York Times* writer John Harwood, competing for Most Woke White Man of the Year, tweeted that "however repugnant their actions, MS-13 gang members are human beings."[245]

He may have sounded like an idiot, but at least Harwood got the context of the "animals" remark right.

---

240   Julie Hirschfield Davis, "Trump Calls Some Unauthorized Immigrants 'Animals' in Rant," *New York Times*, May 16, 2018: https://www.nytimes.com/2018/05/16/us/politics/trump-undocumented-immigrants-animals.html.

241   Eugene Scott, "In reference to 'animals,' Trump evokes an ugly history of dehumanization," May 16, 2018: https://www.washingtonpost.com/news/the-fix/wp/2018/05/16/trumps-animals-comment-on-undocumented-immigrants-earn-backlash-historical-comparisons/?utm_term=.dbd158ea3fbe.

242   Chuck Schumer, Twitter.com, May 16, 2018: https://twitter.com/senschumer/status/996892735989780480?lang=en.

243   Eric Swalwell, Twitter.com, May, 16, 2018: https://twitter.com/repswalwell/status/996926889515257856?lang=en.

244   Tim Hains, "Nancy Pelosi: 'Calling People Animals Is Not A Good Thing,'" RealClearPolitics.com, May 17, 2018: https://www.realclearpolitics.com/video/2018/05/17/nancy_pelosi_ms-13_gang_members_are_not_animals.html.

245   John Harwood, Twitter.com, May 17, 2018: https://twitter.com/johnjharwood/status/997068578116513793?lang=en.

Because the media can't be depended on for context, here is exactly what was said during the conversation at the White House between Trump and the sheriff:

> *Sheriff Mims: Thank you. There could be an MS-13 member I know about—if they don't reach a certain threshold, I cannot tell ICE about it.*
>
> *Trump: We have people coming into the country, or trying to come in—and we're stopping a lot of them—but we're taking people out of the country. You wouldn't believe how bad these people are. These aren't people. These are animals. And we're taking them out of the country at a level and at a rate that's never happened before.*

The blatant mischaracterization of the exchange can only have happened because the news media deliberately lied or because they really are that stupid.

Trump's critics are so self-deluded that the "animals" controversy went through a second cycle almost a full year later after some random person on Twitter republished the video clip of the White House meeting and falsely stated that it was illegal immigrant asylum seekers who Trump had referred to as "animals."

South Bend, Indiana, mayor Pete Buttigieg, 2020 Democratic presidential nomination candidate and probably the most boring gay man alive, reacted to the microwaved clip, indignantly tweeting, "You do not refer to human beings as animals. You just don't."[246]

New York senator Kirsten Gillibrand, another 2020 Democratic presidential candidate, tweeted, "No human being is an animal. We have to be better than this."[247]

---

246 Pete Buttigieg, Twitter.com, April 6, 2019: https://twitter.com/PeteButtigieg/status/1114480551694618624.

247 Kirsten Gillibrand, Twitter.com, April 6, 2019: https://twitter.com/SenGillibrand/status/1114523135599104000.

CBS skid mark Dan Rather called Trump's comment "despicable" and said that he'd "seen this playbook before, words weaponized into bloodshed."[248]

The immigration debate is not a winning one for Democrats or the media. A July 2019 study by the liberal Center for American Progress admitted as much. It explicitly said that Democrats "have ceded powerful rhetorical ground" on the subject by openly advocating for open borders and doing precisely nothing to so much as signal that they believe America is a sovereign nation that deserves clear, established boundaries.[249] Democrats were presumably at least already somewhat aware that they had hurt themselves in their aggressive advocacy for open borders. That's why they repeatedly turn to misrepresenting facts or flat-out lying in order to make their case.

In April 2018, Attorney General Jeff Sessions announced that there had been a 203 percent increase in illegal border crossings from the year before. He said the administration would respond to the surge by prosecuting aliens to the full extent of the law, which was, until that point, a novel concept.[250] This meant that rather than simply catching illegal border crossers and beginning the process to return them to their home countries, they would instead be prosecuted as criminals. But because everyone south of Texas had figured out how to skirt border laws by bringing their children with them to function as legal shields, the crackdown also meant that adult aliens would have to be sent to jails and their children would be sent to separate detention centers for their own processing.

---

248 Dan Rather, Twitter.com, April 5, 2019: https://twitter.com/DanRather/status/1114368182330974208?s=19.

249 Tom Jawetz, "Restoring the Rule of Law Through a Fair, Humane, and Workable Immigration System," Center for American Progress, July 22, 2019: https://www.americanprogress.org/issues/immigration/reports/2019/07/22/472378/restoring-rule-law-fair-humane-workable-immigration-system/.

250 "Attorney General Announces Zero-Tolerance Policy for Criminal Illegal Entry," Department of Justice, April 6, 2018: https://www.justice.gov/opa/pr/attorney-general-announces-zero-tolerance-policy-criminal-illegal-entry.

That's what happens with any person who is arrested. It's no different than for a crack addict busted on possession. If the addict has children, they can't accompany their parent to the lockup.

Sessions called this a zero-tolerance policy, though it wasn't as though the Justice Department had just created some vast new rule out of whole cloth. All Sessions did was make the crazy decision to start enforcing a law that had already existed.

It's like if one college professor grades on a curve and one just gives students what they earn on their tests. One may be offering leniency, but that doesn't mean the other one is operating in an alternative universe because he follows standard procedure.

And yet the full enforcement of immigration law was characterized by the media as if it were a cruel anomaly. Everything the national media said about it was an attempt to mislead everyone into believing that the Trump administration was ruthlessly ripping babies out of their mothers' arms.

A *New York Times* article on June 18, 2018, referred to the zero tolerance measure as Trump's "policy of separating children from their parents at the border."[251]

The liberal news site Vox declared that Trump had "created family separation."[252]

Rachel Maddow looked like she might vomit from overexertion as she tried to force out a tear on her show while reading from a report about "babies and other young children" sent to migrant detention centers.[253]

Maddow's colleague Stephanie Ruhle choked up earlier in the day talking about the same thing. And just so that there was no confusion

---

251 Katie Rogers and Sheryl Gay Stolberg, "Trump Resisting a Growing Wrath for Separating Migrant Families," *New York Times*, June 18, 2018: https://www.nytimes.com/2018/06/18/us/politics/trump-immigration-germany-merkel.html.

252 Dara Lind, "What Obama did with migrant families vs. what Trump is doing," Vox.com, June 21, 2018: https://www.vox.com/2018/6/21/17488458/obama-immigration-policy-family-separation-border.

253 Rachel Maddow, "Rachel Maddow Show," MSNBC, June 19, 2018.

about Ruhle's level of sincerity and compassion, she wore an under-stated pin on her top that said, in all capital letters, "LOVE."[254]

People who cross the border without authorization have broken a law, and the Justice Department under Sessions chose to enforce that law. Family separations under the Obama and George W. Bush administrations happened as well. True, they were far more limited, but only because Obama and Bush declined to prosecute viola-tors, instead largely turning them loose into the country on merely a promise that they would show up for their court hearings some-time in the future (a practice that was eventually adopted by the Trump administration).

After mixing the country into a frothy mess with a barrage of reports on illegal-immigrant moms locked up away from their children, the press began pushing narratives that weren't just excessively hostile, but were also demonstrably false.

In late May 2018, liberal journalists on social media passed around a photo that showed migrant children sleeping in "cages" on the floors of detention centers at the border, only to find out that the images were from the Obama years.[255]

The following month, the Associated Press reported at great length on a lawsuit wherein a juvenile detention center for illegal alien minors was accused of neglect and abuse of its detainees.[256] The suit targeted the Shenandoah Valley Juvenile Center in Virginia, and the complaint, filed in October 2017, alleged that detainees were stripped naked and

---

254 "MSNBC Live with Stephanie Ruhle," MSNBC, June 19, 2018.

255 Siraj Hashmi, "Remember those brutal immigrant detention centers liberals tried to pin on Trump? It was all Obama," *Washington Examiner*, May 29, 2018: https://www.washingtonexaminer.com/opinion/remember-those-brutal-immigrant-detention-centers-liberals-tried-to-pin-on-trump-it-was-all-obama.

256 Michael Biesecker, Jake Pearson, and Garance Burke, "Governor orders probe of abuse claims by immigrant children," Associated Press, June 21, 2018: https://apnews.com/afc80e51b562462c89907b49ae624e79.

left in their rooms, called derogatory names like "Mexican monkey," and physically assaulted. Two detainees cited in the complaint said they had been stabbed by a staff member with a pen.

The initial version of the AP report attempted to tie the lawsuit solely to Trump's immigration enforcement, noting: "Many of the children were sent there after U.S. immigration authorities accused them of belonging to violent gangs, including MS-13;" and "President Donald Trump has repeatedly cited gang activity as justification for his crackdown on illegal immigration." The article noted that the allegations in the complaint spanned from 2015 to 2018, but it conveniently neglected to mention that the time period overlapped with Obama's presidency, which ended in January 2017. Nowhere was Obama specifically mentioned in the AP report, though Trump was name-checked several times.

You have to go beyond the AP report and read the actual complaint to see that it said "John Doe," the lawsuit's main plaintiff, arrived at the detention center in April 2016, which, again, was when Obama was president. It was six weeks after his arrival when the plaintiff "first disclosed...that he had engaged in self-harm" and that "prior to his arrival in the United States, Doe had not engaged in self-harm." Doe attributed his new destructive tendency to the detention center, saying that he "learned this behavior while in...custody."[257]

It was only after I directly asked a spokesperson for the AP why the report didn't include any reference to Obama that the story was updated to make one single mention of the former president's administration. By contrast, there were four mentions of Trump throughout the article.[258]

---

257   John Doe and Nelson Lopez v. Shenandoah Valley Juvenile Center Commission, United States District Court for the Western District of Virginia Harrisonburg Division filing, Oct. 4, 2017: https://www.documentcloud.org/documents/4529878-Shenandoah-Complaint.html.

258   Eddie Scarry, "AP report on alleged illegal immigrant abuse at detention centers omits Obama was president at time," *Washington Examiner*, June 21, 2018: https://www.washingtonexaminer.com/news/ap-report-on-alleged-illegal-immigrant-abuse-at-detention-centers-omits-obama-was-president-at-time.

Maybe the detention facilities for illegal alien minors do suck. Maybe they're everything that the lawsuit against the Virginia facility says they are. And if they are, that didn't start with Trump. Yet the only reason the public was alerted about their conditions in the first place was because reporters and commentators needed a new thing that would hopefully make you hate the president—the "privileged"—as much as they do.

Time magazine was forced to issue a massive correction that same month after it mischaracterized what was happening in a photo it had published of a crying Honduran child who was brought into the country illegally. The photo ran on the magazine's cover and it was accompanied by a menacing image of Trump towering over the toddler. *Time* described the child as having been taken away from her illegal alien mother by U.S. Border Patrol, though that's not at all what happened.

"The original version of this story misstated what happened to the girl in the photo after she was taken from the scene," the magazine's correction said. "The girl was not carried away screaming by U.S. Border Patrol agents; her mother picked her up and the two were taken away together."[259]

Astonishingly, the magazine stood by its cover art, even after the story behind it was revealed as fraudulent. Editor-in-Chief Edward Felsenthal reasoned that even if the image didn't reflect the truth, it captured a "moment" in the immigration debate. (In other words, the cover was a crock, but it expressed how journalists *felt*.) "The June 12 photograph of the 2-year-old Honduran girl became the most visible symbol of the ongoing immigration debate in America for a reason," Felsenthal said in a statement to the *Washington Post*. "Under the policy enforced by the administration, prior to its reversal this week, those who crossed the border illegally were criminally prosecuted, which in

---

259 "'All I Wanted to Do Was Pick Her Up.' How a Photographer at the U.S.-Mexico Border Made an Image America Could Not Ignore," *Time*, June 19, 2018: http://time.com/longform/john-moore-getty-zero-tolerance-immigration-policy/.

turn resulted in the separation of children and parents. Our cover and our reporting capture the stakes of this moment."[260]

This is how the debate over privilege and victimhood works. The culture fascists maintain that something is true because they say so. And even if it's demonstrably not true, they'll insist that it *reflects* an otherwise *larger* truth. Facts are beside the point.

There are a few instances where journalists let their guard down and tell the truth about immigration in this country, but otherwise, the countless problems that stem from the endless tide of migrants rarely come up in the national media's coverage. If a journalist does happen to hit the truth a little too squarely, they're forced to repent. That's what happened to Tom Brokaw in January 2019, after he said on NBC's *Meet the Press* that too many immigrants were failing to properly assimilate.

"I also happen to believe that the Hispanics should work harder at assimilation," said Brokaw. "That's one of the things that I've been saying for a long time, you know, that they ought not to be just codified in their communities but make sure that all of their kids are learning to speak English and that they feel comfortable in the communities."[261]

If he hadn't said "Hispanics," you might have easily thought he was talking about Minnesota Democrat Ilhan Omar. But otherwise, nothing he said should have been controversial.

Every honest person knows what Brokaw was talking about. If you move to Italy, you learn to speak Italian and live fluidly among Italians. If you move to Japan, you learn to bow instead of shake hands. And if you move to Spain, you move somewhere else because you inevitably tire of only eating eggs and fried potatoes.

---

260 Aaron Blake, "Time magazine's major mistake on the crying-girl cover," *Washington Post*, June 22, 2018: https://www.washingtonpost.com/news/the-fix/wp/2018/06/22/time-magazines-major-screw-up-on-the-crying-girl-cover/?utm_term=.6acd6cc058f6.

261 Tom Brokaw, *Meet the Press*, NBC, Jan. 27, 2019.

You're expected to do pretty much nothing to be an American. Show up and you're more or less welcome to the party. But is it too much to ask that we share a common language and some sense that we all belong to the same country, which, presumably, strives for common greatness? There's a resistance to assimilation among far too many immigrants, and that's evident in Central American-born gangs in Maryland, Spanish interpreters for low-income patients in our biggest cities, and the tendency for Democrats to scream "raaaaciiiist" at anyone who might so much as think about holding her purse a little tighter when walking around Los Angeles at night.

For anyone who was born and grew up in America only speaking English, Brokaw's remarks were nothing out of the ordinary. According to the American Academy of Arts and Sciences, 80 percent of America speaks only English.[262] And yet Brokaw was instantly rebuffed by PBS reporter and noted culture fascist Yamiche Alcindor, who is black and who was seated next to Brokaw on the show's panel. "I grew up in Miami, where people speak Spanish, but their kids speak English," she prattled with an air of self-righteousness. "And the idea that we think Americans can only speak English, as if Spanish and other languages wasn't always part of America, is, in some ways, troubling."

No one said Americans "can only speak English." Brokaw said immigrants should put a priority on learning English. But this is what the culture fascists do when they have no rebuttal: They simply mischaracterize the point they've been confronted with and question the integrity of the person who made it.

The purpose of learning a country's language is that it requires people to immerse themselves in that culture, consuming its songs, movies, TV shows, and books. And, more important, mastering a country's language means interacting with the native, mainstream

---

262 American Academy of Arts & Sciences, "The State of Languages in the U.S.: A Statistical Portrait," December, 2016: https://www.amacad.org/publication/state-languages-us-statistical-portrait.

population. That's an idea you can no longer say aloud in America, lest the culture fascists in the media slap you for it.

Just hours after that edition of *Meet the Press* aired, Brokaw apologized. And then he apologized again. And again. And again.

"I feel terrible a part of my comments on Hispanics offended some members of that proud culture," he tweeted, using the authorized vernacular required by America's culture fascists when discussing topics related to privilege and victimhood.[263] "I am sorry, truly sorry, my comments were offensive to many," he continued in a separate tweet. "The great enduring American tradition of diversity is to be celebrated and cherished."[264]

He tweeted another apology: "Finally, I am sorry - I never intended to disparage any segment of our rich, diverse society which defines who we are."[265]

And another: "Finally, I am sorry I failed to convey my strong belief that diversity - dynamic and inclusive is what makes America."[266]

And, as required, in yet one more tweet, he thanked the culture fascist who properly checked his privilege. "Yamiche, thank u for your comments. let's go forward together."[267]

In a bonus tweet, he made his deference clear. "Great Yamiche is a wonderful colleague," he wrote, "and an important voice."[268]

The neutering of Brokaw was complete.

---

263 Tom Brokaw, Twitter.com, Jan. 27, 2019: https://twitter.com/tombrokaw/status/1089663227829592065?lang=en.

264 Tom Brokaw, Twitter.com, Jan. 27, 2019: https://twitter.com/tombrokaw/status/1089704096687419393?lang=en.

265 Tom Brokaw, Twitter.com, Jan. 27, 2019: https://twitter.com/tombrokaw/status/1089704217432993792?lang=en.

266 Tom Brokaw, Twitter.com, Jan. 27, 2019: https://twitter.com/tombrokaw/status/1089704218846466050.

267 Tom Brokaw, Twitter.com, Jan. 27, 2019: https://twitter.com/tombrokaw/status/1089704096687419393?lang=en.

268 Tom Brokaw, Twitter.com, Jan. 27, 2019: https://twitter.com/tombrokaw/status/1089704220314533894?lang=en.

Even after that rousing struggle session, Brokaw, having *checked his privilege*, needed to endure yet more public humiliation.

USA Today's in-house Latino, Raul Reyes, wrote the next morning that Brokaw had been "bigoted, misguided, and deeply disappointing."[269]

A *New York Times* story spanked Brokaw for having made his assimilation comments "nonchalantly."[270] (Perhaps he should have made the comments in Spanish.)

Brokaw's own employer, NBC, released a statement well after his apology, calling his on-air comments "inaccurate and inappropriate."[271]

Brokaw spoke the truth on network television, and the veteran newsman was forced to kneel at the altar of grievance. This is business as usual among the press, where there is only one acceptable position in the immigration debate: uncontrolled open borders, no questions allowed.

⌘　⌘　⌘

Never listen to a Democrat who says with a straight face that "everyone believes in border security." To a normal person, "border security" should mean something like a sealed-tight border that no one can cross without permission.

That's not what Democrats mean when they make evasive promises about "border security." When Democrats say "border security," they mean opening more ports for legal entry, increasing the number

269　Raul Reyes, "Before Tom Brokaw 'Meet(s) the Press' he should meet the Latinos," *USA Today*, Jan. 28, 2019: https://www.usatoday.com/story/opinion/2019/01/28/tom-brokaw-assimilation-meet-press-racism-apology-hispanics-latinos-column/2700595002/.

270　Sandra E. Garcia, "Tom Brokaw Apologizes for Comments About Hispanics and Assimilation," *New York Times*, Jan. 28, 2019: https://www.nytimes.com/2019/01/28/business/media/tom-brokaw-hispanics-assimilation.html.

271　Rob McLean and Brian Stelter, "NBC calls Tom Brokaw's assimilation comments 'inaccurate and inappropriate'," Jan. 27, 2019: https://www.cnn.com/2019/01/27/media/tom-brokaw-nbc-meet-the-press/index.html.

of refugees that we allow in from broken countries, and, worst of all, eliminating penalties for anyone who crosses into the U.S. without authorization.

Once upon a time, Democrats were able to claim with some feasibility that at the very least, they imagined America had some sense of boundaries, even if those borders and their function were a little fuzzy. Not anymore. Under President Trump, Democrats have dropped the act altogether. When Democrats say "border security" now, they mean "welcoming committee," complete with free healthcare and family services for every single sick and poor person coming up from Central America.

Watch the CNN interview with Representative Xochitl Torres Small, Democrat of New Mexico, that aired on December 27, 2018, and you come away with two things: a splitting migraine and the inescapable conclusion that Democrats want Border Patrol agents to function as nothing more than caretakers and babysitters for illegal immigrants.

Torres Small said on the show that the immediate priority for border security should be fixing up detention facilities and dumping more taxpayer resources into caring for illegal immigrants. "All of our safety depends upon having an agency that's quickly able to adapt to changing circumstances, and that's exactly what we have here," she babbled. "So we have to prioritize, of course, medical equipment, as well as personnel, appropriate facilities for these families that are being detained, because that's important to save children's lives, to make sure that detainees are safe and healthy." She also said she's "willing to work with anyone to make sure that we have real border security and that we are relying on this border that keeps all of our communities vibrant."

Yeah, I don't know what the hell she's saying either, but it doesn't sound anything like "Here's how to halt the waves of destitute foreigners currently breaking into our country."

Torres Small invited then Homeland Security secretary Kirstjen Nielsen to her district "to evaluate the medical conditions of these holding cells so that we can work together to fix what we can control," and repeated that the Border Patrol agency should "enforce our laws and reflect our values."[272]

She said nothing about preventing the hordes of migrants showing up at the border with their children, overwhelming authorities and our resources. No, instead we're supposed to eagerly redirect more American taxpayer funds to a border that Democrats want transformed into a charity center.

After the Trump administration in December 2018 ordered that migrants seeking asylum at legal ports of entry would need to wait in Mexico, Democrats suddenly discovered that our neighbor down south may not be the dreamy oasis they had been pretending it was right up until that point.

On CNN, Representative Luis Gutiérrez suffered a conniption. "God," he said on *Cuomo Prime Time*, "why should they have to wait on the other side of the border when they could be victimized again?… You know what we're going to have there? We're going to have illness. Right? You're going to have more murder, more rape, more harm coming to people that are fleeing."[273]

This came from a member of the same party that called Trump a racist for warning about rapists and drug dealers crossing the border from Mexico. Democrats and their friends in the media swore up and down in 2015, right after Trump announced his first presidential campaign, that there wasn't a single rapist coming in from Mexico. Now here was Gutiérrez in a panic attack over all the rape and illness to the immediate south of Texas. What changed?

Nothing. Gutiérrez wasn't honestly worried about anything. He was simply doing more advocacy on behalf of every single migrant who wants in, regardless of the skillset or capacity to make America a better place for the people who already live here.

---

272 CNN, *New Day*, Dec. 27, 2018.
273 CNN, *Cuomo Prime Time*, Dec. 20, 2018.

Beto O'Rourke was considered a viable contender for the 2020 Democratic presidential nomination. Not only did he say he opposed building more border barriers, but he advocated for tearing down any and all existing structures.[274]

California senator Kamala Harris, another 2020 Democratic presidential candidate, saw similarities between Immigration and Customs Enforcement agents and members of the Ku Klux Klan.

Ocasio-Cortez, who quickly became the unofficial leader of the House Democratic caucus, has said that ICE should be abolished altogether.[275] She has also called illegal immigrant detention centers "concentration camps" and directly compared our immigration laws to Nazi Germany. "The United States is running concentration camps on our southern border, and that is exactly what they are, they are concentration camps," she said in one of her insipid social media rants. "I want to talk to the people that are concerned enough with humanity that 'Never Again' means something."[276]

What "never again" means is, never again will the world witness the attempted mass extermination of a race, religion, or people. What it doesn't mean is that America is required to put up every illegal immigrant at the nearest Ritz-Carlton.

By the way, I've toured the detention facilities in Texas, and they're fine—which isn't a good thing. Accompanying my tour in summer 2019 was Acting Secretary of Homeland Security Kevin McAleenan, and he and the border agents were very proud and eager to note that detainees are given three hot meals per day, plus all the snacks they want, recreation

---

274   Caitlin Yilek, "Beto O'Rourke says he'd 'absolutely' take down the existing border wall in El Paso," *Washington Examiner*, Feb. 14, 2019: https://www.washingtonexaminer.com/news/beto-orourke-says-hed-absolutely-take-down-the-existing-border-wall-in-el-paso.

275   Alexandria Ocasio-Cortez, Twitter.com, Jan. 27, 2019: https://twitter.com/AOC/status/1089686929086599168.

276   Tim Pearce, "'I don't use those words lightly': AOC compares US southern border to the Holocaust," *Washington Examiner*, June 18, 2019: https://www.washingtonexaminer.com/news/i-dont-use-those-words-lightly-aoc-compares-us-southern-border-to-the-holocaust.

time, medicine, toiletries, and bathing facilities. It's all free, and it all serves as nothing but an even greater incentive for everyone south of Texas to drop themselves into the care of the American taxpayer.

At the first Democratic presidential primary debate in June 2019, former Housing and Urban Development secretary Julián Castro challenged his rivals to pledge that if elected president, they would decriminalize unauthorized entry into the U.S. Such a rule would, in essence, erase whatever sense of a border we currently have. Ohio representative Tim Ryan agreed with the idea. Senator Amy Klobuchar of Minnesota said she would look at the proposal, as though it were a complicated math problem.

The next day on CNN, Castro pretended he hadn't said what he said, as is the Democratic way when it comes to their unpopular immigration proposals.

"I'm for decriminalizing, not legalizing," he said. (*Mom, it's not that I failed the test, I just didn't pass!*) Castro added that there would still be "civil penalties" and a "process" for illegal aliens, but he described neither.

Then he *really* got lame. "Also, 'open borders' is a right-wing talking point," said Castro, who up until then had been very proud to support open borders. "We have 654 miles of fencing. We have thousands of border personnel. We have planes. We have helicopters. We have boats. We have guns. We have security cameras. Nobody has called for open borders."[277]

The only thing missing was that always present promise of "border security."

White House adviser Stephen Miller did God's work when he dispelled the myth of the Democrat who believes in border security. In December 2018, Miller was asked by CNN's Wolf Blitzer how the White House intended to get $5 billion from Congress for President Trump's "wall." Blitzer regurgitated the tired and false talking point

---

277 CNN, *New Day*, June 27, 2019.

that though Democrats won't fund more walls on the southern border, they "all say they support border security."

Miller replied with what every Republican should have said every time they've been confronted with that specious argument. "Like what?" said Miller. "With all due respect, Wolf, they voted against [imprisoning illegal immigrants caught entering the country a second time], they voted against ending sanctuary cities, they voted against deporting MS-13 gang members, they voted against deporting violent criminals, they voted time and time against a physical border wall to stop illegal entry. Where is the evidence that [Democrats] keep supporting that they're for border security?"

Blitzer then thoughtfully said, "Wow, all of that is true, and I hadn't thought of it that way."

I'm kidding. He said, "Stephen, I want to move on."[278]

While watching, by the way, I suspected Miller might have exaggerated at least the parts about Democrats' voting against ending sanctuary cities and deporting MS-13 members. Then I looked it up. Both claims are true.[279, 280]

The next day, Trump threw the federal government into a partial shutdown after Democrats in Congress refused a White House request for the wall money. It was $5.7 billion, which amounts to pennies for a government that spends trillions. The requested $5.7 billion was effectively nothing given that the "wall" project, if intended to cover the one thousand miles Trump promised, was going to cost closer to thirty billion dollars.

278   CNN, *The Situation Room*, Dec. 20, 2018.
279   Jenna Portnoy, "House passes Comstock bill targeting immigrant members of MS-13 gang," *Washington Post*, Sep. 14, 2017: https://www.washingtonpost.com/local/virginia-politics/house-passes-comstock-bill-targeting-immigrant-members-of-ms-13-gang/2017/09/14/71e97ce0-9956-11e7-b569-3360011663b4_story.html?utm_term=.586a5559d5c0.
280   Alexander Bolton, "Dems block Senate vote on sanctuary cities," TheHill.com, Feb. 13, 2018: https://thehill.com/homenews/senate/373622-senate-dems-block-vote-on-sanctuary-cities.

Twelve days into the government shutdown, Trump hosted an event at the White House featuring border agents who pleaded their case for a border wall.

Both CNN and MSNBC either downplayed the event or ignored it altogether.

After brief remarks on wanting to work with the new Democrat-controlled House, Trump introduced National Border Patrol Council president Brandon Judd, who said, "I can personally tell you, from the work that I have done on the southwest border, that physical barriers—that walls actually work."

National Border Patrol Council vice president Arturo Del Cueto was introduced thereafter to say, "It has nothing to do with political parties. You all got to ask yourself this question: If I come to your home, do you want me to knock on the front door, or do you want me to climb through that window?"

And then there was Hector Garza, another vice president and an agent who works on the Texas border, who said, "We're talking about murderers, rapists, people that commit very serious crimes in this country," and, "[I]f we had a physical barrier, if we had a wall, we would be able to stop that."

If you were watching MSNBC live, you missed everything they said. Dingbat anchor Katy Tur interrupted the feed from the White House to say, "The president clearly [wants] to take the day's narrative back from Speaker Nancy Pelosi, back from the new Democratic Congress…and back to the border and his demand for a wall." By "the day's narrative," Tur meant the ceremonies and speeches that Democrats were giving as they took control of the House, which were, no doubt, a TV ratings riot when compared to the chaos at the southern border.[281]

Judd, the National Border Patrol Council president, said at the press event that he had worked on the border in Naco, Arizona, where there was no physical barrier, and as a consequence, "illegal immigration

---

281   Katy Tur, *MSNBC Live with Katy Tur*, MSNBC, Jan. 3, 2019.

and drug smuggling was absolutely out of control." Instead of hearing that crucial information, Tur treated MSNBC viewers to anti-Trump writer Bret Stephens to say that the president should simply change his mind altogether about the wall and instead insist on "security." Ah, yes. That tried and true promise of "security" that has proven so helpful in years past. Every Republican and Democrat before Trump campaigned on "security." Trump campaigned on specific and tangible solutions and, against all odds, he won. Perhaps it's time lawmakers stop talking about "security" and concentrate on the specific and tangible solutions.

Even when Trump came back to the lectern at the White House, MSNBC still refused to cover the rest of the immigration event.

CNN carried it live, but rather than debate the merits of immigration once it ended, analysts on set took turns complaining that the event had been wrongly labeled a press briefing. Trump "didn't even take questions," moaned Brianna Keilar.[282] The next day on CNN, a screen graphic referred to the gathering of border agents as a "publicity stunt."

That's weird, because Hunter Walker, White House correspondent for Yahoo! News, also called it a publicity stunt.[283] So did the liberal Talking Points Memo website.[284]

Funny how they all said the same thing, almost as if they were working in unison.

That episode was more or less a repeat of what CNN and MSNBC did during the summer of 2018, when Trump hosted a White House event highlighting families who had seen loved ones killed by illegal immigrants.

282 Brianna Keilar, *CNN Newsroom*, CNN, Jan. 3, 2019.

283 Hunter Walker, Twitter.com, Jan. 3, 2019: https://twitter.com/hunterw/status/1080960892819386370.

284 Nicole Lafond, "Trump Trots Out Border Patrol Agents As Shutdown Over His Wall Drags On," Talking Points Memo, Jan. 3, 2019: https://talkingpointsmemo.com/news/trump-trots-out-border-patrol-agents-shutdown-over-wall-drags-on.

Before each of the victims' family members gave separate thanks to Trump and made remarks about their personal experiences, Trump accused the news media of having ignored their loss and their grief. "Because the news media has overlooked their stories," he said, "I want the American people to hear directly from these families about the pain they have had to endure, losing not only their loved ones [but] great people."

In a turn of dramatic irony that Shakespeare himself couldn't have written, as the victims' families began telling their stories, CNN anchor Brooke Baldwin interrupted the stream to complain about Trump's "attacks on the media" and then turn the programming over to yet more coverage of illegal-immigrant family members who had been separated from one another at the border.[285]

American parents who had their children killed or murdered by illegals were at the White House. But CNN chose instead to devote its airtime to the plight of aliens who showed up in the country unannounced.

In the lead-up to the 2018 midterm elections, the media put every ounce of energy toward blocking President Trump from using the immigration issue to the advantage of Republicans. Fighting the GOP is supposed to be the Democratic Party's job, but liberals can always count on the media to lend a helping hand.

Weeks ahead of Election Day, Trump sounded the alarm about a caravan of thousands of migrants that had originated in Central America and was headed toward the border with the intent of arriving in America and claiming asylum.

"Asylum" is the magic word. Everyone south of Texas knows that saying it to a border agent instantly secures them legal protection to remain in the country once they've set foot on U.S. territory. In the Rio Grande Valley border sector of Texas, just a few feet of water separate Mexico from the U.S., and all of Latin America has figured out that if

---

285 *CNN Newsroom with Brooke Baldwin*, CNN, June 22, 2018.

they simply drift across on a raft, they have to do nothing more than find a border patrol agent and tell him they want asylum. There's a background check on the aliens, but if they have no criminal history, they're told to show up for a future hearing and then released into the country, where—surprise!—nearly half of them vanish, never bothering to show up for their court date.[286]

Trump, ahead of the election, shouted day after day that the caravan of nearly ten thousand migrants, mostly from Guatemala, El Salvador, and Honduras, was on its way to the U.S. He rightfully noted that we hadn't the faintest clue as to who they were or what they would do once they got inside the country.

The media's response was to deny, downplay, and dismiss—and of course describe any anyone worried about the caravan as racist.

New York Times liberal Charles Blow said Trump's rhetoric on the caravan "encapsulates a sentiment" about "America…being invaded and overrun by people who are not white and not European, which risks the maintenance of American heritage, which is white heritage."[287]

Or maybe, *just maybe*, it's a matter of objecting to the thousands of people from poverty-stricken, crime-ridden countries barging into our country and handing American taxpayers the bill for all of the healthcare and other government services they'll need. Blow and the rest of the media know that's what the issue is really about, but to acknowledge it would derail their narrative on privilege and victimhood.

Washington Post writer Max Boot went on CNN and accused Trump of demagoguery and of "really pandering to the fears of Trump

---

286 John Kruzel, "Majority of undocumented immigrants show up for court, data shows," PolitiFact.com, June 26, 2018: https://www.politifact.com/punditfact/statements/2018/jun/26/wolf-blitzer/majority-undocumented-immigrants-show-court-data-s/.

287 Charles Blow, "Count me among the mob," *New York Times*, Oct. 21, 2018: https://www.nytimes.com/2018/10/21/opinion/trump-midterm-mob.html.

supporters and Fox News viewers who tend to be older, white, male who are alarmed about the supposed invasion of dark-skinned newcomers coming to America."[288]

Chris Cuomo pleaded with his viewers, "Please, don't see these people as Trump does, monsters on the march. See them as they are: desperate, leaving behind whatever they had, and whomever they knew, all for a better chance at life, a real life."[289]

Some in the media laughably suggested that though the mass of migrants was real, it was too far away to matter.

On Fox News, overt Trump hater Shepard Smith said, "The migrants…are more than two months away, if any of them actually come here. But tomorrow is one week before the midterm election, which is what all of this is about. There is no invasion; no one's coming to get you. There's nothing at all to worry about."[290]

Washington Post columnist Eugene Robinson wrote, "There is in fact no emergency, no invasion, no reason to panic."[291]

A *New York Times* report accused Trump and his supporters of attempting "to push alarmist, conspiratorial warnings about the migrant caravan." The report diligently noted that the caravan was "more than 2,000 miles from the border."[292] A separate article in the *Times* described Trump's focus on the caravan as "political opportunism."[293]

---

288 *Reliable Sources*, CNN, Oct. 21, 21, 2018.

289 *Cuomo Prime Time*, CNN, Oct. 18, 2018.

290 *Shepard Smith Reporting*, Fox News, Oct. 29, 2018.

291 Eugene Robinson, "Don't tell me that 'both sides' need to do better," *Washington Post*, Oct. 29, 2018: https://www.washingtonpost.com/opinions/dont-tell-me-that-both-sides-need-to-do-better/2018/10/29/78eb0d8e-dbb2-11e8-b732-3c72cbf131f2_story.html?utm_term=.5d4c7253ca6f.

292 Jeremy W. Peters, "How Trump-Fed Conspiracy Theories About Migrant Caravan Intersect With Deadly Hatred," *New York Times*, Oct. 29, 2018: https://www.nytimes.com/2018/10/29/us/politics/caravan-trump-shooting-elections.html.

293 Azam Ahmed, Katie Rogers, and Jeff Ernst, "How the Migrant Caravan Became a Trump Election Strategy," *New York Times*, Oct. 24, 2018: https://www.nytimes.com/2018/10/24/world/americas/migrant-caravan-trump.html.

Washington Post blogger Philip Bump wrote, "The perception is conveyed that a flood of people is rapidly approaching the U.S. border with Mexico. It is not."[294]

This would be like dismissing the concerns of Floridians who had been told by weather reports that a Category 5 hurricane was looming offshore. *Don't panic! It's still got a long way to go!*

Sure, the caravan was far away, but it was expected to show up eventually. And it did.

The *New York Times* reported on November 14, 2018, that the "first wave" of the caravan had made its way to the California–Mexico border. So much for all the comfort about it being too far away. The *Times* said that the Central American migrants had "begun arriving in the northern Mexico border city of Tijuana, setting up a potential confrontation with the American authorities that has been brewing for weeks."[295]

Huh. If only someone somewhere had warned about this "confrontation" that had "been brewing for weeks." Oh well!

Days later, another wave of migrants showed up at the Tijuana border and hundreds of them attempted to bum-rush U.S. authorities, who reported that rocks and bottles had been thrown at border agents.[296] Agents fired tear gas to keep the horde of migrants at bay, scattering the crowd and forcing them back into Mexico.

---

294 Philip Bump, "That caravan has a long way to go before it gets close to the U.S.," *Washington Post*, Oct. 22, 2018: https://www.washingtonpost.com/politics/2018/10/22/that-caravan-has-long-way-go-before-it-gets-close-us/?utm_term=.e6836a9d581c.

295 Kirk Semple and Elisabeth Malkin, "First Wave of Migrants in Caravan Reaches U.S. Border in Tijuana," *New York Times*, Nov. 14, 2018: https://www.nytimes.com/2018/11/14/world/americas/migrants-caravan-tijuana-border.html.

296 Sarah Kinosian and Joshua Partlow, "U.S. closes major crossing as caravan migrants mass at border in Mexico," *Washington Post*, Nov. 26, 2018: https://www.washingtonpost.com/world/the_americas/us-closes-major-crossing-as-caravan-migrants-mass-at-border-in-mexico/2018/11/25/f94aabe0-f0ea-11e8-99c2-cfca6fcf610c_story.html?utm_term=.5a619459e619.

The Mexican interior ministry said in a statement that it would be deporting the aggressors.[297] The ministry added that the actions of the migrants violated Mexico's legal migration framework and could have led to a "serious incident."

Tijuana mayor Juan Manuel Gastélum Buenrostro said in a post on Facebook that he wouldn't permit the behavior to threaten his city's relationship with the U.S.[298]

While the media couldn't be brought to even fake interest in Americans who'd had their families torn apart by illegal immigrant criminals, they were beside themselves over the confrontation at the border—the same confrontation that so many of them had insisted was too far into the future to be cause for concern.

CNN's Ana Navarro said on air that the U.S. needs an immigration policy "that does not involve tear-gassing children."[299]

A *Washington Post* story began by focusing on the images of migrant parents with their children, running to avoid the tear gas: "Reuters photographer Kim Kyung-Hoon shot the images, which provoked outrage and seemed at odds with President Trump's portrayal of the caravan migrants as 'criminals' and 'gang members.'"[300]

CNN legal analyst Jeffrey Toobin allowed that "certainly people shouldn't throw rocks." But, he said, the *real* issue was that "these people are poor, they're desperate, they want to come to find a better

---

297   "Mexico to deport migrants who 'violently' tried to cross the U.S. Border," Reuters, Nov. 25, 2018: https://www.reuters.com/article/us-usa-immigration-mexico/mexico-to-deport-migrants-who-violently-tried-to-cross-the-u-s-border-idUSKCN1NU12A.

298   Emanuella Grinberg and Mariano Costillo, "US authorities fire tear gas to disperse migrants at border," CNN.com, Nov. 25, 2018: https://www.cnn.com/2018/11/25/us/san-ysidro-port-of-entry-closed/index.html.

299   Ana Navarro, *New Day*, CNN, Nov. 26, 2018.

300   Tim Elfrink and Fred Barbash, "'These children are barefoot. In diapers. Choking on tear gas,'" *Washington Post*, Nov. 26, 2018: https://www.washingtonpost.com/nation/2018/11/26/these-children-are-barefoot-diapers-choking-tear-gas/?utm_term=.ae5676416b6d.

life, which is why immigrants always come." He added that the clash at the border, all things considered, went "pretty well."[301]

Tell that to the communities in Maryland, Philadelphia, and Boston devastated by Central American gangs. I suspect they might not look at thousands more illegal immigrants flooding into the country and say that things are going "pretty well."

And how quickly we went from "There is no emergency" at the border to "What about the children?"

The news media spoke of immigration in dire terms throughout all of 2017 and 2018, instigating hysteria over "family separations" and "children in cages." But when the White House said in January 2019 that Trump might declare a national emergency on the border in order to free up funds for wall construction,[302] it was as if the last two years had never happened. The media immediately began denying that there was any problem at the border at all.

Crisis? What crisis?

Previously in shock, journalists were suddenly unable to see a single problem at the border. What about the family separations? What about the cages? What about the concentration camps?

Nope! None of that apparently rose to the level of an "emergency," even after Democrats and liberals in the media had just spent the past two years having a meltdown about all of it.

Trump followed through and scheduled a prime-time speech from the Oval Office to officially declare the border crisis a national emergency. The hysteria intensified.

MSNBC's Joe Scarborough called on the national TV networks to boycott the address, asking on his show, "Why in the world would

---

301   Jeffrey Toobin, *New Day*, CNN, Nov. 26, 2018.
302   Boris Sanchez, "Trump inclined to declare national emergency if talks continue to stall," CNN.com, Jan. 5, 2019: https://www.cnn.com/2019/01/05/politics/trump-national-emergency-border-wall-shutdown/index.html.

the networks run Donald Trump's address tonight when we know that Donald Trump is going to be using it to spread these lies?" He continued, "And at this point, I've got to say, how stupid are Americans who still believe there's a crisis on the southern border?"[303]

On the same program, *Washington Post* columnist Karen Tumulty said, "We are headed to this extraordinary situation where the president declares a state of emergency, which does not exist, and the law does not really explain what we do if the president manufactures an emergency." Tumulty evidently had not read her own paper just days before, which at the time said, "Record numbers of migrant families are streaming into the United States, overwhelming border agents and leaving holding cells dangerously overcrowded with children, many of whom are falling sick."[304]

What crisis?

What's more, Tumulty evidently did not recall her own reporting from 2014. That year, with coauthor David Nakamura, she wrote on the "the current crisis on the Southwest border, where authorities have apprehended tens of thousands of unaccompanied Central American children."[305]

So, was there a "crisis" in 2014 but not in 2019, even though the number of border crossings, particularly by unaccompanied minors, had exponentially increased over that time? Funny how that works.

---

303 Joe Scarborough, *Morning Joe*, MSNBC, Jan. 8, 2019.

304 Nick Miroff and David Nakamura, "After years of Trump's dire warnings, a 'crisis' has hit the border but generates little urgency," *Washington Post*, Jan. 5, 2019: https://www.washingtonpost.com/world/national-security/ after-years-of-trumps-dire-warnings-a-crisis-has-hit-the-border-but-generates- little-urgency/2019/01/05/9a79a0e0-103d-11e9-8938-5898adc28fa2_story. html?utm_term=.5127dc8f7e41.

305 Karen Tumulty and David Nakamura, "Border crisis scrambling the politics of immigration policy," *Washington Post*, July 12, 2014: https://www. washingtonpost.com/politics/border-crisis-scrambling-the-politics-of- immigration-policy/2014/07/12/78b6ab16-0920-11e4-8a6a-19355c7e870a_ story.html?utm_term=.c85a7c115e8b.

When the administration in 2018 decided it was time to fully enforce immigration law, treating aliens as criminals, the media repeatedly called the situation a crisis. *USA Today* called it a crisis.[306] So did the *Washington Post*.[307] Even the liberal magazine *The Nation* called it a crisis.[308]

But all of that was before the Christmas miracle of 2019, when both Democrats and the media looked at the border and said, basically, "This all looks just fine to us!"

CNN's John Avlon said that the White House claim that there was an emergency on the border was "unrelated to reality."[309] Representative Jerry Nadler, Democrat of New York, told reporters at the time, "There is no crisis on the border."[310]

The *New York Times* editorial board cleverly declared that the crisis wasn't at the border; it was in the Oval Office and of Trump's "own making."[311]

When Barack Obama was president, even he referred to the ungodly numbers of migrants showing up in the U.S.—many of them just children without their parents—as a crisis.

"We now have an actual humanitarian crisis on the border that only underscores the need to drop the politics and fix our immigration

---

306   Aaron Hegarty, "Timeline: Immigrant children separated from families at the border," *USA Today*, June 27, 2018: https://www.usatoday.com/story/news /2018/06/27/immigrant-children-family-separation-border-timeline/734014002/.

307   Editorial board, "The family-separation crisis is not over," *Washington Post*, June 21, 2018: https://www.washingtonpost.com/opinions/ the-family-separation-crisis-is-not-over/2018/06/21/a03b8bb8-757b-11e8- 805c-4b67019fcfe4_story.html?utm_term=.b67e186424af.

308   John Washington, "The Family-Separation Crisis Is Not Over," *The Nation*, Sep. 5, 2018:https://www.thenation.com/article/ the-family-separation-crisis-is-not-over/.

309   John Avlon, *New Day*, CNN, Jan. 8.

310   Alfredo Corchado, "Trump's border crisis is disingenuous, nonexistent, say Dems as they tour border facilities," *Dallas Morning News*, Jan. 7, 2019: https://www.dallasnews.com/news/immigration/2019/01/07/ trumps-border-crisis-disingenuous-nonexistent-say-dems-fact-finding-visit.

311   Editorial board, "The crisis is in the Oval Office," *New York Times*, Jan. 8, 2019: https://www.nytimes.com/2019/01/08/opinion/president-trump-speech.html.

system once and for all," Obama said in the Rose Garden on June 30, 2014. "In recent weeks we've seen a surge of unaccompanied children arrive at the border, brought here and to other countries by smugglers and traffickers."[312]

Liberals were quick to note that Obama had called it a "humanitarian crisis," as though putting the word "humanitarian" in the mix changes the equation. Even so, the emergency predates Obama's speech.

Here's the *New York Times* on June 5, 2014: "The unanticipated surge in migrants in recent weeks has created a political, practical and humanitarian crisis for the Obama administration."[313]

What changed between 2014 and late 2018? Nothing changed, other than how the media characterized the issue. Under Obama, it was fine to call it what it was. Under Trump, it's privilege and victimhood. There is finally a president who at least in theory wants to secure the border, but pointing out the problem at the border has become tantamount to a hate crime.

In February 2019, Trump delivered a national address on the border crisis, and once again, he laid out the case for additional funding from Congress that would go toward enhanced border technology, medical resources to handle the obscene influx of children migrants, and the $5.7 billion for a physical barrier at the border. Two of those three were things that Democrats wanted (and that doesn't take into account that until 2015, Democrats had been in favor of building more physical barriers at the border). Trump said that the rich and powerful don't erect gates and walls around their homes because they hate everyone outside

---

312 "Transcript: President Obama's June 30 remarks on immigration," *Washington Post*, June 30, 2014: https://www.washingtonpost.com/politics/transcript-president-obamas-remarks-on-immigration/2014/06/30/b3546b4e-0085-11e4-b8ff-89afd3fad6bd_story.html?utm_term=.53fdf724f423.

313 Richard Fausset and Ken Belson, "Faces of an Immigration System Overwhelmed by Women and Children," *New York Times*, June 5, 2014: https://www.nytimes.com/2014/06/06/us/faces-of-an-immigration-system-overwhelmed-by-women-and-children.html.

them, but rather "because they love the people on the inside." He said that the border is under siege by drug smugglers, gang members, and human traffickers, all of which is 100 percent true, no matter how many times Democrats and the media ignore it or lie about it.

If you hate Trump, but have at least seen the reports on the illegal aliens inundating the Border Patrol and all of our taxpayer-funded resources, you might think, *Okay, Democrats, I'm ready to hear you prove him wrong.* Or maybe, *Okay, Democrats, I'm ready to hear an alternative solution.* But that's not what House speaker Pelosi and Senate minority leader Schumer did. Instead, they complained about the government shutdown being Trump's fault.

Pelosi accused Trump of spreading "misinformation and even malice." Schumer said Trump was using the government shutdown "to manufacture a crisis, stoke fear, and divert attention from turmoil" in his administration.

Okay, if they say so. But what about the things Trump was asking for? Statler and Waldorf were apparently unprepared to offer any substantial rebuttal to a very reasonable set of requests over a deadly serious problem. They never really got around to answering why they would oppose funding for those things.

Pelosi must have thought she got a deep dig in by mentioning Trump's campaign gag about Mexico's paying for the wall, a burn so good that Schumer repeated it later with a jagged smirk. (Apologies to Schumer in advance if that is simply the position in which his face rests.)

Okay, again, fine. Trump didn't get Mexico to directly pay for more wall construction. Now what about the illegal aliens dumping themselves into southern Texas by the thousands, clogging up the immigration courts, backlogging the asylum process, and turning border agents into nannies?

Pelosi repeated the trope about Democrats' believing in border security while at the same time "honoring our values," the Democrat code phrase for "Give illegals free food, housing, and healthcare." The closest either Pelosi or Schumer got to proposing a real solution to the border chaos was when Pelosi encouraged "innovation" that would "detect unauthorized crossings." Yes, and I encourage more innovation that would detect when a person has HIV, but that wouldn't really help the people dying of AIDS right now. Detecting unauthorized border crossers is useless if all of our agents are busy changing diapers. The goal should be to shut illegal border crossings down altogether.

Our problem at the border isn't that we don't know when aliens are illegally invading the country. The problem is that we don't have a system in place to stop them. We simply can't absorb all of Latin America's most destitute people. And yet our laughable immigration laws and wide-open border suggest that it's precisely what we're here to do.

There was, however, an upside to Democrats demanding equal air time to rebut Trump's immigration address. Everyone got to see for the umpteenth time that they're not serious about the border.[314]

The same is true for the national news media and Hollywood, America's ruling class of culture fascists. Their gated communities and high-rise apartment buildings are safe from illegal immigrant gangbangers, drug dealers, and child molesters pushing their way across the border and into ordinary public schools and neighborhoods. The culture fascists don't care what happens once Central America's poorest and sickest people dump themselves into the U.S. That's not their problem. It's yours. And if you won't deal with it, well, that's because you're a racist.

The immigration debate isn't really even about immigration. It's about checking the privileged. It's about reinforcing social justice.

---

314   Susan Ferrechio, "Democrats demand 'equal air time' to parry Trump's border security speech," *Washington Examiner*, Jan. 7, 2019: https://www.washington examiner.com/news/congress/democrats-demand-equal-air-time-to-parry-trumps-border-security-speech.

CHAPTER 7

THE CLOTHES DON'T MAKE THE MAN, AND THEY CERTAINLY DON'T MAKE THE MAN A WOMAN

Mixing up and confusing sexes and genders and biological differences is a hallmark of the social justice movement, and it has led to the creation of scores of privileged victims.

Anyone can understand a person who says he doesn't mentally connect with his biological sex, the same way anyone can understand a person who says he feels intensely disgusted by any part of his body, regardless of genitalia. It sounds unhealthy, but there's at least comfort in knowing that there's a good chance those feelings can be addressed by different therapies and medications. Hopefully, over time, the person suffering from the dysphoria or depression will find balance.

And besides, any man or woman is entitled in this country to dress, behave, and describe himself or herself in whatever way he or she likes. That's freedom.

That, however, doesn't satisfy the social justice movement in its perverse crusade to remake the country in such a way that not only are people free to feel and dress as they please, but everyone else is supposed to submit to it and accommodate it as deemed necessary. Social justice goes so far as to redefine what it means to be born with observable, scientifically understood qualities and features determined by an individual's biological makeup. The movement insists that an individual's unique perspective—their *truth*—overrides any biological reality.

We're expected to accept this as a new normal.

Don't ask whether it's appropriate for a biologically male adult to share a public restroom with a teenage girl. Don't ask about the fairness of a biologically male high school student competing in a young women's weightlifting league. Don't ask about the potential hazard of a biological woman showering in a men's locker room. Don't ask if pumping prepubescent boys and girls full of chemicals in order to suppress and synthesize their natural growth is in the best interest of children not mature enough to understand the lifelong consequences.

The questions are null and void, because the phrase "biological sex" has been scrapped from the lexicon by social justice. There is no biology or science to the body, according to the social justice mob. There are only self-professed identities, and they are legion. There are now: the cis-gender people, meaning people who identify with their biological sex; the transgendered, as in the men and women who attempt to live as the opposite sex; the non-binary, those who claim to be neither male nor female; the gender fluid, who pick and choose their gender depending on their immediate feelings; and the "queer," which, as far as I can tell, means whatever an individual wants it to mean.

Ryan T. Anderson, a senior researcher at the conservative Heritage Foundation, has exhaustively studied the ins and outs of transgenderism (including the outs that, after surgery, become the ins). He wrote in 2018 on the inconsistencies and oddities of the trans activist crowd that rightfully confound normal people.

"Regardless of whether they identify as 'cisgender' or 'transgender,' the activists promote a highly subjective and incoherent worldview," says Anderson.[315]

There is a glaring contradiction at play when transgender individuals insist that the biological makeup of a person is irrelevant while they at the same time take on the stereotypical traits of either men or women. It's the same contradiction that occurs when a trans woman— that is to say, a man who claims to be a woman—insists on reminding everyone that he's not a *real* woman.

In June 2018, trans woman Charlotte Clymer, a political activist, complained to the *Washington Post* that she had been discriminated against at a Cuban restaurant in Washington, D.C. (with really good dancing nights) because she was asked to show her ID when she tried to use the restroom. "In D.C., a city celebrated for its LGBTQ culture, inclusivity, and protections, it stunned me that a business could so openly discriminate against transgender people," said Clymer.[316]

Isn't this precisely the opposite of what anyone trying to live as a legitimate female would do—go to a national newspaper to out herself as a man?

Perhaps there really are trans women out there who live discreet lives and pray each day that no one detects their biological maleness. But Clymer (and trans activists like her) is not one of those people. A cursory look at her Twitter profile shows her paying tribute to "queer vaginal wall art"[317] and posting photos of herself in ridiculous costumes

---

315 Ryan T. Anderson, "Understanding and Responding to Our Transgender Moment," *Fellowship of Catholic Scholars Quarterly 41*, no. 1 (Spring 2018): https://papers.ssrn.com/sol3/papers.cfm?abstract_id=3172277.

316 Amy B. Wang, "Transgender woman says she was asked for ID to use restroom, then kicked out of D.C. restaurant," *Washington Post*, June 24, 2018: https://www.washingtonpost.com/news/local/wp/2018/06/24/ transgender-woman-says-she-was-asked-for-id-to-use-restroom-then-kicked-out-of-d-c-restaurant/?utm_term=.95e04db5e893.

317 Charlotte Clymer, Twitter.com, June 4, 2019: https://twitter.com/cmclymer/ status/1136078605035945989.

with captions like, "My favorite part about this tweet is knowing I can both look this glamorous and kick your mediocre, racist, misogynist, anti-LGBTQ ass if the occasion ever presented itself."[318]

This doesn't strike me as the behavior of a man who simply wants to be recognized as a woman. It looks like performance art. It's dress-up.

Says Anderson, "They say that there are no meaningful differences between man and woman, yet they rely on rigid sex stereotypes to argue that 'gender identity' is real, while human embodiment is not."[319]

In other words, why act like the mustard and relish matter if you insist that the hot dog doesn't?

The problems with transgenderism aren't limited to bathroom use. The psychological issues that trans people encounter, made no less difficult by a culture that says everyone should ignore those very issues, turn their lives into hell. This is particularly true of trans people who physically alter their genitals through surgeries that can be described as nothing short of mutilation.

To this date, there has been only one major scientific study on the long-term effects of sex-reassignment surgery. Over the course of thirty years, six Swedish doctors and scientists tracked the outcomes of 324 transgender people who had received reassignment surgeries—191 male-to-female subjects and 133 female-to-male subjects. Each subject was cross examined with ten random control subjects whose birth sex was matched up with the trans subject's after the subject had had their operations and hormone therapy. For example, a natural, biological woman was the control subject for a man who had had sexual reassignment surgery to become a "woman."

The results were devastating.

Subjects who underwent surgery were more likely than the control subjects to receive inpatient care for a psychiatric disorder, to

318 Charlotte Clymer, Twitter.com, June 2, 2019: https://twitter.com/cmclymer/status/1135335887888375808.
319 Ryan T. Anderson, "Understanding and Responding to Our Transgender Moment."

be convicted of a crime, and to develop cardiovascular disease. The mortality rate by suicide was most striking: Transgender subjects were almost twenty times more likely to have committed suicide within ten years after their operations.[320]

"This study found substantially higher rates of overall mortality, death from cardiovascular disease and suicide, suicide attempts, and psychiatric hospitalisations in sex-reassigned transsexual individuals compared to a healthy control population," the authors conclude. "This highlights that post surgical transsexuals are a risk group that need long-term psychiatric and somatic follow-up." They note that surgery and hormone therapy may provide some relief for transgender people, but that such treatment is "apparently not sufficient to remedy the high rates of morbidity."

In what world is this something to celebrate?

A 2009 survey by the Massachusetts Department of Public Health shows similar problems for people identifying as transgender. Nontransgender heterosexuals, gays, and lesbians all reported feeling some level of depression for about four days per month. Transgender adults reported double that amount. Among nontransgender hetero-sexuals, gays, and lesbians, between 2 and 4 percent said they had considered suicide within the past year. For transgender people, it was 30 percent. Among nontransgender heterosexuals, gays, and lesbians, between 12 and 14 percent reported that they had been violently victimized by an intimate partner. For transgender subjects, it was 35 percent.[321]

320   Cecilia Dhejne et al., "Long-Term Follow-Up of Transsexual Persons Undergoing Sex Reassignment Surgery: Cohort Study in Sweden," *PLoS ONE* 6, no. 2 (Feb. 22, 2011): https://journals.plos.org/plosone/article/file?id=10.1371/journal.pone.0016885&type=printable.

321   "The health of lesbian, gay, bisexual and transgender (LGBT) persons in Massachusetts," Massachusetts Department of Public Health, July 2009: https://www.masstpc.org/wp-content/uploads/2012/10/DPH-2009-lgbt-health-report.pdf.

The report concludes that overall, the trans people "had worse outcomes with respect to self-reported health, disability status, depression, anxiety, suicide ideation, and lifetime violence victimization."

That these findings largely mirror the results of the study in trans-friendly Sweden says everything. The psychological issues that accompany gender dysphoria are deadly serious, and they're overlooked by the social justice movement's pathological lie that these people need nothing more than understanding and acceptance.

No, they need help.

Feminist trans woman and writer Andrea Long Chu described her lived experience in a November 2018 op-ed in the *New York Times*. Gender dysphoria, she wrote, "feels like being unable to get warm, no matter how many layers you put on. It feels like hunger without appetite. It feels like getting on an airplane to fly home, only to realize mid-flight that this is it: You're going to spend the rest of your life on an airplane. It feels like grieving. It feels like having nothing to grieve."[322]

She wrote that her transitioning process has thrown her deeper into psychological turmoil. "I feel demonstrably worse since I started on hormones," Long Chu said. "One reason is that, absent the levees of the closet, years of repressed longing for the girlhood I never had have flooded my consciousness. I am a marshland of regret. Another reason is that I take estrogen—effectively, delayed-release sadness, a little aquamarine pill that more or less guarantees a good weep within six to eight hours." She added, "I was not suicidal before hormones. Now I often am."

These are not the thoughts of a well and stable person. These are not the thoughts of a person who simply needs affirmation.

Long Chu wrote in the op-ed that she would soon undergo surgery to have her penis made into a "vagina," and she admitted that she didn't

---

322 Andrea Long Chu, "My New Vagina Won't Make Me Happy," *New York Times*, Nov. 24, 2018: https://www.nytimes.com/2018/11/24/opinion/sunday/vaginoplasty-transgender-medicine.html.

expect it to make her happy. Still, she said she was entitled to have all of those feelings and desires, even if they're unhealthy. "I still want this, all of it," she wrote. "I want the tears; I want the pain. Transition doesn't have to make me happy for me to want it."

True, but the transition also shouldn't mean the rest of society has to reorganize itself to accommodate those feelings.

There are countless cases of transgender people who say they experience conflicting and tumultuous emotions like Long Chu's. But sometimes those feelings come when it's too late.

In 2004, an article in the British *Guardian* newspaper told the horrifying story of Marissa Dainton, a thirty-six-year-old trans woman who over the course of just eleven years had gone from man to "woman" and back to man before once again transitioning to "woman." Dainton's first procedure involved cutting up the penis to create a "vagina." When she decided she wanted to once again be a man, she then had a second surgery to remove the artificial vagina. It left her with a flat, smooth area resembling no human genitalia at all. "What happened to me should be a lesson in the need to make sure you're really ready before changing gender," Dainton said.

Imagine already going through the inner turmoil of believing that your biological sex does not comport with your feelings about your gender, only to have different doctors load up your system with unnatural chemicals and then agree to manipulate the physical makeup of your body.

The same *Guardian* article quoted Claudia (no last name given), a trans woman in Britain, who was immensely regretful about having a sex-reassignment surgery that she thought would save her troubled relationship with a man. But he broke up with her just one year after the surgery. Claudia said she felt betrayed by the psychiatrist who she believed had hastily cleared her for the procedure.

"My psychiatrist told me, you look great, you can 'pass,'" said Claudia, referring to her convincing female appearance. "I've come to realize that human life is made up of connecting, not 'passing.' I can 'pass' in a shop, I can 'pass' on the street. But when you tell a man your background, if you're lucky, he'll walk away. Nothing can prepare you for that. I feel notorious in any group. You can say you're Napoleon but unless the whole world agrees with you, you patently are not Napoleon. I'm not a woman, I'm a thing—a chimera."

You will never hear the social justice movement or the culture fascists in Hollywood and the national news media say today that this experience is far too common among people who undergo unnecessary, irreversible surgery on their genitalia. The 2005 film *Transamerica* stars Felicity Huffman as Bree, a reserved trans woman who drives across the country to have her penis converted to a vagina. In the movie, Bree tells her psychiatrist that once the procedure is over, "I will be a woman." At the movie's end, you see her in a bathtub, satisfied with her new gash and optimistic about the future ahead. Someone might tell Bree, though, that she's now twenty times more likely to commit suicide.

In February 2019, Walt Heyer wrote in *USA Today* that as a forty-two-year-old man, he attempted to transition to female. He said that he consulted a psychiatrist about the sexual abuse he had experienced as a child at the hands of his teenage uncle. The doctor told him that his gender dysphoria, however, was unrelated to the childhood trauma and that a sex change "was the only solution."

Heyer began taking estrogen, and he scheduled the surgical procedures to change his penis, his chest, and other features to make him appear more like a natural woman. He changed his name to Laura. Soon after, though, he said the trauma from his childhood resurfaced and he became suicidal.

"Why hadn't the recommended hormones and surgery worked?" he wrote. "Why was I still distressed about my gender identity? Why wasn't I happy being Laura?"

Heyer eventually decided to revert back to his old self, as best as possible, though he knew that some of the physical changes were permanent. He had his implants removed, and he began new hormone treatment to stabilize his body.

"I lived as 'Laura' for eight years," he wrote, "but, as I now know, transitioning doesn't fix the underlying ailments."[323]

Heyer didn't get into the details of his surgical reversion, but as you could expect, it's easy to remove an appendage from the body. It's impossible to grow a new one. Men with gender dysphoria who regret their bottom-half surgeries have no good options.

Urological surgeon James Bellringer has performed hundreds of male-to-female sex changes, and he told the *Guardian* that reversing the surgery is ultimately impossible. "The erectile tissue has been taken out, so you need a prosthetic," he said. "The urethra's gone, so you'd have to construct one out of a tube of skin. The tip of the penis will have been made into a neo-clitoris and I don't think you could put it back in its original place. It would probably be at the base of the artificial phallus." In short, he said, "It's a mess."

A pretty penis is hard enough to come by, but imagine a mutilated "penis" that you'll never cum by.

Now that social justice has sunk its claws into the medical field, prepubescent children, with all of their insecurity and uncertainty about life, are encouraged by witless celebrities to undergo hormone therapy and even transitional surgery if they profess to be transgender. To object to this way of thinking earns you a struggle session with the culture fascists.

In summer 2019, actor Mario Lopez said in an interview that he believed it to be dangerous for parents to affirm children, especially prepubescent ones, who claim to be transgender. "I think parents need to allow their kids to be kids but at the same time, you gotta be the adult in the situation," he said. "Pause with that and—I think the formative years is when you start having those discussions and really start making these declarations."

---

323 Walt Heyer, "Hormones, surgery, regret: I was a transgender woman for 8 years—time I can't get back," *USA Today*, Feb. 11, 2019: https://www.usatoday.com/story/opinion/voices/2019/02/11/transgender-debate-transitioning-sex-gender-column/1894076002/.

Liberals on social media naturally swarmed. They accused Lopez of bigotry. He then apologized for his "ignorant and insensitive" remarks, and he vowed to "better educate" himself.[324]

Real Housewives crazy lady Cindy Barshop used the opportunity to make the controversy about herself. She ran to *People* magazine to declare that one of her twin daughters, who were just nine years old, was transgender. She posted a photo on Instagram with the pair of them at a pool, with one of them wearing a bikini and the other one topless.[325] If this isn't cause for concern, what is?

Charlize Theron is another actress who thinks she's doing her adopted child a favor by playing along with his insistence that he's a girl. In April 2019, she told the *Daily Mail* that her son at age three told her he's actually a girl. "So there you go," Theron said. "I have two beautiful daughters who, just like any parent, I want to protect and I want to see thrive."[326]

It's sick. A three-year-old boy can barely wipe his own ass, but he's entrusted with the responsibility to declare his personal preferences on sex?

A June 2016 study by the Williams Institute at the University of California, Los Angeles estimated that the number of people in the U.S. claiming to identify as transgender had doubled from the previous

---

324 Rachel DeSantis, "Mario Lopez Apologizes for 'Ignorant and Insensitive' Comments About Parenting Transgender Kids," People.com, July 31, 2019: https://people.com/tv/mario-lopez-criticized-comments-parenting-transgender-kids/.

325 Tamara Palmer, "Inspired by Mario Lopez, RHONY Alum Cindy Barshop Revealed One of Her 9-Year-Old Twins Is Transgender," People.com, Aug. 2, 2019: https://www.bravotv.com/the-real-housewives-of-new-york-city/personal-space/cindy-barshop-twin-child-jesse-is-transgender.

326 Gabbrielle Donnelly, "Charlize: My child I thought was a boy is... a girl! For the first time, the Hollywood actress reveals why her adopted child Jackson is wearing dresses. And her inspiration? Her own mother—who shot her father," DailyMail.co.uk, April 18, 2019: https://www.dailymail.co.uk/news/article-6938233/Charlize-Theron-child-thought-boy-girl.html.

decade, bringing the total in 2016 to 1.4 million.[327] That figure has grown in large part due to the number of children whose whimsies about sexuality are now taken with grave severity, as is prescribed by the social justice mob and enforced by our culture fascists.

Little data exists about the ubiquity of transgender people in America. But one 2017 study, also by the Williams Institute, said that 150,000 Americans ages thirteen to seventeen identified as transgender.[328] A separate study by the University of Minnesota in 2018, only in that state, put the number higher.[329] In the United Kingdom, the National Health Service saw 1,419 referrals for gender identity issues at one clinic in the span of a year between 2015 to 2016. Between 2016 and 2017, the same clinic saw referrals increase by 42 percent, to 2,016.[330]

The Atlantic in 2018 published an extensive report on children experiencing gender dysphoria and found that youth clinicians in the U.S. are also "reporting large upticks in new referrals" of transgender patients. Waiting lists for appointments at those clinics "can stretch to five months or longer," the report said.

One young girl profiled by the magazine was fourteen-year-old "Claire" (not her real name), who recalled having internalized feelings

---

327 Andrew R. Flores et al., "How Many Adults Identify as Transgender in the United States," The Williams Institute of the University of California, Los Angeles, June 2016: https://williamsinstitute.law.ucla.edu/wp-content/uploads/How-Many-Adults-Identify-as-Transgender-in-the-United-States.pdf.

328 Jody L. Herman et al., "Age of Individuals Who Identify as Transgender in the United States," The Williams Institute of the University of California, Los Angeles, January 2017: https://williamsinstitute.law.ucla.edu/wp-content/uploads/TransAgeReport.pdf.

329 Lindsey Tanner, "More U.S. teens identify as transgender, survey finds," *USA Today*, February 5, 2018: https://www.usatoday.com/story/news/nation/2018/02/05/more-u-s-teens-identify-transgender-survey-finds/306357002/.

330 Tavistock and Portman NHS Foundation Trust, "GIDS referrals increase slows in 2016/17," Tavistock and Portman NHS Foundation Trust, April 27, 2017): https://tavistockandportman.nhs.uk/about-us/news/stories/gids-referrals-increase-slows-201617/.

that she was male. She had pleaded for her parents to help her find hormone therapy, and she eventually asked them to support her in undergoing a double mastectomy to remove her breasts. The feelings grew over the course of several years, but one day in late 2017, Claire looked in the mirror and realized that the changes she was making to her appearance, which by that point was considerably more masculine, weren't helping her feelings of anxiety and depression. "I was still miserable, and I still hated myself," she said. With more consideration, she determined that at their core, her feelings were driven by an inability to fit in with many of the girls she knew at school. But in time, she found some who shared her interests. "It was kind of sudden when I thought, 'You know, maybe this isn't the right answer—maybe it's something else.' But it took a while to actually set in that yes, I was definitely a girl."[331]

The article addressed the quandary of parents confronted with children who claim to be transgender and a culture that tells the parents to act on those claims with haste, erring on the side of affirming the children.

"How can parents tell?" wrote the author of the article, Jesse Singal. "How can they help their children gain access to the support and medical help they might need, while also keeping in mind that adolescence is, by definition, a time of fevered identity exploration?"

Under normal circumstances, the answers would be left to the parents' judgment. But we're no longer living under normal circumstances. We're living under social justice. Now powerful transgender groups like the Human Rights Campaign say things like "being transgender is not a phase."[332]

Even if you believe that, it's abhorrent that any responsible adult would immediately move to get his or her child on medication that

---

331 Jesse Singal, "When Children Say They're Trans," *The Atlantic*, July 2018: https://www.theatlantic.com/magazine/archive/2018/07/when-a-child-says-shes-trans/561749/.

332 Human Rights Campaign, "Transgender Children & Youth: Understanding the Basics," HRC.org: https://www.hrc.org/resources/transgender-children-and-youth-understanding-the-basics.

blocks puberty, or consider sending a daughter to a surgeon so that her breasts can be removed. As *The Atlantic* said, "Researchers have just begun tracking the kids engaged in this process, and we don't yet have comprehensive data about their long-term outcomes."

It's true that there are studies showing that hormone therapy and "reassignment" surgery result in a low number of patients who exhibit regret. But that ignores the 20 percent increase in postoperative transgender people likely to commit suicide.

This would be like promising three chronically anxious patients that you can cure them of their worries with a pill that makes them grow an extra tongue. If one patient commits suicide, another lives but regrets the treatment, and the third lives and is happy, you could technically consider that a 50 percent satisfactory rate. One of the subjects may have killed himself but, hey, out of the two who lived, at least one was happy.

This is the new normal. "Affirming care," wrote Singal, "has quickly become a professional imperative: Don't question who your clients are—let them tell you who they are, and accept their identity in a nurturing, encouraging manner."

Paul McHugh, M.D., a professor of psychiatry at the Johns Hopkins University School of Medicine, argues that even with surgery and hormones dumped into their bodies, mental hardship is the norm for transgender people, and that such people are best treated with psychotherapy rather than surgery. "Transgendered men do not become women, nor do transgendered women become men," Dr. McHugh wrote in 2015. "All…become feminized men or masculinized women, counterfeits or impersonators of the sex with which they 'identify.' In that lies their problematic future. When 'the tumult and shouting dies,' it proves not easy nor wise to live in a counterfeit sexual garb."[333]

In essence, the clothes don't make the man, and they certainly don't make the man a woman.

---

333 Paul McHugh, "Transgenderism: A Pathogenic Meme," ThePublicDiscourse.
    com, June 10, 2015: https://www.thepublicdiscourse.com/2015/06/15145/.

Jesse Singal's article in *The Atlantic* recounted the experience of Max Robinson. At age seventeen, with the consent of her parents, Robinson had her breasts removed after expressing dysphoric feelings about her gender.

"Max was initially happy with the results of her physical transformation," wrote Singal. "Before surgery, she wasn't able to fully pass as male. After surgery, between her newly masculinized chest and the facial hair she was able to grow thanks to the hormones, she felt like she had left behind the sex she had been assigned at birth."

But as Dr. McHugh said, there's no guarantee that the high of going through the process is permanent. In fact, it's likely not. And that's what Robinson experienced.

"[T]hat feeling didn't last," Singal wrote. "After her surgery, Max moved from her native California to Portland and threw herself into the trans scene there. It wasn't a happy home. The clarity of identity she was seeking—and that she'd felt, temporarily, after starting hormones and undergoing surgery—never fully set in. Her discomfort didn't go away."

Robinson thereafter admitted to having misinterpreted her feelings. She now maintains that her "sense of self isn't entirely dependent on how other people" see her. She also believes that the doctors who administered "care" were too eager to listen to her, rather than have her listen to them.

Dr. McHugh says that transgendered people are done no favors by the current American culture, which encourages them to pursue an impossible kind of self-fulfillment rather than the appropriate medical treatment. "The idea that one's sex is fluid and a matter open to choice runs unquestioned through our culture and is reflected everywhere in the media, the theater, the classroom, and in many medical clinics," says Dr. McHugh. "It has taken on cult-like features: its own special lingo, internet chat rooms providing slick answers to new recruits, and clubs for easy access to dresses and styles supporting the sex change. It is doing much damage to families, adolescents, and children."

Jesse Singal's *Atlantic* article profiled a third transgendered person, a woman, who said that she ventured to become a man but that she eventually came to regret the decision. Carey Callahan, thirty-six and living in Ohio, said that she had felt like a man for four years. She said, though, that after taking hormones for nine months, she found that her mental state never fully changed. She worked at a clinic for transgender people in 2014 and 2015, and during that time, she said, she began feeling differently about the transitioning process. "People had said often to me that when you transition, your gender dysphoria gets worse before it gets better," she said. "But I saw and knew so many people who were cutting themselves, starving themselves, never leaving their apartments. That made me doubt the narrative that if you make it all the way to medical transition, then it's probably going to work out well for you."

The trans issue is dangerous on a social level, a medical level, and now a political level. To wit, the U.S. military is expected to function as a laboratory for the social justice movement's weird human experiments.

President Trump in summer 2017 announced that the armed forces would no longer accommodate the rooming needs, hormone treatments, and surgical procedures sought by men and women attempting to live as the opposite sex. To be sure, the policy change doesn't ban transgender people from serving their country, any more than people who on their own time enjoy wearing clown makeup might be banned from working at Goldman Sachs.

The "ban" is simply a notice that the military would cease mixing transgender individuals in with troops who are not of the same biological sex. It further made clear that the Pentagon's budget would no longer cover hormone therapy and funding for sex-transition surgeries.

Trump's announcement about the policy was nonetheless characterized by Democrats and the news media as an attack on the LGBT community, and they accused him of backtracking on a 2016 campaign promise to support gays, lesbians, and transgender people.[334]

There was absolutely nothing inconsistent between Trump's action on the military trans "ban" and what he said about gays during the election. It's true that after the Orlando gay-nightclub shooting in 2016, Trump delivered a speech vowing to protect gays, lesbians, and trans people—and everyone else, too—from the threat of Islamic terrorism. But what does that have to do with telling the military it is no longer responsible for turning penises into vaginas and needlessly tinkering with hormones? Nothing, but where there is Trump, so too must there be victims.

As is the social justice way, trans people derive all of their clout from their portrayal as perpetual victims.

The Human Rights Campaign (HRC), an advocacy group for gay and trans people, sends out routine notices about transgender people as victims of violence. The purpose is to convince the public that trans women are permanent targets for bloodshed by intolerant bigots. Evidence backing up that idea, however, is scarce. Many, if not most, assaults against trans women are committed by significant others or by repeat criminal offenders, like drug dealers. Motivations for the assaults often have nothing to do with the victim being transgender.

In September 2018, *The Advocate*, a gaycentric magazine, compiled a list of trans people killed that year. The first one was Christa Leigh Steele-Knudslien, age forty-two, who was stabbed to death by her own husband. *Her own husband.* He went to the police after the incident to turn himself in.[335]

Another entry was for Phylicia Mitchell, who was forty-six when she was shot dead in Cleveland. When the suspect, Gary Sanders, was

334 Maggie Haberman, Twitter.com, July 26, 2017: https://twitter.com/maggieNYT/status/890197516368654337.
335 "These are the trans people killed in 2018," *The Advocate*, Sep. 19, 2018: https://www.advocate.com/transgender/2018/9/19/these-are-trans-people-killed-2018#media-gallery-media-0.

apprehended, a local news report said that the violent confrontation was the result of his "collecting a drug debt."[336]

Dallas trans woman Carla Patricia Flores-Pavón was another entry. She was strangled to death in May 2018, and after police took the suspect into custody, they said the motive was likely not prejudice and that the homicide was the outcome of a violent robbery.[337]

Trans man Nino Fortson was listed for having died after a public altercation that included two men and two women, according to the *Atlanta Journal-Constitution*. A witness said that Fortson had been the first to pull out a gun and fire it before she was shot.[338]

The HRC also included the following in its list of violence against transgender people in 2018:

- Victoria "Viccky" Ramos Gutierrez, age thirty-three, of Los Angeles, was stabbed to death during an attempted robbery.[339]

- Honduran trans woman Roxsana Hernández Rodriguez, age thirty-three, had been detained by Immigration and Customs Enforcement and on May 25 was pronounced dead, apparently due to dehydration and complications from HIV. (It's worth noting that others who weren't transgender have also died after making the life-threatening trek to the U.S. from Central America.)[340]

---

336 Adam Ferrise, "Man charged in slaying of Cleveland transgender woman," Cleveland.com, April 10, 2018: https://www.cleveland.com/metro/2018/04/man_charged_in_slaying_of_clev_1.html.

337 Richie Duchon, "Police make arrest in killing of transgender woman in Dallas," NBC News, May 17, 2018: https://www.nbcnews.com/feature/nbc-out/police-make-arrest-killing-transgender-woman-dallas-n875206

338 Raisa Habersham, "Transgender man shot, killed in northwest Atlanta," AJC.com, May 17, 2018: https://www.ajc.com/news/crime—law/transgender-man-shot-killed-northwest-atlanta/ngBzxSDnCrxm5scgsuIgQO/.

339 Nicole Santa Cruz, "Man is charged in the stabbing death of Pico-Union house fire victim," *Los Angeles Times*, Jan. 16, 2018: https://www.latimes.com/local/crime/la-me-fire-homicide-20180116-story.html.

340 Scott Bixby, "Trans Woman Was Beaten in ICE Custody Before Death, Autopsy Finds," Nov. 26, 2018, Daily Beast: https://www.thedailybeast.com/trans-woman-roxsana-hernandez-rodriguez-beaten-in-ice-custody-before-death-pathologist-finds.

- Sasha Wall, age twenty-nine, of Chesterfield County, South Carolina, was shot to death and found in early April in her car on the side of a highway. Police said, "Everything's pointing to [the indication that] it was a breakup-like argument."[341]

- Michelle Washington, age forty, of Philadelphia was found dead on a sidewalk on May 19 after having been shot. Detectives said it didn't appear that Washington was targeted for her trans identity and that she likely didn't know her attacker. They said her murder was probably the result of a robbery.[342]

- An unidentified twenty-one-year-old trans woman in Cleveland was shot in the head and had to be transported to the hospital for treatment on April 1, 2019. (The incident was still included for some reason in the HRC's 2018 catalog.) The altercation, according to a local report, took place after the victim got into an argument with her mother over a tax return check. John Booth, age sixty-one, reportedly intervened and shot the trans woman.[343]

None of these deaths was the result of some widespread antipathy for trans people. There is no evidence that they're targeted en masse simply because they're trans. But why should that stop the trans lobby from pretending they all were? For trans people to be targeted for their sexuality is to achieve higher rank on the intersectionality scale. And that, of course, opens up all kinds of doors in America.

Transgender people have been turned into yet one more set of privileged victims, and the culture fascists who made it that way expect

---

341 Teddy Kulmala, "Police have a 'very strong' lead in killing of transgender SC woman," *The State*, April 30, 2018: https://www.thestate.com/news/local/crime/article210131529.html.

342 Laura Smythe, "Transwoman shot to death in North Philadelphia on Sunday," Epgn.com, May 20, 2019: http://www.epgn.com/news/breaking-news/14675-transwoman-shot-to-death-in-north-philadelphia-on-sunday.

343 Adam Ferrise, "Argument over tax check led to shooting of transgender woman in Cleveland, police say," Cleveland.com, April 15, 2019: https://www.cleveland.com/metro/2019/04/argument-over-tax-check-led-to-shooting-of-transgender-woman-in-cleveland-police-say.html.

complete submission from everyone else. Their suffering, after all, demands that they be revered. Their grievance, naturally, entitles them to be seen and heard.

That explains why, among the first things Democrats did after taking the House back in 2019, was pass a bill that, in part, said trans people "could not be denied access to a restroom, locker room or dressing room based on their gender identity."[344]

It's just one more way that the social justice movement has sought to erase American norms, institutions, and conventions and, by consequence, bring down those who sit at the top and elevate those who dwell at the bottom.

---

344 Ashley Killough, "Houses passes Equality Act to increase protections for sexual orientation and gender identity," CNN.com, May 17, 2019: https://www. cnn.com/2019/05/17/politics/houses-passes-equality-act/index.html.

CHAPTER 8

VICTIM STATUS FOR HER AND HER AND #METOO, PLEASE!

Nothing pure goes uncorrupted by America's social justice movement. The very concept of privilege itself was innocent, a simple observation that men—white men in particular—might consider whether they have inherent advantages in certain situations and that they might express more empathy for anyone who doesn't. But then the social justice mob seized on the idea, turning it into a weapon for shaming and stigmatizing.

The same fate has met #MeToo.

The #MeToo movement kicked off in 2017 with serious accusations against movie mogul Harvey Weinstein, related to his pattern of appalling and abusive behavior. Over a number of years, he had repeatedly groped and exposed his hoggish nude body to young aspiring actresses and other women hoping to break into the movie industry. He duped them into believing that he would advance their careers if only they'd touch him or watch him shower.

The *New York Times* in October 2017 broke the blockbuster story that Weinstein "for decades" had paid off an untold number of women accusing him of sexual harassment.

"Across the years and continents," the *Times* article said, "accounts of Mr. Weinstein's conduct share a common narrative: Women reported to a hotel for what they thought were work reasons, only to discover that Mr. Weinstein, who has been married for most of three decades, sometimes seemed to have different interests."[345]

Women employed by Weinstein, and who traveled around the globe with him, described his "appearing nearly or fully naked in front of them, requiring them to be present while he bathed or repeatedly asking for a massage or initiating one himself."

When these women sought a coveted, close working relationship with Weinstein so that they might get an intimate look at the movie industry, I suspect that seeing his fat ass hop into a tub wasn't what they had in mind.

Famous men might be wrongfully accused of sexual misconduct for any number of reasons: the accuser wants money or attention, or perhaps the accuser is getting even for a perceived slight from the past. If the man accused denies the charge and there's no evidence outside of an uncorroborated account, the allegation often ends up in a stalemate.

Fortunately for America, Weinstein rid us of any of those uncomfortable scenarios with his personal situation by simply admitting to his long history of predatory behavior.

"I appreciate the way I've behaved with colleagues in the past has caused a lot of pain, and I sincerely apologize for it," he said in a statement to the *Times* for its initial report. "Though I'm trying to do better, I know I have a long way to go."

Weinstein expanded on those feelings in a separate statement he sent to the paper shortly after the story was published. "I realized some time ago that I needed to be a better person and my interactions with the people I work with have changed," it said.[346]

---

345 Jodi Kantor and Megan Twohey, "Harvey Weinstein Paid Off Sexual Harassment Accusers for Decades," *New York Times*, Oct. 5, 2017: https://www.nytimes.com/2017/10/05/us/harvey-weinstein-harassment-allegations.html.

346 Statement from Harvey Weinstein, *New York Times*, Oct. 5, 2017: https://www.nytimes.com/interactive/2017/10/05/us/statement-from-harvey-weinstein.html.

At the bottom of that statement, as though he knew this was just the thing that would cleanse his soul and restore his reputation, Weinstein said that he would make up for his perverse conduct by attacking the National Rifle Association.

"I am going to need a place to channel [my] anger so I've decided that I'm going to give the NRA my full attention," the statement said.

And the women who had been violated by Weinstein's hairy, fleshy body said in unison, "I forgive you, Harvey."

Not really. The same day as that statement was published, Weinstein's lawyer issued yet another one to *The Hollywood Reporter*, this time saying that the *Times* story was "saturated with false and defamatory" claims about Weinstein and that the legal team planned to sue the paper.[347]

Someone should have told Weinstein and his team that this isn't how denials work. You do them first, and if you plan to admit to wrongdoing, that comes later--usually *much* later.

But wait, there's more! Five days after the *Times* report, journalist Ronan Farrow released a 2015 audio recording wherein Weinstein is heard admitting to groping the breast of twenty-two-year-old model Ambra Battilana Gutierrez. He's also heard pleading for Gutierrez to come and wait inside his hotel room while he showers, something he did to women often, according to the *Times*. Gutierrez, clearly in distress, is heard on the tape repeatedly resisting Weinstein.[348]

The recording device was reportedly strapped to Gutierrez as part of a New York police sting operation after she had filed a report. The confrontation between her and Weinstein took place at a luxury hotel frequented by Weinstein in New York.

---

347 Eriq Gardner, "Harvey Weinstein to Sue N.Y. Times, Says His Attorney," *Hollywood Reporter*, Oct. 5, 2017: https://www.hollywoodreporter.com/thr-esq/harvey-weinstein-lawsuit-new-york-times-is-being-prepared-says-his-attorney-1046170?utm_source=twitter.

348 Ronan Farrow, "From Aggressive Overtures to Sexual Assault: Harvey Weinstein's Accusers Tell Their Stories," *New Yorker*, Oct. 10, 2017: https://www.newyorker.com/news/news-desk/from-aggressive-overtures-to-sexual-assault-harvey-weinsteins-accusers-tell-their-stories.

Gutierrez: What do we have to do here?

Weinstein: Nothing. I'm going to take shower. You sit there and have a drink—water.

Gutierrez: I don't drink. Can I stay [at] the bar?

Weinstein: No, you must come here now.

Gutierrez: No, I don't want to.

Weinstein: I'm not doing anything with you, I promise.

Weinstein continues begging her to come to his room, insisting that she will embarrass him at the hotel if she doesn't. Gutierrez rejects his beckoning, over and over.

Weinstein: Go to the bathroom.

Gutierrez: Please, I don't want to do something [that] I don't want to.

Weinstein: Go to the bath—hey, come here. Listen to me.

Gutierrez then asks Weinstein why he had touched her breast the previous day.

Weinstein: Oh, please, I'm sorry....Come on in. I'm used to that.

Gutierrez: You're used to that?

Weinstein: Yes, come in.

What happened to Weinstein was a major comeuppance for powerful men—major Democratic donors no less—who had sexually taken advantage of women. It followed the summer 2016 ousting of Roger Ailes as CEO of Fox News. Ailes was fired after anchor Gretchen Carlson accused him of demoting her for rebuffing his aggressive advances, a claim similar to one shared thereafter by Megyn Kelly, who said that Ailes had grabbed her and attempted to kiss her mouth.

This is what #MeToo is about. Like the very concept of privilege, it served a valuable purpose before it was sharpened into a shiv, used for political gain, and for settling personal grudges.

Sexual harassment and misconduct should be precisely defined by incidents of gross behavior, wherein a person is violated in such a way that any reasonable person could understand who is the victim and who is the alleged perpetrator. That's no longer the case. What we have now is a culture that allows women to allege sexual assault or harassment, regardless of any supporting evidence, and then we all watch as the accused are turned into outcasts.

Fox News's ousting of star anchor Bill O'Reilly technically predates the national rise of #MeToo, but his fate should have been a cautionary tale about what such a movement would become: an insatiable monster that robs men of due process.

Just six months before the fall of Weinstein, the *New York Times* reported that O'Reilly and Fox had paid out millions of dollars in settlements for sexual harassment claims over the course of several years.

The paper "found a total of five women who have received payouts from either Mr. O'Reilly or the company in exchange for agreeing to not pursue litigation or speak about their accusations against him," with payments totaling roughly $13 million.[349]

The *Times* said that the women accusing O'Reilly of misconduct "either worked for him or appeared on his show," a very clever phrasing that mixed together claims of workplace sexual harassment and ones involving women who were employed by neither O'Reilly nor Fox. And yes, there is a difference, just as there's a difference between calling a woman you work with a bitch and saying it to a random person who cuts you off in traffic. Only one of those is professional misconduct, and the other is just kind of a rude thing to do.

"Mr. O'Reilly would create a bond with some women by offering advice and promising to help them professionally," the *Times* said. "He

---

349   Emily Steel and Michael S. Schmidt, "Bill O'Reilly Thrives at Fox News, Even as Harassment Settlements Add Up," *New York Times*, April 1, 2017: https://www.nytimes.com/2017/04/01/business/media/bill-oreilly-sexual-harassment-fox-news.html?module=inline.

then would pursue sexual relationships with them, causing some to fear that if they rebuffed him, their careers would stall."

The careful wording here obscures whether the *Times* is referring to women employed by Fox or women who wanted to use O'Reilly's show and airtime to promote themselves.

Are we talking about women who worked at Fox and therefore might legitimately feel that they were being harassed by a colleague who held power over their employment, or are we talking about the leggy opportunists who only wanted O'Reilly to promote them on his show but who were cut off once they declined alleged romantic advances?

This is the difference between the right to feel secure in your working environment and feeling entitled to use someone for your own advancement without anything in return.

In the *Times* report, Wendy Walsh, a psychologist who had appeared on O'Reilly's show, said that O'Reilly promised her that he could get her a contract at the network, a cushy gig that involves getting paid thousands of dollars for doing the hard labor of wearing nice makeup and shooting the shit on national television.

Walsh said that in 2013, she met O'Reilly for dinner at a hotel in Los Angeles and that afterward, he invited her to his room. She declined but suggested they go to the hotel bar. She said that once they got there, O'Reilly grew cold, insulted her purse, and told her that she could "forget any career advice he had given her and that she was on her own."

And yet, she remained a guest on O'Reilly's show for four months before her bookings dried up.

Where's the sexual harassment here, exactly? She wasn't O'Reilly's or Fox's employee, there was no legal agreement between any parties, and she was, according to the report, no longer booked because the network saw that ratings for her segments were lagging.

Nowhere in the world, least of all in the national news business, is it required that you give opportunities away out of the kindness of your heart to people who are otherwise talentless bores and have nothing to offer in return. Assume that O'Reilly had kept booking Walsh on his show, which would have suffered because of it. She would get all the benefits and have offered nothing. That's fair? How long was he required to keep booking her before it would no longer have been considered sexual misconduct to let her go?

MSNBC's *Morning Joe* cohosts Mika Brzezinski and Joe Scarborough literally sleep together. Does anyone honestly believe they would boost each other's careers so cheerfully if they weren't?

If it's fine to get a career lift from having consensual sex, why is it a problem to see nothing at all happen from declining sex?

Let's assume Walsh's story, which O'Reilly denies along with the rest, is true. It boils down to him showing interest in her, wooing her with potential financial gain (which she wasn't entitled to), and then getting turned down. Once he saw the relationship was going nowhere, he cut ties.

Why would he be expected to still offer Walsh career advancement that he never owed her from the start?

As noted by the *Times*, Walsh never received a settlement from O'Reilly or Fox, but her grievances were aired out in the report anyway. It was one more accusation that could pad the numbers against O'Reilly.

Speaking of settlements, the whole point of one is that both sides reach an agreement to drop the issue and either deny that any wrongdoing occurred or remain silent about all of it. That's not how they work anymore. Now, either the plaintiff's lawyer or someone close to the plaintiff leaks it all to the news media. Any defendant who agrees to a settlement now will not only be out of a large sum of money, but they can expect for the details of the suit to become public anyway, regardless of whether silence was part of the deal.

O'Reilly's settlements are all laughable in their details and circumstances. It was only after the ousting of Roger Ailes, a fraught period for the network, that former anchor Laurie Dhue, and Juliet Huddy, who had been a morning host at Fox, came forward with their own allegations.

The *Times* reported that Dhue, who is open about her struggles with alcoholism, had not complained during or after her tenure at Fox about any harassment. It wasn't until the Ailes episode that she accused both him and O'Reilly of misconduct and received a $1-million-plus settlement.

Huddy, who often appeared on O'Reilly's show, claimed that after a lunch meeting in 2011, he took her to his home in New York and gave her a tour. At the end, before departing and to Huddy's "shock and disgust," he attempted to kiss her. She was so "repulsed," as a 2017 letter her lawyers wrote to Fox put it, that she "instinctively recoiled and actually fell to the ground."[350] The letter adds that O'Reilly seemed amused and didn't offer to help her up.

The language used in the letter, written like an overwrought script for a Lifetime movie, was obviously chosen with the intent of making it public. Naturally, that's exactly what happened.

After Huddy's "I've fallen and can't get up" incident, she alleged that just a week later, O'Reilly asked her to dinner and a Broadway show, and she agreed to join him because "he had total control over her work assignment." Then, according to Huddy, O'Reilly "moved close to [me] in a way that made [me] feel uncomfortable" and tried to hold her hand before she pulled away. After all of that, she says, he gave her a key to his hotel bedroom.

Huddy says she resisted going to his room, asking that he come claim the key in the lobby. She said, however, that she eventually relented and went to O'Reilly's room, where she was greeted at the door by O'Reilly in his underwear. This was the number-one-rated cable news star answering a hotel room door, where he could have been seen by anyone at any moment, in his underwear? Did Shonda Rhimes write Huddy's claims for her?

Huddy received a settlement of nearly $2 million, according to the *Times*.[351]

---

350 Emily Steel and Michael S. Schmidt, "Fox News Settled Sexual Harassment Allegations Against Bill O'Reilly, Documents Show," *New York Times*, Jan. 10, 2017: https://www.nytimes.com/2017/01/10/business/media/bill-oreilly-sexual-harassment-fox-news-juliet-huddy.html?module=inline.
351 Emily Steel and Michael S. Schmidt, "Bill O'Reilly Thrives at Fox News."

The culture fascists had been going after O'Reilly for years because he had an impact and, though in his sixties, had shown no interest in retirement. They finally got him. Almost twenty days after the *Times* report was printed, he was out at Fox.

There were other claims against O'Reilly, but public details were scant. One woman claimed to have recordings of phone calls with O'Reilly, but the *Times* report devoted just one paragraph to that revelation.

Nonetheless, what happened to O'Reilly was purely a matter of knocking down an influential person who had power in our culture, particularly in politics. As a white man, he was deemed to hold privilege, so he had to be taken out. Get rid of the "privileged" to elevate the "oppressed" and train the national attention on yet more oppression and grievance. The reach of the social justice movement is absolute, and though liberals have embraced it, even their own can be taken down without notice.

The canceling of beloved NBC *Today* host Matt Lauer epitomizes that fact.

The network announced on the morning of November 29, 2017, that the longtime anchor had been fired. NBC knew that reports were coming about complaints that he had sexually harassed or assaulted women who worked there. The *New York Post* said that much of NBC's decision to terminate Lauer rested on the claims of one NBC staffer who had been working at the 2014 Winter Olympics in Sochi, Russia, which Lauer had covered for the network. The lawyer for the staffer said that the woman had been sexually harassed by Lauer and that she had evidence that other women had, too, though the report contained no details about the allegations.[352]

Variety magazine published a piece just hours after the announcement of Lauer's firing. It detailed claims by women who said that Lauer

---

352 Emily Smith and Yaron Steinbuch, "Matt Lauer allegedly sexually harassed staffer during Olympics," *New York Post*, Nov. 29, 2017: https://pagesix.com/2017/11/29/matt-lauer-allegedly-sexually-assaulted-female-staffer-during-olympics/.

had exposed himself to them, made inappropriate comments in their presence and, in some cases, forced himself on them. The *New York Times* had its own story with similar details.

A day later, Lauer released a statement expressing "sorrow and regret for the pain I have caused," though he added that "some of what is being said about me is untrue or mischaracterized."

Perhaps by "some" he meant almost everything that was reported, which was either absurd or ungodly stupid or, at the very least, should have invited more questions about what exactly happened before anyone could make the call that he be ripped out of the anchor chair. But most people, particularly those in his position with massive public pressure, don't know that an immediate apology does nothing more than feed the social justice beast. It wins you no favor, earns you no quarter.

The *Times* reported on one such incident of Lauer's alleged conduct, detailing the story of an NBC employee who said that in 2001, Lauer asked that she come to his office so that he could discuss a news item. When she arrived, according to the report, he asked her to unbutton her shirt.[353]

She ran away mortified.

Just kidding. The *Times* report said that the woman went ahead and did as Lauer asked—just as any uninterested person would do! Lauer then came out from behind his desk, according to the report, pulled the woman's pants down, bent her over the chair, and the two had sex.

This is without question inappropriate for the workplace, but where was the assault, harassment, or abuse? If it wasn't consensual, was it a rape? Where is the police report or at least some indication that this was criminal? There is none.

The *Times* said the woman fainted at some point, that she woke up on the floor of Lauer's office, and that Lauer had an assistant take her to see a nurse.

---

353   Ellen Gabler, Jim Rutenberg, Michael M. Grynbaum, and Rachel Abrams, "NBC Fires Matt Lauer, the Face of 'Today,'" *New York Times*, Nov. 29, 2017: https://www.nytimes.com/2017/11/29/business/media/nbc-matt-lauer.html?smid=tw-nytimes&smtyp=cur&_r=0.

To recap: This woman went into Lauer's office, unbuttoned her blouse at his request, and then proceeded to have sex with him until she passed out. Aside from sounding like a weird morning TV-inspired porno, the most bothersome thing about this anecdote is that there's no indication that it was nonconsensual.

Variety reported on a former employee who said everyone on the *Today* staff felt intense pressure to be liked by Lauer. "There is such shame with Matt Lauer not liking you," she said. "I did this special with him and we are traveling and I had a cold sore on my lip and I heard him say to Bryant Gumbel, 'She has this really ugly cold sore on her lip,' like that was something to be ashamed of. He was just really cruel."

Okay, again, where does the sexual assault come in? It's an unprofessional comment to make at work, certainly, but why is this lumped in with #MeToo accusations of sexual assault and harassment?

Maybe Lauer was an asshole and maybe that would have been enough to fire him. That doesn't make him a serial sexual harasser.

The *Times* report with the story about the woman passing out also said that "the on-set environment [of *Today*] could sometimes resemble a boys' club" with "jokes about women's appearances," including one floor director's remarking on a woman's breasts, saying he "wanted some milk." The report said that "two former employees recalled colleagues playing a crude game in which they chose which female guests or staff members they would prefer to marry, kill or have sex with."

All of this is in a story about Lauer, and yet none of that behavior was attributed to him.

The one incident in the *Variety* report that could even remotely be considered sexual harassment or assault concerns a woman who said Lauer asked her to come to his office, and when she arrived, he showed her his penis. When she declined the advancement, he "reprimanded" her.

Active punishment of an underling who declines a sexual advance from her superior would absolutely qualify as workplace harassment. If Lauer exposed himself and the woman left the room with no subsequent punishment, that would still be harassment.

But we don't know. There's an accusation and there's a denial that it happened. That's it.

Every one of the accusations against Lauer was made anonymously except one. That woman came forward publicly to say that she'd had a sexual relationship with Lauer, who was married throughout all of this, when she was an employee at NBC. And she said it was consensual.[354]

Even the NBC staffer who was ultimately responsible for Lauer's firing should be suspect. The *New York Post*, the same outlet that broke her story the day that Lauer got fired, followed up with a report a year and a half later that the woman was shopping a potential tell-all book to potential buyers. One source, according to the report, said that the relationship between Lauer and the woman had not been a fling; "it was an affair."

Lauer, a legendary morning show anchor, was out of a job. But the privileged victim who ultimately took him down might get very rich with a book deal.[355] It's the elevation of our worst people.

Oh, by the way, the woman who had the affair with Lauer and effectively ended his career with her claim about the 2014 Sochi Olympics, more or less admitted that it was consensual in Ronan Farrow's book *Catch and Kill* released in late 2019. Though the woman, who revealed her identity as Brooke Nevils, laughably told Farrow that Lauer raped her in his hotel room at the Olympics, she also said that she had sex with him multiple times thereafter. "It was completely transactional," she said.[356]

354 Ramin Setoodeh, "Inside Matt Lauer's Secret Relationship With a 'Today' Production Assistant (EXCLUSIVE)," *Variety*, Dec. 14, 2017: https://variety.com/2017/tv/news/matt-lauer-today-secret-relationship-production-assistant-1202641040.

355 Sara Nathan, "Accuser who got Matt Lauer fired is shopping tell-all book," *New York Post*, March 12, 2019: https://pagesix.com/2019/03/12/accuser-who-got-matt-lauer-fired-is-shopping-tell-all-book/.

356 Kate Aurthur and Ramin Setoodeh, "Ronan Farrow Book Alleges Matt Lauer Raped NBC News Colleague," *Variety*, Oct. 8, 2019: https://variety.com/2019/tv/news/matt-lauer-rape-nbc-ronan-farrow-book-catch-kill-1203364485/.

Perhaps Lauer and O'Reilly should have been fired for comments they made at work or because enough of their colleagues no longer liked or respected either of them. But their stories aren't in the same vein as Weinstein. Theirs weren't #MeToo. Theirs were "Me…and them, and them, and her as well."

To drive home just how sick #MeToo has become, consider that a single anonymous claim nearly derailed the stratospheric success of comedian Aziz Ansari. In January 2018, an obscure website called Babe published the account of "Grace" (not her real name), who said that she'd met Ansari the year before at an Emmy Awards after-party. The two exchanged numbers and later went on a date.[357]

Grace said that after the two had dinner, they went back to Ansari's home in New York and made out and groped each other, though Grace said she wasn't interested in the encounter. She said that he initiated sex with her multiple times and she consistently pulled away, eventually telling him she didn't want to go that far. He respected the boundary, though she said that he continued making comments about sex and suggested she perform oral sex on him, which she did. Finally, she said she went to get her phone in the kitchen to call for an Uber. She said that Ansari hugged her goodbye and called the Uber himself so that she could leave.

That's it. "Aggressive" kissing and her consented-to performance of fellatio constituted Grace's #MeToo moment. Ansari shrunk from his mainstream career for more than a year, doing mostly low-key stand-up shows around the country, before he released a special on Netflix. In that show, *Right Now*, he addressed the issue, telling the audience that after Babe published the story, he felt scared, embarrassed, and "ultimately, I just felt terrible that this person felt this way." He said that it made him more thoughtful and that he hoped he had become a "better person" since the encounter with Grace.

---

357 Katie Way, "I went on a date with Aziz Ansari. It turned into the worst night of my life," Babe.net, Jan. 13, 2018: https://babe.net/2018/01/13/aziz-ansari-28355.

And this is all because she gave him a reluctant blowjob instead of going home early. Ansari sounds like an awkward date and perhaps not very smooth with women. In other words, he sounds like a fairly standard straight man. But he also sounds like someone who tries to be a gentleman, and not like someone who would have known he was making Grace uncomfortable.

#MeToo and everything it stands for has quickly become like one of those Cialis ads you see on TV so often that your immediate reaction is to roll your eyes and walk away.

As such, it would be a great waste of your time for me to go over the multiple allegations against President Trump, but because I don't want to be accused of glossing them over, I'll say with great sensitivity that all of the women who made claims against him were probably full of shit. There isn't a shred of substantial evidence to corroborate a single one of those claims. (And no, a photograph showing the accuser and Trump having met one time isn't corroborating evidence.)

But to pick one case at random, let's look at the real-life crash test dummy known as E. Jean Carroll. In June 2019, *New York* magazine published the first-person account of Carroll, a longtime advice columnist, who claimed that Trump had raped her in a New York Bergdorf Goodman department store more than two decades before. Carroll alleged in great dramatic detail that Trump all but forced her into a fitting room, pulled down her tights, and penetrated her with his penis. After a struggle, she got loose from his grip and left the store. Carroll said this happened after she and Trump had been laughing and teasing each other, gallivanting throughout the store, including the fitting room. It was an apparent riot and yet Carroll said that no store attendant noticed them.[358]

The reason for Carroll's delay in coming forward twenty-three years after the alleged rape? "Receiving death threats, being driven from my

---

358   E. Jean Carroll, "Hideous Men," *New York*, June 21, 2019: https://www.thecut.com/2019/06/donald-trump-assault-e-jean-carroll-other-hideous-men.html.

home, being dismissed, being dragged through the mud, and joining the 15 women who've come forward with credible stories about how the man grabbed, badgered, belittled, mauled, molested, and assaulted them, only to see the man turn it around, deny, threaten, and attack them, never sounded like much fun," she reasoned. "Also, I am a coward."

Oh, one more thing: She had a book to sell! Carroll's first-person account in *New York* magazine was an excerpt from her book that was to be released just a few days later. The story was of course picked up by the *New York Times*, the *Wall Street Journal*, the *Washington Post*, *USA Today*, CNN, MSNBC, and Fox News. That couldn't have been bad for presales.

This is, however, the formula of the privileged victim. First, claim to have been a victim on the basis of race, gender, or sexuality, and then—profit!

This wasn't how #MeToo started, and it's not what it was intended for. #MeToo was supposed to address people like onetime Democratic Minnesota senator Al Franken, another one who flat-out admitted he had behaved inappropriately with women. On November 16, 2017, Los Angeles-based radio personality Leeann Tweeden claimed in graphic terms that during an overseas USO tour of the Middle East in 2006, Franken had forced his tongue into her mouth while they were practicing a skit they were going to perform for American troops. She also said that on the flight back to the U.S., he groped her while she was sleeping. To support the allegation, Tweeden produced a photograph in which Franklin is seen with his flipper-like hands cupped around Tweeden's breasts over her Kevlar vest while she lies there, apparently unconscious.

Following Tweeden's account, several other women came forward with similar stories about Franken's having touched them inappropriately, on both their behinds and their breasts. There were photographs in nearly all of these cases showing that Franken had at least been present with his accusers at the locations that the women had identified as the places of their alleged assaults.

Franken apologized for all of it. Regarding the allegations related directly to Tweeden, he said in a statement that he felt "ashamed" and "disgusted."[359] At a press conference with reporters several days later, he said, "It's been clear that there are some women—and one is too many—who feel that I have done something disrespectful and it's hurt them and for that, I am tremendously sorry."[360]

Less than a month later, Franken said he would be resigning from his Senate seat.

This is what #MeToo was for, and this is how American justice works. You have an accusation and substantial evidence—a recording, a photograph, a witness. You might even have a confession, and finally some action is taken to help remediate the wrong.

Social justice infected the cause and turned it into a crusade against the "privileged," which is to say, men. Every claim of sexual misconduct is to be assumed true, and every man accused is to be punished. With great irony, Hillary Clinton, wife of accused rapist Bill Clinton[361], endorsed that sick standard, tweeting in November 2015: "Every survivor of sexual assault deserves to be heard, believed, and supported."[362]

⌘　⌘　⌘

College campuses across the country were afflicted with the disease long before #MeToo was recognized as a national movement. Starting at some point in the past ten years, young men have been expected to ask

---

359　Politico, "Full text: Al Franken apologizes for allegedly groping woman," Nov. 16, 2017: https://www.politico.com/story/2017/11/16/full-text-al-franken-apologizes-for-allegedly-groping-woman-244978.

360　Seung Min Kim, "'Ashamed' Franken apologizes in Senate over groping allegations," Politico, Nov. 27, 2017: https://www.politico.com/story/2017/11/27/al-franken-apologizes-sexual-harassment-260986.

361　Eliza Relman, "These are the sexual-assault allegations against Bill Clinton," Business Insider, June 4, 2018: https://www.businessinsider.com/these-are-the-sexual-assault-allegations-against-bill-clinton-2017-11.

362　Hillary Clinton, Twitter.com, Nov. 22, 2015: https://twitter.com/hillaryclinton/status/668597149291184128?lang=en.

with every pump of intercourse whether his female partner continues to consent.

Seriously. The nonprofit TeenSource.org website tells young people that initial consent to sexual activity "doesn't mean forever. Either partner can change their mind at any time."[363]

True, if you begin to have sex and don't like it, you should feel entitled to end the experience by simply saying so. But social justice has expanded the concept of consent to include feelings about regret. Ever feel a little icky after a sexual encounter that you had consented to? The #MeToo movement says that encounter is now tantamount to assault.

Columbia University student Emma Sulkowicz told school officials in April 2013 that she was raped by co-ed Jean-Paul Nungesser. The two had had sex twice before, according to Sulkowicz herself, but she said that in August 2012, Nungesser hit and choked her before anally penetrating her. He denied it.[364] Though Facebook messages between the two after the alleged rape showed that Sulkowicz was still interested in seeing Nungesser—"I want to see yoyouououyou," she wrote in September, two weeks after the supposed rape—the school wouldn't permit those messages as part of Nungesser's defense. And yet he was still found by administrations to not have been responsible for whatever happened between him and Sulkowicz.[365]

Still, Sulkowicz put on a show in 2014 by carrying a mattress around campus in protest of Columbia's decision, garnering national media attention for the display. She later filed a police report, though

---

363 "Consent is sexy + safe. remember: consent is continuous. learn more about consent," Teen Source, 2017: https://www.teensource.org/blog/2017/03/consent-sexy-safe-remember-consent-continuous-learn-more-about-consent.

364 Emma Bogler, "Frustrated by Columbia's inaction, student reports sexual assault to police," *Columbia Spectator*, Dec. 28, 2016: https://www.columbiaspectator.com/news/2014/05/16/frustrated-columbias-inaction-student-reports-sexual-assault-police/.

365 Cathy Young, "Columbia Student: I Didn't Rape Her," Daily Beast, Feb. 3, 2015: https://www.thedailybeast.com/columbia-student-i-didnt-rape-her.

investigators hit a wall when Sulkowicz abruptly stopped cooperating with them. There were never any charges, though I imagine that wasn't of much comfort to Nungesser, whose reputation had still been stained by a horrible rape accusation.[366] Meanwhile, Sulkowicz was made a hero, showered with uncritical national media attention in *Time* magazine, profiled favorably as an artist in the *New York Times*, and described by journalists as an international sensation.[367] Senator Kirsten Gillibrand, Democrat of New York, invited Sulkowicz to be her guest at the 2015 State of the Union address.[368] It's the elevation of mediocrity.

Nungesser sued the school in a gender discrimination lawsuit. It was settled in 2017.[369]

Freshman Peter Yu at Vassar College had sex with a co-ed in 2012. A year later, she told school administrators that the encounter was not consensual.

The two had gotten together on the night of a booze-fueled party, and the next day, Yu's accuser sent him a Facebook message to say, "don't worry" because she was "really drunk" and "I'm really sorry I led you

366   Kate Taylor, "Columbia Settles With Student Cast as a Rapist in Mattress Art Project," *New York Times*, July 14, 2017: https://www.nytimes.com/2017/07/14/nyregion/columbia-settles-with-student-cast-as-a-rapist-in-mattress-art-project.html.

367   Vanessa Grigoriadis, "Meet the College Women Who Are Starting a Revolution Against Campus Sexual Assault," *New York* magazine, Sep. 21, 2014: https://www.thecut.com/2014/09/emma-sulkowicz-campus-sexual-assault-activism.html.

368   Katie Van Syckle, "Alleged Columbia Rapist 'Dismayed and Disappointed' by Accuser's SOTU Invitation," *New York*, Jan. 20, 2015: http://nymag.com/intelligencer/2015/01/alleged-columbia-rapist-dismayed-by-sotu-honor.html?gtm=bottom&gtm=bottom.

369   T. Rees Shapiro, "Columbia University settles Title IX lawsuit with former student involving 'mattress girl' case," *Washington Post*, July 13, 2017: https://www.washingtonpost.com/news/grade-point/wp/2017/07/13/columbia-university-settles-title-ix-lawsuit-with-former-student-involving-mattress-girl-case/?utm_term=.97173842b6d3.

on," adding that she nonetheless "had a wonderful time last night."[370] Yu was expelled in 2013, given the school's policy that a drunk person cannot properly consent.[371]

That same year, an unnamed male student at the University of Colorado Boulder was accused of sexual misconduct and suspended from the school for three semesters, even after his accuser told university administrations that she "may have stretched the truth" about her own claim and that she was "pissed off" at the male student for being "just another douchy [sic] frat dude."[372]

The accused male voluntarily withdrew from the school, sued, and won a $15,000 settlement.[373]

In February 2012, an Amherst College student took a co-ed back to her dorm and performed oral sex on him. Two years later, she accused him of sexual assault and he was expelled.[374]

It's now set up so that having a drink and spending a night with a man is on the same plane as sexual assault, simply because maybe a girl isn't feeling so proud the next day.

The Justice Department in 2016 issued a survey wherein students at nine colleges were asked about their encounters with sexual abuse.

---

370 Larry Neumeister, "Federal Court Backs Vassar's Ouster of Student in Rape Case," NBCNewYork.com, April 15, 2015: https://www.nbcnewyork.com/news/local/Federal-Court-Vassar-College-Student-Rape-Case-299801741.html.

371 Tyler Kingkade, "Judge Dismisses Lawsuit Against Vassar College Filed By Student Expelled For Sexual Assault," *Huffington Post*, April 15, 2015: https://www.huffpost.com/entry/vassar-lawsuit-gender_n_7071694.

372 Ashe Schow, "No such thing as evidence of innocence in campus sexual assault hearings," *Washington Examiner*, April 27, 2015: https://www.washingtonexaminer.com/no-such-thing-as-evidence-of-innocence-in-campus-sexual-assault-hearings.

373 Sarah Kuta, "CU-Boulder paying 'John Doe' $15K to settle Title IX lawsuit stemming from sexual assault case," *Daily Camera*, Feb. 20, 2015: https://www.dailycamera.com/2015/02/20/cu-boulder-paying-john-doe-15k-to-settle-title-ix-lawsuit-stemming-from-sexual-assault-case/.

374 Ashe Schow, "Man receives sex act while blacked out, gets accused of sexual assault," *Washington Examiner*, June 11, 2015: https://www.washingtonexaminer.com/man-receives-sex-act-while-blacked-out-gets-accused-of-sexual-assault.

Liberal news outlets like HuffPost got their sticky hands on the survey's results and reported on them in a way that suggested there was a massive problem with sex and violence on college campuses. HuffPost said the study "proves" that "an average of 21 percent of female undergraduates… had been sexually assaulted since starting their higher education."[375]

But what the survey actually did was ask women students to check any number of four options to define what would constitute sexual assault. The fourth option offered that sexual assault can take place when a woman is "unable to provide consent" due to being "incapacitated, passed out, unconscious, blacked out, or asleep," regardless of whether she "voluntarily used alcohol or drugs."[376]

What does "incapacitated" mean? Is it getting a buzz, feeling loose, and saying yes when a student otherwise might not? Is it getting wasted and remembering nothing until someone reminds the student? The survey didn't say. And it's ludicrous to suggest that any regretful encounter is a matter of sexual assault solely because a woman had been "incapacitated" from having voluntarily consumed alcohol or drugs.

Even if you were to assume it's true that nearly a quarter of female college students are sexually assaulted at school (and there's no reason you should), the overwhelming majority of women who responded to this particular survey said they notified no one of their alleged incident because, well, they weren't that concerned with it.

Around 80 percent of survey respondents said they did not tell school administrators, call a crisis hotline, or alert police because they "did not need assistance, did not think the incident was serious enough to report, or did not want any action taken."[377]

---

375 Tyler Kingkade, "There's No More Denying Campus Rape Is A Problem. This Study Proves It," *Huffington Post*, Jan. 20, 2016: https://www.huffpost.com/entry/college-sexual-assault-study_n_569e928be4b0cd99679b9ada.

376 Bureau of Justice Statistics Research and Development Series, "Campus Climate Survey Validation Study Final Technical Report," January 2016, 64: https://www.bjs.gov/content/pub/pdf/ccsvsftr.pdf.

377 Bureau of Justice Statistics Research and Development Series, "Campus Climate Survey Validation Study Final Technical Report," January 2016, 111–112: https://www.bjs.gov/content/pub/pdf/ccsvsftr.pdf.

It sounds like after a few deep breaths, the bulk of these women realized they could stop worrying and that they would just make better choices in the future.

The number of women in the survey who said they never told anyone about their "assault" out of fear of being victim-blamed was far lower than those who simply didn't think the incident rose to a serious level of concern. Only around 18 percent said that the reason they never alerted any of the aforementioned authorities or hotlines was because they had felt that "other people might think that what happened was at least partly her fault or that she might get in trouble for some reason."

So, of even the quarter of students who said they had been sexually assaulted, based on an absurdly low standard for what circumstances constitute assault, most of them didn't even view themselves as victims.

Does that sound like the results of a survey that justifies the headline "There's No More Denying Campus Rape Is A Problem. This Study Proves It"? Of course not.

It's not just that accusations of rape and sexual assault can now be based on simple regret. They're now a convenient weapon of retaliation for hurt feelings and rejection.

In September 2014, two students at Allegheny College in Pennsylvania, known only in court documents as John and Jane Doe, had a relationship that included sex. Jane would even sleep in the same bed as John. She texted him multiple times that month about their relationship, though he mostly ignored the messages. She eventually told school administrators that John assaulted her.

John Doe was found by the school to be responsible for the allegation, though a friend of Jane's was on the record as having told John that Jane was acting out because she had been rejected. "[Jane] is upset because [John] will not talk to her anymore and she can't stand being at the same school with him," the friend said. "She doesn't want to leave

Allegheny, so the only way to get him out was to claim that he raped her and to press charges."[378]

John did, however, sue Allegheny College in 2017 and won a settlement, the details of which have been sealed.[379]

Something very similar happened to Tom Rossley's son, who also is identified in court documents only as John Doe, and his accuser as Jane. John is afflicted with some neurological disorders that, though mild, make him somewhat slow when processing human interaction. One night in October 2015, he and Jane, who he had been friendly with before, had drinks at a bar before returning to his frat house. There, Jane performed oral sex on John before the two went to his room to either have sex or go to sleep, depending on whom you ask.

Jane later accused him of sexual assault. And though she said during a court hearing that she did in fact willingly perform the fellatio, she admitted she did it without ever having received verbal consent from John. She said she merely thought she was "giving him what he wanted." (Yes, these cases can get excruciatingly absurd, but that's the point.)

John confirmed that he never gave his consent regarding the oral sex. And despite filing his own report against Jane, he was rebuffed by the school, which determined that the claim had been made merely in retaliation to Jane's.[380] In other words, the school determined that

---

378   Ashe Schow, "Allegheny College Settles With Student Peer Says Was Accused In Revenge For Not Dating Girl He Slept With," TheFederalist.com, July 11, 2017: https://thefederalist.com/2017/07/11/allegheny-college-settles-student-peer-says-falsely-accused-assault-revenge-not-dating-girl-slept/.

379   Keith Gushard, "Settlement reached with Allegheny College regarding alleged civil rights violation," *Meadville Tribune*, July 11, 2017: https://www.meadvilletribune.com/news/local_news/settlement-reached-with-allegheny-college-regarding-alleged-civil-rights-violation/article_ab5c2144-aa67-586b-91a7-58da209e7ec0.html.

380   Ashe Schow, "Lawsuit: Father fired after defending disabled son from campus kangaroo court," Townhall.com, March 20, 2017: https://townhall.com/watchdog/Iowa/2017/03/20/father-fired-defending-disabled-son-campus-kangaroo-court-n10491.

it would believe Jane, but that John was being disingenuous. John was expelled.

In 2014, two male students at the University of Findlay, a private university in Ohio, were expelled after a female student accused the two of them of sexual assault. The male students were roommates Justin Browning and Alphonso Baity, and the female was identified in court documents only as M.K.[381]

M.K. reportedly had sexual relations with Browning, Baity, and others all in one night. At some point, she was with several of them simultaneously. Only ten days later did she accuse Browning and Baity of inappropriate behavior. Though every witness who had been present on the night of the alleged multiple sexual encounters said that M.K. had consented to all of it and had even bragged to others that it happened, Browning and Baity were immediately expelled.

The two men sued the university for racial discrimination. They settled in January 2019.

Sexual assault and rape accusations are deadly serious. But in the social justice ideology, they're simply tools in the fight against the privileged. It has turned every sexual encounter on college campuses into a game of Russian roulette. It has warped the #MeToo movement. And it's all reinforced by the culture fascists in the media, in Hollywood, and in academia.

Due process has been given the shaft by social justice, but the sham is occasionally exposed and it may have reached a turning point in the fall of 2018.

---

381 Ashe Schow, "She Accused Them Of Sexual Assault After Allegedly Bragging About Their Encounter. Now They've Settled With The School That Expelled Them," DailyWire.com, Feb. 19, 2019:https://www.dailywire.com/news/43684/she-accused-them-sexual-assault-after-allegedly-ashe-schow.

CHAPTER 9

#METOO IS TOLD TO GO SCREW ITSELF

Brett Kavanaugh's confirmation to the Supreme Court in 2018 was, if nothing else, a blow to the social justice movement's grip on our culture and proof on a national scale that getting slandered by #MeToo doesn't have to be a reputational death sentence.

America now knows once and for all that being accused of privilege isn't a death sentence. It isn't automatic defeat.

The conclusion of the Kavanaugh confirmation was like the climax of 1986's *The Labyrinth*, wherein Jennifer Connelly as Sarah destroys Jareth, played by David Bowie, having realized the simple truth, "You have no power over me." The epiphany on its own starts the collapse of Jareth's maze trap.

The *New York Times* reported on September 13, 2018, more than two months after Kavanaugh was nominated by President Trump, that Senator Dianne Feinstein, Democrat of California, had given the FBI a letter detailing a woman's claim regarding Kavanaugh and a sexual assault. After receiving the letter, Feinstein alerted her Democratic colleagues on the Senate Judiciary Committee about the allegation. The letter had originally been delivered in July to Representative Anna Eshoo, Democrat of California, who then forwarded it to Feinstein.[382]

Feinstein said in a statement that Kavanaugh's accuser, whose name was still not yet public, had "strongly requested confidentiality, declined to come forward or press the matter further."

The next day, citing anonymous sources "familiar with the contents of the letter," the *Times* reported that the note recounted an alleged incident from more than thirty years prior, wherein Kavanaugh and "a male friend" (later identified as the conservative writer Mark Judge), both drunk at a house party in Maryland, trapped his accuser in a bedroom upstairs. While the party music was blaring, the letter said, Kavanaugh forced his accuser onto the bed, climbed on top of her and then, while holding his hand over her mouth, attempted to remove her clothes. The woman said that she was eventually able to break free and leave the room.[383]

All parties involved were in high school at the time of the alleged assault.

Two days after that second *Times* report and less than a week before the Senate Judiciary Committee was scheduled to advance Kavanaugh's nomination for a full floor vote, the *Washington Post* reported the identity of his accuser, Christine Blasey Ford. Included in the *Post*'s report was an interview with Debra Katz, a lawyer Ford had obtained prior to the story's publication.[384]

382   Nicholas Fandos and Catie Edmondson, "Dianne Feinstein Refers a Kavanaugh Matter to Federal Investigators," *New York Times*, Sep. 13, 2018: https://www.nytimes.com/2018/09/13/us/politics/brett-kavanaugh-dianne-feinstein.html.

383   Nicholas Fandos and Michael S. Schmidt, "Letter Claims Attempted Assault by a Teenage Brett Kavanaugh," *New York Times*, Sep. 14, 2018: https://www.nytimes.com/2018/09/14/us/politics/kavanaugh-assault-allegation-letter.html.

384   Emma Brown, "California professor, writer of confidential Brett Kavanaugh letter, speaks out about her allegation of sexual assault," *Washington Post*, Sept. 16, 2018: https://www.washingtonpost.com/investigations/california-professor-writer-of-confidential-brett-kavanaugh-letter-speaks-out-about-her-allegation-of-sexual-assault/2018/09/16/46982194-b846-11e8-94eb-3bd52dfe917b_story.html?utm_term=.f8c335482323.

Ford, who has a doctorate in psychology and who was employed as a professor at Palo Alto University, provided the *Post* with what she said were notes from a 2012 couple's therapy session she attended with her husband, wherein she said that she told the therapist about the alleged assault.

Ford said she remembered both Kavanaugh and Mark Judge "manically" laughing while Kavanaugh forced himself on her; that it felt like Kavanaugh had attempted to rape her; and that "I thought he might inadvertently kill me."

Ford told the *Post* that on Katz's advice, she had taken a polygraph test to substantiate her claims. The *Post* article said that the exam "concluded that Ford was being truthful when she said a statement summarizing her allegations was accurate." (Mind you, any polygraph expert worth a grain of salt will admit that the tests are completely subjective, and are about as reliable as a Scientology "auditing," a palm reading, or a Cher farewell tour.)

The *Post*'s story did, however, disclose a very important detail that almost no one talked about during the entire Kavanaugh controversy: Ford had actually initiated contact with the newspaper regarding her story in July, two months before the *New York Times* broke the story about the letter received by Senator Dianne Feinstein.

Ford "contacted the Post through a tip line in early July," the paper said in the story, "when it had become clear that Kavanaugh was on the shortlist of possible nominees to replace retiring justice Anthony M. Kennedy but before Trump announced [Kavanaugh's] name publicly."

So, before Ford's name was ever made public, she had contacted her state representative, pinged a national newspaper, gotten a lawyer, and taken a polygraph test. And yet she claimed that she had wanted to remain anonymous. Her initial outreach to the media took place before Kavanaugh was even the official nominee.

I don't know about you, but these are precisely the steps I would take if I wanted to keep a low profile, especially right before accusing a Supreme Court nominee of an attempted rape and possible manslaughter!

Setting aside whether Ford was assaulted by anyone, all evidence suggests she came forward because she was upset that Kavanaugh, who had a long history in Republican politics, might take the place of Anthony Kennedy, a swing vote in controversial cases that Democrats didn't want to see replaced by a more reliable conservative.

The political stakes were high and, like all hysterical liberals who still hadn't accepted the 2016 election results, Ford was devastated that Trump was filling a second Supreme Court seat in his first term.

Immediately after the *Post* story was published, Senator Chuck Grassley, Republican of Iowa and head of the Senate Judiciary Committee, delayed the vote on Kavanaugh until the nominee and Ford could offer testimonies on the allegation to the committee. Debra Katz said on CNN that her client, Ford, was willing to testify.[385] Grassley then scheduled a hearing for Ford to take place a week later.

Grassley said he would accommodate Ford in whatever capacity she wished. He said her testimony could be given in public or private. After a report that Ford, who lived in California, said she feared flying, Grassley said he would even arrange for committee staffers to travel to her, if she preferred.[386]

In response, Ford and her attorney began making ridiculous demands.

They wanted Kavanaugh to testify first, though it would be fairly difficult for him to defend himself from charges that he would not have yet heard. They said more witnesses should be brought in, though all of the ones Ford identified as witnesses, including a longtime friend, denied having any memory of the party where she said the incident

---

385 *New Day*, CNN, Sep. 17, 2018.

386 Elana Schor and Burgess Everett, "Grassley extends deadline on Kavanaugh accuser's decision to testify," Politico, Sep. 21, 2018: https://www.politico.com/story/2018/09/21/trump-kavanaugh-christine-blasey-ford-charges-834664.

happened.[387] And they said an FBI investigation, unlimited by time or budget, should take place first, though Kavanaugh had already been through six FBI background checks.[388]

Even if another investigation were conducted, Ford lacked crucial leads for the FBI to follow, like exactly where and when the assault allegedly took place. She couldn't remember how she got to the party or how she got home once she left. She had said that after she got away from the room where Kavanaugh supposedly assaulted her, she immediately ran outside the house. It was unlikely she got home by foot, however, given that she lived several miles away from the general area where she said the party was held. Altogether, Ford's memory was about as useful as a book on parenting by Casey Anthony.

Grassley refused all of Ford's attorney's demands, but the stall that they caused gave the news media ample time to show what the real problem was: It wasn't that a woman had made an uncorroborated, unproven (and unprovable) accusation about an attempted rape. It was that Kavanaugh was a man. A white one. And all the Republicans who sat on the committee where white men, too.

Right after Ford's identity was revealed, *New York* magazine's Irin Carmon bemoaned the political consequences that women might face should Kavanaugh be confirmed. She didn't seem to care about the real-life hell he was about to experience as a man accused of an attempted rape in the national media. "The only thing less accountable than a powerful white man against a woman's word," wrote Carmon, "is one with a lifetime appointment."[389]

---

387   Burgess Everett, "Woman denies attending party where alleged Kavanaugh assault occurred," Politico, Sep. 22, 2018: https://www.politico.com/story/2018/09/22/kavanaugh-ford-woman-party-letter-836913.

388   Fred Lucas, "FBI's Previous Probes Would Have Looked Into Kavanaugh's Drinking," DailySignal.com, Oct. 2, 2018: https://www.dailysignal.com/2018/10/02/fbis-previous-probes-would-have-looked-into-kavanaughs-drinking/.

389   Irin Carmon, "Will Brett Kavanaugh Face Any Consequences? Women Will," *New York*, Sep. 16, 2018: https://www.thecut.com/2018/09/brett-kavanaugh-accuser-consequences.html?utm_campaign=thecut&utm_source=tw&utm_medium=s1.

The *New York Times*' editorial board kicked off the quickly tiresome comparison to Justice Clarence Thomas' confirmation and the Anita Hill hearings of 1991, noting that "twenty-seven years later, Clarence Thomas remains on the court and the Republican side of the Judiciary Committee remains all male."[390]

The *Times* presumably omitted the "white" factor because the privilege narrative gets complicated when you consider it was all white men who confirmed Thomas, who is black. But don't worry! CNN political commentator Maria Cardona was there to finish the job. Asked by anchor Brooke Baldwin whether the white male senators on the Senate Judiciary Committee now "get it" all these years after the Thomas hearings, Cardona replied, "Wow, male white privilege does not dull with age, does it?"[391]

That same day, Joy Behar of ABC's *The View* referred to "these white men" on the Senate who were "protecting a man who's probably guilty."[392]

Jess McIntosh, executive editor of the liberal Shareblue Media website, made the original comparison between the Kavanaugh controversy and Anita Hill's hearings during a segment on MSNBC. "It's still all white men on the Republican side," she said. "There is no change between 1991 and 2018 if you look at the Republican side of the Senate Judiciary Committee. It was all white men then; it's all white men now."[393]

You see, it's now presumed to be an inherent problem to be a white man in power. No explanation necessary.

CNN anchor Anderson Cooper questioned whether there would be any "political strategy" if Senate Republicans were to choose outside counsel, a woman, to interrogate Ford during any testimony. CNN

---

390 Editorial board, "Why America Needs to Hear Brett Kavanaugh's Accuser," *New York Times*, Sep. 17, 2018: https://www.nytimes.com/2018/09/17/opinion/kavanaugh-allegations-blasey-ford.html.

391 *CNN Newsroom*, CNN, Sep. 19, 2018.

392 *The View*, ABC, Sep. 19, 2018.

393 *MSNBC Live with Stephanie Ruhle*, MSNBC, Sep. 21, 2018

chief political analyst Gloria Borger proved she was worthy of her title, telling Cooper, "Look, it's all political. I mean, they're not dumb. They understand that you have all of these white men who would be questioning this woman.... The optics of it would look terrible."[394]

It's the standpoint knowledge feature of the social justice movement. The noted white men of the committee could not possibly have a full grasp of the issue at hand. How could they? They're white men. The implication is that only other women, preferably nonwhite ones, would have the inherent moral authority to understand the full weight of what Ford was claiming to have experienced. Notice that by contrast, no one was asking whether Kavanaugh, accused of a horrific crime, was being properly understood. He was deemed as a white male to hold privilege and was therefore undeserving of consideration.

There was no end to the "white men" mantra.

- "[The] worst-case scenario [is] for a bunch of white men on the Senate Judiciary Committee cross-examining Dr. Ford."[395]

- "At the end of the day, if they have a bunch of white men once again defending another white man…"[396]

- "It is a lineup of white guys over the age of 50."[397]

- "Once again, it will be all white men on the Republican side of the Judiciary Committee questioning both Judge Kavanaugh and Doctor Ford."[398]

- "If she testifies in front of the Judiciary Committee, where 11 members are white men, even if they try so carefully, it will still be viewed as an interrogation."[399]

---

394 *Anderson Cooper 360*, CNN, Sep. 20, 2018.
395 MSNBC's Joe Scarborough, *Morning Joe*, Sep. 17, 2018.
396 Axios Editor-in-Chief Jim VandeHei, MSNBC's *Morning Joe First Look*, Sep. 17, 2018.
397 MSNBC's Stephanie Ruhle, *Velshi & Ruhle*, Sep. 18, 2018.
398 CNN's Poppy Harlow, *CNN Newsroom*, Sep. 18, 2018.
399 MSNBC Republican Susan Del Percio, *MTP Daily*, Sep. 19, 2018.

- "Kavanaugh reeks of white entitlement."[400]

- "The Hour of Angry White Male Rage had come 'round at last."[401]

- "No longer is this about Brett Kavanaugh and Christine Blasey Ford, or what he may have done to her in suburban Maryland in 1982.… [I]t is about showing that white men in power are not going anywhere."[402]

- "Kavanaugh Borrows From Trump's Playbook on White Male Anger."[403]

- "And now, for an entire generation of women going forward, they will not be able to look at the Supreme Court the same way, particularly post that Kavanaugh performance that, as a man, I was embarrassed for him; it was the ultimate display of white entitlement."[404]

- "What Thursday's hearing drove home, however, was that white male rage isn't restricted to blue-collar guys in diners."[405]

- "I hate Mitch [McConnell] - what a slimy creep - the cast of cocoon joins him SHUT UP OLD WHITE. MEN."[406]

400 Toure Neblett, Twitter.com, Sep. 27, 2018: https://twitter.com/Toure/status/1045421950233915393.

401 Charles Pierce, "This Was the Hour of White Male Rage," *Esquire*, Sep. 28, 2018: https://www.esquire.com/news-politics/politics/a23499571/brett-kavanaugh-hearing-republicans-white-male-rage/.

402 Zack Beauchamp, "Lindsey Graham, Brett Kavanaugh, and the unleashing of white male backlash," Vox.com, Sep. 28, 2018: https://www.vox.com/policy-and-politics/2018/9/28/17913774/brett-kavanaugh-lindsey-graham-christine-ford-backlash.

403 Jeremy Peters and Susan Chira, "Kavanaugh Borrows From Trump's Playbook on White Male Anger," *New York Times*, Sep. 29, 2018: https://www.nytimes.com/2018/09/29/us/politics/brett-kavanaugh-trump-men.html.

404 Donnie Deutsch, MSNBC's *Morning Joe*, Oct. 1, 2018.

405 Paul Krugman, "The Angry White Male Caucus," *New York Times*, Oct. 1, 2018: https://www.nytimes.com/2018/10/01/opinion/kavanaugh-white-male-privilege.html.

406 Rosie O'Donnell, Twitter.com, Oct. 4, 2018: https://twitter.com/Rosie/status/1047919092160778241.

Ford's well-timed accusation, her lawyer's absurd demands, and the media pressure on the Judiciary Committee to jump through countless hoops to satisfy an allegation that was impossible to prove or disprove, all made for a convenient delay in Kavanaugh's confirmation.

During the several-day lag:

- Journalist Ronan Farrow found a woman (with no corroborating witnesses) to say that Kavanaugh had flashed his penis at her during a freshman-year party at Yale.[407]

- Shyster lawyer Michael Avenatti found a woman to imply that Kavanaugh had once been in a rape gang.[408]

- The *New York Times* scrutinized the sophomoric language in one of Kavanaugh's high school yearbooks, producing an article that would usher the term "boofing" into America's lexicon.[409]

- And the *Washington Post* investigated whether Kavanaugh as a teenager had ever gotten drunk.[410]

That's what you can expect when social justice hijacks the Supreme Court confirmation process.

---

407   Ronan Farrow, "Senate Democrats Investigate a New Allegation of Sexual Misconduct, from Brett Kavanaugh's College Years," *New Yorker*, Sep. 23, 2018: https://www.newyorker.com/news/news-desk/senate-democrats-investigate-a-new-allegation-of-sexual-misconduct-from-the-supreme-court-nominee-brett-kavanaughs-college-years-deborah-ramirez.

408   Tina Nguyen, "Is Avenatti's 'gang rape' bombshell the end of Brett Kavanaugh?," *Vanity Fair*, Sep. 26, 2018: https://www.vanityfair.com/news/2018/09/avenatti-gang-rape-bombshell-the-end-of-brett-kavanaugh.

409   Kate Kelly and David Enrich, "Kavanaugh's Yearbook Page Is 'Horrible, Hurtful' to a Woman It Named," *New York Times*, Sep. 24, 2018: https://www.nytimes.com/2018/09/24/business/brett-kavanaugh-yearbook-renate.html.

410   Aaron C. Davis, Emma Brown, and Joe Heim, "Kavanaugh's 'choir boy' image on Fox interview rankles former Yale classmates," *Washington Post*, Sep. 25, 2018: https://www.washingtonpost.com/investigations/2018/09/25/ea5e50d4-c0eb-11e8-9005-5104e9616c21_story.html?utm_term=.b9376b019373.

At the hearing, eleven days after Ford was first identified by the *Post*, sex-crimes prosecutor Rachel Mitchell was called in to question Ford on behalf of Republicans. Ford was able to say with "100 percent" certainty that Kavanaugh had been her aggressor more than three decades prior, leading even Fox News anchor Chris Wallace to call Ford "extremely credible."[411]

By the end, however, Ford was unable to answer fundamental questions about her allegation. She couldn't say how she had gotten to the house party. She couldn't say where the house was specifically located. She couldn't say how she had left the party. She couldn't say who, if anyone, would have accompanied her home, seven miles away. She couldn't say why the friend she identified as a witness couldn't corroborate that the party had ever taken place at all. Ford had the memory of a goldfish with advanced Alzheimer's.

Mitchell produced a report with her conclusions four days later, definitively stating that the lack of evidence and corroboration for Ford's accusation would make a case such as hers impossible to prosecute.

"A 'he said, she said' case is incredibly difficult to prove," wrote Mitchell. "But this case is even weaker than that."[412] She said that Ford had "not offered a consistent account of when the alleged assault happened," referring to key discrepancies in what Ford said in her testimony, what she told the *Washington Post*, and what she said during her polygraph exam.

Most devastating to Ford's credibility was her back-and-forth with Mitchell during the hearing, wherein she restated her fear of flying yet admitted that she frequently flew to far-flung destinations for pleasure.

---

411 Fox News live coverage of the Christine Blasey Ford and Brett Kavanaugh hearing, Sep. 27, 2018.

412 Alex Johnson and Frank Thorp V, "Evidence doesn't support claims against Kavanaugh, Judiciary Committee questioner says," NBC News, Oct. 1, 2018: https://www.nbcnews.com/politics/supreme-court/evidence-doesn-t-support-claims-against-kavanaugh-judiciary-committee-prosecutor-n915236.

From the hearing:

> *Mitchell: May I ask, Doctor Ford, how did you get to Washington?*
>
> *Ford: In an airplane.*
>
> *Mitchell: Okay. It's—I ask that, because it's been reported by the press that you would not submit to an interview with the committee because of your fear of flying. Is—is that true?*
>
> *Ford: Well, I was willing—I was hoping that they would come to me, but then I realized that was an unrealistic request.*

Ford's answer indicated that she either didn't know about Senator Chuck Grassley's offer to send staff to California to interview her there so that she wouldn't have to fly—a fact that was reported in the media—or Ford's own lawyers misled her.

More of that exchange:

> *Ford: Yes. So that was certainly what I was hoping, was to avoid having to get on an airplane, but I eventually was able to get up the gumption with the help of some friends, and get on the plane.*
>
> *Mitchell: Okay. When you were here in the mid—mid-Atlantic area back in August, end of July, August, how did you get here?*
>
> *Ford: Also by airplane. I come here once a year during the summer to visit my family.*
>
> *Mitchell: Okay.*
>
> *Ford: I'm sorry, not here [in Washington]. I go to Delaware.*
>
> *Mitchell: Okay. In fact, you fly fairly frequently for your hobbies and your—you've had to fly for your work. Is that true?*

Ford: Correct, unfortunately.

Mitchell: You—you were a consulting biostatistician in Sydney, Australia. Is that right?

Ford: I've never been to Australia, but the company that I worked for is based in Australia, and they have an office in San Francisco, California.

Mitchell: Okay.

Ford: I—I don't think I'll make it to Australia.

Mitchell: It is long. I also saw on your C.V. that you list the following interests of surf, travel, and you—in parentheses, Hawaii, Costa Rica, South Pacific islands, and French Polynesia. Have you been to all of those places?

Ford: Correct.

Mitchell: By airplane?

Ford: Yes.

Mitchell: And your interests also include oceanography, Hawaiian and Tahitian culture. Did you travel by air as a part of those interests?

Ford: Correct.

Mitchell: All right. Thank you very much.

Ford: Easier for me to travel going that direction when it's a vacation.

Ford maintained she had a fear of flying despite frequently traveling by air to places like Hawaii, Costa Rica, and the Pacific Islands—*so that she could surf.*

It's like her travel agent was Peter Pan.

After Ford's three hours of testimony, Kavanaugh was introduced to defend himself.

He rightly said that the delay on his confirmation vote had resulted in his and his family's reputations having been "totally and permanently destroyed by vicious and false additional accusations."

He frequently choked back tears and swallowed hard. He accused Democrats and the media of "a calculated and orchestrated political hit, fueled with apparent pent-up anger about President Trump." He said that his treatment was a form of "revenge on behalf of the Clintons."

The appearance was almost unseemly. But when you look at it from his perspective (which the media would never do), there doesn't seem to have been a more appropriate reaction. Kavanaugh had just spent two weeks in near silence while Democrats threw his name and reputation into a dumpster, doused it in kerosene, and lit it with a match. The media did its part in the abuse by dragging Kavanaugh's name through the mud, with multiple stories publishing more allegations of inappropriate conduct and college binge drinking, none of which was ever substantiated and which were, in fact, disputed by Kavanaugh's friends and associates.

The *New York Times* found fault in his having used slang and inside jokes in a high school yearbook.[413]

The *Washington Post* went back decades for evidence that Kavanaugh drank beer as a teen.[414]

It's a shock that Kavanaugh didn't show up for the hearing, flip the table over, and grab his crotch in front of the committee before walking out. Who would have blamed him for it?

---

413   Kate Kelly and David Enrich, "Kavanaugh's Yearbook Page Is 'Horrible, Hurtful' to a Woman It Named," *The New York Times*, September 24, 2018: https://www.nytimes.com/2018/09/24/business/brett-kavanaugh-renate.html.

414   Aaron C. Davis, Emma Brown, and Joe Heim, "Kavanaugh's 'choir boy' image on Fox interview rankles former Yale classmates," *The Washington Post*, September 25, 2018: https://www.washingtonpost.com/investigations/2018/09/25/ea5e50d4-c0eb-11e8-9005-5104e9616c21_story.html?utm_term=.b7a9dd06240e.

The purpose of the hearing for Democrats wasn't to fulfill the Senate's power of "advice and consent" role on judicial nominations. It was to humiliate Kavanaugh so badly that Trump would withdraw his name from consideration. And not just because Kavanaugh held conservative views and would tilt the ideological balance of the court, but because as a white male of "privilege," he deserved to be reduced.

Kavanaugh had provided the Senate committee with an old calendar he still had from the summer of 1982, the year Ford said the assault took place.

Senator Cory Booker, Democrat of New Jersey, noted that the calendar showed that Kavanaugh had—pause so the camera can dramatically zoom in—drunk alcohol on weekdays.

"Judge Kavanaugh, you drank on weekdays as well in high school, not just weekends. Is that correct?" asked Booker.

"Weekdays?" replied Kavanaugh.

"Yes, sir," said Booker, somehow maintaining a straight face while asking a Supreme Court nominee for details about his favorite alcoholic beverage as a teenage boy.

Kavanaugh asked if Booker was specifically referring to the summer months, when school would have been out of session.

"You drank on weekdays, yes or no, sir?" demanded Booker.

"In the summer when we went over to Timmy's house on July first, that would indicate, yes," said Kavanaugh.

The calendar had the word "skis" written on it, and Booker, with just the gravitas that the situation called for, asked Kavanaugh to verify that the word was short for "brewskis."

"Sir—sir, I just need a yes or no. That—brewskis, right?"

Kavanaugh said he wanted to "explain the context," which was presumably that yes, a high school kid might have beers with friends on a summer weekday. (The legal drinking age in Maryland was eighteen at the time.)

Booker wouldn't allow it.

"You just said sir that you drank on weekdays. That's all I was looking for," he said.

Let's try this method of interrogation on Booker in a hypothetical interrogation.

> *Interrogator: Senator, you've faced rumors about your sexuality in the past, haven't you?*
>
> *Booker: Yes, but I—*
>
> *Interrogator: No, no, sir, I just wanted a yes or no and you said yes. That will be all.*

Here's a question Kavanaugh got from Senator Amy Klobuchar: "Drinking is one thing, but the concern is about truthfulness, and in your written testimony, you said sometimes you had too many drinks. Was there ever a time when you drank so much that you couldn't remember what happened, or part of what happened the night before?"

The questions pertaining to Kavanaugh's high school and early college years were in some way meant to reflect on his fitness to serve as a Supreme Court justice who was in his fifties.

Here are questions that weren't asked, but perhaps should have been:

- "Judge Kavanaugh, does the phrase 'Drink, motherfucker, drink' mean anything to you?"
- "Judge Kavanaugh, what's your beer pong record?"
- "Judge Kavanaugh, will you pull my finger?"
- "Judge Kavanaugh, have you ever used the phrase 'tig ol' bitties'?"

Kavanaugh at the time was a well-respected federal judge on the U.S. Court of Appeals for the District of Columbia Circuit. He had graduated from Yale Law School. He had served as counsel in George W. Bush's White House and clerked for Supreme Court Justice Anthony Kennedy. If Kavanaugh was able to do all of this as an out-of-control drunk, I'd like to immediately change my preference from vodka and Sprite to whatever it is he's having.

The hearing was a freakshow through and through.

But thank God for Senator Lindsey Graham.

The day after Kavanaugh and Ford completed their testimonies, Graham finally said what any sane person should have said from the beginning. Before voting to advance Kavanaugh's nomination, Graham said in a speech, "I know I'm a single white male from South Carolina and I'm told I should shut up, but I will not shut up, if that's okay."

He knew that this was as much about reducing Kavanaugh for his "privilege" as it was about the ideological balance of the Supreme Court. "So, if this is the new standard, the accusation proves itself… God help us all," said Graham. "If the new standard for the committee is that there is no presumption of anything, that you have to prove why somebody would accuse you…God help us all."

The committee advanced Kavanaugh's nomination through a vote along party lines, though Senator Jeff Flake, Republican of Arizona, asked for yet one more delay on the full Senate vote so that the FBI could further investigate Ford's allegation.

The hysteria continued.

ABC News chief political analyst Matthew Dowd penned a column to say that the hearing made him realize that much of the chaos could have been avoided "if white male Christians had more readily stepped back, and turned over leadership to those who are not the same sex, or the same color, or the same religion as us." He said that white men like him should begin to "take it upon ourselves to step back and give more people who don't look like us access to the levers of power."[415]

No doubt beaming with pride, Dowd added that "we as white male Christians should do what real leadership demands and practice a level of humility which demonstrates strength by stepping back from the center of the room and begin to give up our seats at the table."

Perhaps Dowd might "do what real leadership demands" and give up his ABC contract to a deaf transgender man. Of course he would

---

415   Matthew Dowd, "Us white male Christians need to step back and give others room to lead," ABC News, Sep. 30, 2018: https://abcnews.go.com/US/leadership-means-making-oneself-dispensable-opinion/story?id=58193412.

never do that, because the point of his column wasn't to propose a serious idea. It was to signal to the social justice mob that he was on their side in the Kavanaugh fight.

After Lindsey Graham's remarks, Zack Beauchamp at Vox wrote that the struggle to defend Kavanaugh was about "showing that white men in power are not going anywhere."[416]

The FBI concluded the weeklong investigation that Democrats and Jeff Flake had asked for and still found nothing that would substantiate Ford's claim. But Democrats didn't take that less-than-ideal outcome lying down. Predictably, they rejected the conclusion and charged that the investigation had been insufficient. "The most notable part of this report is what's not in it," said Senator Feinstein. "It looks to be a product of an incomplete investigation that was limited, perhaps by the White House."[417]

Of course. As with the never-ending chase for the Russia-collusion ghost, it couldn't possibly be that there really was no *there* there. It must have been something else: a lack of time, a lack of resources, anything but the truth.

But Republicans finally moved ahead with the vote. When Kavanaugh was finally confirmed on October 6, 2018, Democrats still refused to give up the fight.

They immediately began talking about impeaching the new Supreme Court justice.[418] Liberal activist and rich white man Tom

---

416 Zack Beauchamp, "Lindsey Graham, Brett Kavanaugh, and the unleashing of white male backlash," Vox.com, Sep. 28, 2018: https://www.vox.com/policy-and-politics/2018/9/28/17913774/ brett-kavanaugh-lindsey-graham-christine-ford-backlash.

417 Judy Woodruff, "FBI report on Kavanaugh raises protests by Democrats," PBS.org, Oct. 4, 2018: https://www.pbs.org/newshour/show/ fbi-report-on-kavanaugh-raises-protests-by-democrats.

418 Alex Seitz-Wald, "Impeaching Kavanaugh rouses progressive Democrats after confirmation," NBC News, Oct. 6, 2018: https://www.nbcnews.com/ politics/elections/impeaching-kavanaugh-rouses-progressive-democrats-after-confirmation-n917376.

Steyer suggested on MSNBC that Kavanaugh's confirmation was illegitimate because it was "a group of very rich, very entitled white men" who ushered it through.[419]

A full year later, the *New York Times* published another claim about Kavanaugh having exposed himself to a woman in college, and several of the Democrats running for the 2020 presidential nomination renewed calls for his impeachment. The story in the *Times*, however, was quickly and easily debunked. The woman who was allegedly faced with the penis couldn't even recall the incident ever having taken place. And she wasn't the one who had relayed the story to the authors of the report. The claim had actually come from a Democrat lawyer.[420]

When major political debates are taken over by the angry social justice movement, this is what happens. The arguments are no longer based on logic, facts, and merit. The arguments are, in fact, replaced altogether by baseless accusations and personal attacks. Truth takes a back seat to victimhood, grievance, and oppression.

When social justice gets involved, a decent man like Kavanaugh watches as his reputation and life's work is nearly vaporized and a Supreme Court seat is all but hijacked by a mob obsessed with white male privilege. But his confirmation showed what can happen when the culture fascists and the social justice movement are shoved back. It's possible to stand up to them and win.

Kavanaugh now sits on the Supreme Court, even though he's a white man.

---

419 *MSNBC Live with Hallie Jackson*, MSNBC, Oct. 8, 2018.

420 Allyson Chiu, "New York Times apologizes for 'inappropriate and offensive' tweet about Kavanaugh sexual misconduct allegation," *Washington Post*, Sept. 16, 2019: https://www.washingtonpost.com/nation/2019/09/16/new-york-times-apologizes-inappropriate-offensive-tweet-about-sexual-misconduct-allegation-against-kavanaugh/.

CHAPTER 10

HOLLYWOOD DIES AND AMY SCHUMER ROLLS OUT OF ITS CORPSE

No one is more committed to fortifying the standing of privileged victims than liberal celebrities. What are the Academy and Grammy Awards programs if not tributes to social justice, celebrations of grievance, and recognitions of various forms of oppression?

Recall that after comedian Kevin Hart failed to sufficiently kneel before the altar of grievance, he was fired from hosting the 2019 Oscars. Almost immediately after it was announced that Hart had landed the coveted gig, some of his old social media posts resurfaced in news reports.

"Yo if my son comes home & try's 2 play with my daughters doll house I'm going 2 break it over his head & say n my voice 'stop that's gay,'" he had tweeted in 2011. In a 2010 tweet, he had joked that actor Damien Dante Wayans looked "like a gay bill board for AIDS." He had referred to someone in another tweet as a "fat faced fag," which is at least kind of funny.[421]

---

421 Seth Abramovitch, "Oscar Host Kevin Hart's History of Anti-Gay Tweets Creates New Problem for Academy," *Hollywood Reporter*, Dec. 6, 2018: https://www.hollywoodreporter.com/news/kevin-harts-past-anti-gay-tweets-creates-problem-academy-1167191.

The usual demands for a public apology followed, and Hart swiftly replied with a "fuck you."

Hart wrote on Instagram on December 6, 2018, "Stop looking for reasons to be negative…. Stop searching for reasons to be angry…. I swear I wish you guys could see/feel/understand the mental place that I am in. I am truly happy people…. there is nothing that you can do to change that…NOTHING."

"I'm almost 40 years old," he said in an Instagram video. "If you don't believe people change, grow, evolve as they get older, I don't know what to tell you. If you want to hold people in a position where they always have to justify or explain their past, then do *you*. I'm the wrong guy, man."[422]

In a separate video posted the same day, Hart said that executives at the Academy had told him to apologize; otherwise, they would find a replacement host. He said that rather than "feed the Internet trolls and reward them," he would decline to apologize and forgo the hosting job.

Several hours later on Twitter, Hart did offer an apology for the gay jokes, referring to his "insensitive words of the past," even while making clear that he would still not host the awards show.[423] "I'm sorry that I hurt people," he wrote. "I am evolving and want to continue to do so."[424]

The apology wasn't necessary because it was never going to satisfy the culture fascists. CNN's Don Lemon had already been calling on Hart to become "an ally" of gays, but even after the apology, Lemon took it upon himself to insist that Hart bend at the knee just a little bit lower.[425]

---

422 Kevin Hart, Instagram, Dec. 6, 2018: https://www.instagram.com/p/BrEFNFal Wgw/?utm_source=ig_embed&utm_campaign=embed_video_watch_again.

423 Kevin Hart, Twitter, Dec. 6, 2018: https://twitter.com/KevinHart4real/ status/1070906075812118529.

424 Kevin Hart, Twitter, Dec. 6, 2018: https://twitter.com/kevinhart4real/status/1 070906121551007745?lang=en.

425 Don Lemon, *CNN Tonight with Don Lemon*, Dec. 6, 2018: https://www. facebook.com/cnn/posts/kevin-call-me-lets-talk-lets-make-you-an-ally-to-the-lgbtq-community-cnns-don-le/10159008466436509/.

On his January 4, 2019 program, nearly three months after the controversy, Lemon continued to obsess over it and attempted to cram more social justice into Hart's mouth. He complained that he hadn't seen any "meaningful outreach to the LGBT community" from Hart and called on him to "do the right thing, to change minds."[426]

In another long monologue on the same show, Lemon said that Hart should use his celebrity to become "the ultimate change agent" and "help change homophobia in the black community."

Isn't that, after all, just what people want from their favorite comedians—social justice crusades?

"I'm a gay black man," said Lemon. "I don't know what it's like to be a white lesbian. I don't know. So, listen, if someone called me and they had an issue, they said, 'Hey Don, you don't know what it's like to be a lesbian, [or] you don't know what it's like to be a white man, [or] you don't know what it's like to be woman,' I would listen to them."

That is the foundation of standpoint knowledge, the assertion that a person who claims to have been oppressed by his race, gender, or sexuality is given exclusive access to a higher, more virtuous truth.

In other words, Lemon thought that if Hart wasn't interested in fully debasing himself and become the black face of gay grievance as a way to appease the social justice mob, he deserved to be shamed.

Days after Lemon's soliloquy, Hart said on SiriusXM radio that it had never been his goal to be a spokesman for the gay struggle. "I don't like the forcing," Hart said. "Don Lemon goes on CNN [and says,] 'You can fix this, become an ally.' That's not my life dream."[427]

---

426 Don Lemon, *CNN Tonight with Don Lemon*, Jan. 4, 2018: https://www.newsweek.com/don-lemon-criticizes-kevin-harts-ellen-degeneres-interview-black-lgbt-1280346.

427 Ross A. Lincoln, "Don Lemon says he spoke to Kevin Hart last weekend," TheWrap.com, Jan. 8, 2019: https://www.thewrap.com/don-lemon-says-he-spoke-to-kevin-hart-last-weekend-video/.

Hart was unaware that, according to social justice, his duty as a straight man was to humble himself before the gays—the oppressed.

It took balls for Hart to stand up to the culture fascists and he paid for it with a struggle session of his own. He declined to grovel, resulting in the loss of the hosting gig and a round of attacks from the media and others in the entertainment industry. Despite the annual Oscar ceremony having devolved into a miserable display of "woke" virtue signaling over the last decade, it's still a glamorous affair that can give a boost to any comedian who is lucky enough to get the job. Hart gave it up, rather than buy into social justice ideology.

For any writer, actor, or singer aspiring to have mainstream success in the entertainment industry, a move like Hart's is unconscionable. But he did it and, more miraculously, he survived. It may have dented Hart's career for a period of time, but it didn't crush him. He's still one of the most in-demand comedians and actors in Hollywood.

Bret Easton Ellis, perhaps the most stimulating, thoughtful novelist of the past thirty years, has sold millions of books and yet he will never be enshrined by the mass entertainment industry the way someone like Stephen King is. The difference: King is a predictable liberal who hits all the right keys, and Ellis, a gay guy with provocative opinions, isn't and doesn't.

Here are some comments from King on politics:

- "[Ted] Cruz, [Rand] Paul and [Marco] Rubio, all running for President. Hey, I thought I was supposed to write the horror stories."[428]

- "Could a woman of Chris Christie's size be taken seriously as a presidential candidate? Just asking, although I think I know the answer." (To be fair, he tweeted this in 2014, more than

---

428   Stephen King, Twitter.com, April 16, 2015: https://twitter.com/StephenKing/status/588785256498606083.

a year before Hillary Clinton, no Slim Jim herself, ran for president a second time and got three million more votes than her opponent.)[429]

- "They [Republicans] can replace the Affordable Care Act with…the UNAFFORDABLE Care Act!"[430]

Virtually every major celebrity in Hollywood talks about politics in that same banal way. They all do it and it's easy because it's the popular thing to do when they're among each other.

Contrast that with what Ellis has said. Ellis was asked by *Rolling Stone* in 2018 if it angered him "on a primal level" that his right to marry another man might be "suddenly taken away" by the Trump administration, a question rooted in the fantasy that the president had shown any real interest in gay issues at all.

His answer was so beautiful you could cry.

"That is suggesting that I believe in identity politics, and that I vote with my penis," Ellis said. "It's suggesting that immigration, the economy and other policies matter so much less than whether I can marry a man. It's not something that I worry about, or is on my mind. That's the problem with identity politics, and it's what got Hillary [Clinton] into trouble. If you have a vagina, you had to vote for Hillary. This has seeped into a bedrock credo among a lot of people, and you've gotta step back. People are not one-issue voters. I am not going to vote as a gay man."[431]

---

429 Stephen King, Twitter,.com Jan. 26, 2014: https://twitter.com/StephenKing/status/423804499107397632.

430 Stephen King, Twitter.com, March 10, 2014: https://twitter.com/StephenKing/status/443146020894310400.

431 Drew Fortune, "Bret Easton Ellis on podcasts, politics and how his dark satire predicted Trump's America," *Rolling Stone*, Aug. 6, 2018: https://www.rollingstone.com/culture/culture-features/bret-easton-ellis-podcasts-politics-dark-satire-trump-america-706549/.

And yet, Ellis, like most people who don't fully understand how social justice operates, is still timid when he's confronted by the ideology.

He was onto something when he mocked the "childlike fascism" of liberals in his 2019 memoir *White*. But he was, perhaps understandably, not so brave when he was asked to defend his views on HBO's *Real Time with Bill Maher* in June 2019, where he appeared as a guest to promote his book.

Ellis was asked about previous comments he had made about the effects of social justice and he froze.[432] Stuttering and stammering, he said that he supported the #Resistance against President Trump but that there was an "overreach" by liberals who could find racism in everything. *New York Times* columnist Charles Blow, a parody of a privileged victim who was also a guest on the program, replied that he knew scores of people who "do the work" that matters to the social justice movement. Nobody had a clue what Blow was talking about, but Ellis shrunk further.

"I think there has been an ironic use of the term 'social justice warrior,'" Ellis pleaded. "And I think it's used ironically when there is a social justice warrior that does overreach and starts doing things like that. What you're talking about is completely authentic and cool, but this stuff that goes on, on Twitter…is a different kind of social justice. It's a fake social justice."

Ellis did this same graceless dance in an April interview with *The New Yorker*. In his book *White*, he blames liberals for their "demented narcissism" in being unable to accept the results of the 2016 election. Yet when confronted with baseline questions about Trump in the interview, Ellis caved and spat out the standard #Resistance lines.[433]

---

432 HBO's *Real Time*, June 8, 2019.
433 Isaac Chotiner, "Bret Easton Ellis Thinks You're Overreacting to Donald Trump," NewYorker.com, April 11, 2019: https://www.newyorker.com/news/q-and-a/bret-easton-ellis-thinks-youre-overreacting-to-donald-trump.

"I do think birtherism was racist and the Tea Party was an abomination," said Ellis. "The hysteria over Trump is what I am talking about. It's not about his policies or supposed racism. It's about what I see as an overreaction to Trump." He also said that he thought Trump was probably a racist.

That's the intimidating effect social justice can have on an otherwise highly successful, highly independent thinker.

Oh, no, I'm not talking about the real *social justice warriors. I'm talking about Twitter!*

If Ellis were talking only about Twitter, he'd have no reason to complain. Twitter is full of nobodies, and its daily users make up a fraction of the general public. It's the *real* social justice monsters who are destroying the country.

Screw the nobodies on Twitter. And I'd say screw Bret Easton Ellis for becoming a shrinking violet when confronted by the social justice mob, but who can blame him? Coming face to face with social justice and its adherents can be terrifying.

Most people would rather not bother with the confrontation. So, views and ideas not in line with the grievance and victimhood scheme go unrepresented in mainstream entertainment. Instead, we're treated to the chubby Amy Schumer grabbing her crotch and lifting up her dress onstage. It's called comedy, but its real purpose is to serve as a form of women's "empowerment" and as a middle finger to "the patriarchy."

Schumer isn't a comedian, an actress, or a writer. She is a walking plus-size embodiment of everything that privileged victims are supposed to be. If that weren't true, every crude "joke" wouldn't have to go back to her fleshy body. Shortly after I made a note to myself that I was going to include her as an example in this book, I ran a Google search to see if she'd been in the news, and the first item that showed up was a March 13, 2019, *New York Times* profile on Schumer, wherein the featured image is her in the nude using moss to cover up her languid breasts.[434]

The March 2019 Netflix stand-up special *Growing* boils down to one hour of Schumer on stage, lifting up her dress to show her underwear and pudgy stomach, and making references to her reproductive organs.

When the punchline is always "I'm fat and don't care," or, "Vagina!" it ceases to be comedy. It is then simply a message reinforced through repetition.

While Schumer was promoting her *I Feel Pretty* movie in 2018, *Time* magazine profiled her so she could pinch off some social justice droppings.

"It's not a perfect movie," Schumer told *Time*. "It would be great if my role had been played by a woman of color and there were more trans people in it, more people with disabilities. But it's a step in the right direction, I hope."[435]

Schumer was the movie's lead actress, and she's also credited as one of its producers. If she had seriously wanted to replace herself with an Indian trans woman with no legs, there was nothing to stop her. Why didn't she?

The answer is obvious: She's a fraud. For all of Schumer's lack of talent, she excels at nodding to the social justice movement, winning its approval in the entertainment industry when she needs it most. Though Schumer's career is in itself a tribute to grievance and victimhood, she's

434 Jason Zinoman, "Amy Schumer doesn't care what you think (that much)," *New York Times*, March 13, 2019: https://www.nytimes.com/2019/03/13/arts/television/amy-schumer-growing-netflix.html?fallback=0&recId=1IQ4mfNkaUEckKM2ma7Az3hYP1c&locked=0&geoContinent=NA&geoRegion=DC&recAlloc=story&geoCountry=US&blockId=home-featured&imp_id=617286123&action=click&module=editorContent&pgtype=Article&region=CompanionColumn&contentCollection=Trending.

435 Eliza Berman, "Amy Schumer knows she'll make more mistakes. But she's ready to listen and learn," *Time*, April 12, 2018: http://time.com/5237435/amy-schumer-knows-she-will-make-more-mistakes/.

smart enough to know that there's always someone to outrank her on the intersectionality scale of oppression. She knows that the best way to remain in the mob's good graces is to signal subservience. It's a delicate dance and she's very good at it.

The *Time* magazine article went on to recall Schumer's previous show on Comedy Central, *Inside Amy Schumer*, and her enduring fame. Hint: Her fame is not due to some unexplained capability.

"A writer…described [my] show as 'sneaking shaved carrots into brownies,' she recalls, and the notion of a stealth agenda stuck with her," *Time* said. "Right now, though, she's more interested in talking about overt agendas."

No kidding! Wait, you mean Schumer's subtle comment about wanting more trans actors wasn't just a candid slip of the tongue?

The article also described Schumer as being "so bummed out by the political climate" that she was doing fewer stand-up comedy shows. "At one point in our conversation," said *Time*, "tears come to her eyes."

The *New York Times* profile on Schumer in March 2019 under-scored that she's not so much a funny entertainer as a vessel for social justice. The *Times* lauded Schumer for her Comedy Central *Inside Amy Schumer* show, dubbing it "a sneakily smart show whose viral sendups of gender double standards and misogyny featured some of the funniest feminist humor in the history of sketch comedy." ("Feminist humor" is an oxymoron if there ever was one.)

There's some irony in that Schumer told the paper, "Being cool is powerful in this industry, but there's nothing more powerful than not giving a fuck." Schumer may not give a fuck about her weight, but she certainly cares what Hollywood demands of her. It's why she checks the "women of color," "trans people," and "people with disabilities" boxes in her interviews. Schumer isn't the transgressive heroine she presents. She's a Hollywood conformist to the fullest.

This is what passes for a leading comedian today, thanks to the social justice movement. The adoring coverage of Schumer doesn't rest on whether she's funny; it rests on whether she advances the cause. She does, and she's rewarded for it despite her mediocre talents, as is standard for privileged victims.

Schumer wasn't even always this predictable. A few years ago, she made an actually humorous joke about Mexicans—"I used to date Hispanic guys, but now I prefer consensual"—and after a snippy critique was printed in the *Guardian*, she felt moved to explain herself, even while maintaining that she would not limit her routine to "safe material."[436]

Her material now is exclusively safe and that's what social justice requires. It's a form of an advanced apology for any perceived privilege.

Apologizing for being white, a man, or straight (or all three) is how you escape the struggle sessions, at least for a while. That's true with the entertainment industry, just like it's true with the news media, academia, and political Washington. If you don't want the Kevin Hart experience, say you're sorry in advance and it can buy you time.

Anne Hathaway did it. At a dinner in September 2018 hosted by the Human Rights Campaign gay advocacy group, she said it was "important to acknowledge, with the exception of being a cisgender male, everything about how I was born has put me at the current center of a damaging and widely accepted myth…that gayness orbits around straightness, transgender orbits around cisgender, and that all races orbit around whiteness…. [T]ogether we are not going to just question this myth, we are going to destroy it."[437]

Actor Armie Hammer promoted his starring role in a satirical Broadway show aptly titled *Straight White Men* in the summer of 2018 by offering his own apology for being a straight white man. "[T]he play is so brilliant and prescient and timely," he said. "It deals so well

---

436 Amy Schumer, Twitter, June 28, 2015: https://twitter.com/amyschumer/status/615182173570633728.

437 Nikki Schwab, "Anne Hathaway denounces white privilege in award speech," *New York Post*, Sep. 16, 2018: https://nypost.com/2018/09/16/anne-hathaway-denounces-white-privilege-in-award-speech/.

with the concepts of toxic masculinity and white privilege, which we're finally reckoning with as a society."[438]

You would think Ashley Graham suffers enough on the oppression scale being classified as a plus-size model, but she can't shut up about all the privilege she gets from being white. "I know I'm on this pedestal because of white privilege," she told *New York* magazine in August 2017. "To not see black or Latina women as famous in my industry is crazy! I have to talk about it. I want to give those women kudos because they are the ones who paved the way for me."[439] (What better way to acknowledge your privilege than to give credit to the people you believe you stepped on to continue savoring it?)

In a podcast talk in late 2018, Graham apologized again for being a white girl, while also bragging about it. "Being a curvy woman hasn't been a new thing," Graham said. "It's been a generation of woman [sic] of color who have had our body type for centuries. And here I am, a white woman in this day and age, getting praised for having a curvy, voluptuous body, and now I've been given a platform to talk about it. But if you talk about any curvy models of color, there aren't any that have been given a platform like mine."[440]

In another interview with *Glamour* magazine, she said, "Because I'm white and because of white privilege, I've been given a platform. But we can't erase all the women who came before me."[441]

Nonwhite women everywhere were no doubt filled with gratitude.

---

438 Adam Green, "Armie Hammer on making his Broadway debut and reckoning with toxic masculinity," *Vogue*, June 19, 2018: https://www.vogue.com/article/armie-hammer-interview-vogue-july-2018-issue.

439 Jada Yuan, "Now this is a supermodel...," *New York* magazine, Aug. 2017: https://www.thecut.com/2017/08/ashley-graham-supermodel.html.

440 Jason Pham, "Ashley Graham opens up about her white privilege as a curvy model," StyleCaster, Dec. 2018: https://stylecaster.com/ashley-graham-white-privilege-curvy-model/.

441 Ana Colone, "Ashley Graham's been having difficult conversations for two decades. Now people are listening," *Glamour*, Nov. 19, 2018: https://www.glamour.com/story/ashley-graham-november-2018-digital-cover-story.

Admittedly, it's not really Graham's fault for being such an insufferable swine. She was saying what she'd been taught that she had to say. Privileged victims owe their benefits to social justice. They know that they had better pay their respects and acknowledge the intersectionality scale of oppression.

Chelsea Handler, who went from legitimately funny comedian to self-consoling bore after the 2016 election, told a Canadian newspaper in September 2018, "I didn't realize that half my career is because I'm white and pretty rather than me picking myself up by my bootstraps and working hard."[442]

What a good social justice foot soldier.

In a December 2017 essay for Goodreads, actress and liberal activist Emma Watson recalled being taken aback when someone had described her as a white feminist. She said she eventually came to realize that she had done something wrong. "It would have been more useful to spend the time asking myself questions like: What are the ways I have benefited from being white?"[443]

If the apologies don't come first, they better come later. In a 2017 podcast interview, singer Katy Perry was asked if she understood why wearing hair braids in literally a split second of a three-year-old music video would be controversial. Perry sheepishly replied, "I have lots of white privilege."[444]

The satirical Onion website perfectly captured the proliferation of anti-privilege sentiment in mass entertainment with a mock review of

442   Eric Volmers, "Comedian Chelsea Handler talks pot, Trump and her own white privilege," *Calgary Herald*, Sep. 14, 2018: https://calgaryherald.com/entertainment/celebrity/chelsea-handler-talks-pot-trump-and-her-own-white-privilege.

443   Emma Watson, "First book of 2018! Why I'm no longer talking to white people about race by Reni Eddo-Lodge," GoodReads.com, Dec. 31, 2017: https://www.goodreads.com/topic/show/19152741-first-book-of-2018-why-i-m-no-longer-talking-to-white-people-about-race.

444   Natalie Wolfe, "Katy Perry responds to appropriating culture on her 72-hour livestream," News.com.au, June 13, 2017: https://www.news.com.au/entertainment/music/music-videos/katy-perry-responds-to-appropriating-cultural-on-her-72hour-livestream/news-story/fd79aaa43f4217b162c014d32860676a.

Super Smash Bros., a video game series in which different characters from Nintendo's world engage in physical combat.

The faux review lampooned the privilege nonsense, calling Kirby, a bulbous and pink pillow-like character, "one of the most offensive and harmful stereotypes in the history of popular entertainment." The fake reviewer continued, "How a backwards, demeaning image like this made it into a game in 2018 is beyond me. It just goes to show that [video game] developers come from a privileged and insulated world."[445]

The satire all too accurately demonstrates the joyless world that the grievance obsessives are forcing on the rest of us.

Executives and top movie producers in Hollywood contribute to the misery by making and remaking the dullest movies possible, all with the aim of reinforcing social justice.

They do it most notably with the endless, god-awful reboots that make gender and race the most important parts of the production. Acting ability and dialogue are afterthoughts when it comes to social justice-driven movie reboots.

Columbia Pictures in 2016 offered up a microwaved remake of the iconic *Ghostbusters* movie but switched out every one of the male roles for female ones. Film review columnist Anthony Lane for the *New Yorker* paid the required respects to the film's "woke" elements—he blamed a portion of the "loathing" for the movie's release on "misogyny"—but then trashed it for all the right reasons.

He described Kate McKinnon's performance as "overkill," which he attributed to the director perhaps not being able to fill any "left-over space."[446]

---

445 *The Onion*, "Review: 'Super Smash Bros. Ultimate' sunk by unforgivable inclusion of Kirby, one of the most offensive harmful stereotypes to ever appear in popular entertainment," Dec. 7, 2018: https://ogn.theonion.com/review-super-smash-bros-ultimate-sunk-by-unforgivab-1830942802.

446 Anthony Lane, "Ghostbusters and Absolutely Fabulous: the movie," *New Yorker*, July 15, 2016: https://www.newyorker.com/magazine/2016/07/25/ghostbusters-and-absolutely-fabulous-the-movie.

Of course there was leftover space. The purpose of remaking the movie wasn't to improve upon the *Ghostbusters* franchise or because someone had written a great script that deserved to be made into a feature film. The purpose was to pat women on the back for being, well, women.

The movie sucked, as evidenced by reports in early 2019 of another *Ghostbusters* movie in the works, but as a sequel to the original and without any relation to the all-female version.

Leslie Jones, one of the actresses in the 2016 *Ghostbusters* reboot, took the news like a champion privileged victim. "So insulting," she tweeted. "Like fuck us. We dint count. It's like something trump would do.... Such a dick move. And I don't give a fuck I'm saying something!!" In another tweet, she said it "makes my heart drop" to know that another *Ghostbusters* movie might go back to an all-male cast because it could send the message that "boys are better."[447]

Well, no. If the second reboot sucks just as bad or even half as bad, audiences will hate that one, too. But the notion that a product should be based on its quality rather than its message doesn't register with privileged victims. And if Jones was worried that an all-male cast would suggest that "boys are better," what message did she think was conveyed by the all-female cast? My guess is that she probably didn't consider it, because part of being a privileged victim is feeling a sense of entitlement born of oppression.

The 2018 *Ocean's 8* spinoff tried the same trick. Producers swapped out the all-male cast of *Ocean's Eleven* for a group of women, including Rihanna. And not that audience reviews are everything, but vast discrepancies for movies meant to mirror each other should say something. *Eleven* has an audience score of 80 percent on Rotten Tomatoes, whereas *8* is at 44 percent.

---

447   Rosemary Rossi, "Leslie Jones calls 'Ghostbusters' sequel 'insulting' and 'a D-Move,' TheWrap.com, Jan. 21, 2019: https://www.thewrap.com/leslie-jones-calls-new-ghostbusters-squel-insulting/.

And yet, as twisted, sick, and nonsensical as social justice can be, it *is* possible to go too far.

Moviemakers Scott McGehee and David Siegel did just that when in 2017 they announced that they were cocreating an adaptation of *Lord of the Flies* but with an all-girls cast. It was, again, another marketing ploy targeting the grievance market, without regard for the whole point behind the *Lord of the Flies* story. Anyone who read the book knows that the entire plot is about the nature of men—specifically men—when left only with their unrestrained, basic instincts. A movie about that kind of requires a cast of…men.

The announcement was widely panned on social media. Even Roxane Gay, a feminist author and literally the biggest social justice mob boss there is, knocked the planned all-female *Lord of the Flies* incarnation, tweeting, "An all women remake of Lord of the Flies makes no sense because…the plot of that book wouldn't happen with all women."[448]

⌘ ⌘ ⌘

Stand-up comedians have probably suffered the most in the entertainment business.

Ask any comedian with a background in stand-up. They know better than anyone the havoc that this sick culture has wrought, even if they don't know why.

It was a stunning display in late November of 2018 when comedian Nimesh Patel was kicked off the stage at Columbia University for telling what was formerly known as a joke, because the spawn of the social justice movement on campus didn't approve.

The setup for Patel's bit was everything you'd think the grievance fetishists of social justice would appreciate: a commentary on the

---

448   Roxane Gay, Twitter, Aug. 30, 2017: https://twitter.com/rgay/status/903067493966766081.

marginalization of both blacks and gays. The punchline was even a tribute to the privileged victim's most sacred tenet—intersectionality.

Patel described his New York neighborhood, where he said there are gay black men who tell him when they don't like his clothes. The joke ended with Patel's observation that being gay can't possibly be a choice, because, after all, who would choose to be gay (aggrieved), on top of already being black (oppressed). "No one looks in the mirror and thinks, 'This black thing is too easy; let me just add another thing to it,'" went the joke.[449]

That's it. That was the punchline. It was funny enough, but Patel had breached social justice protocol in making light of those who claim to have been victimized by nature of their race, gender, or sexuality.

Student leaders of Columbia's Asian American Alliance, which had invited Patel for their annual cultural event, stormed the stage to ask that he wrap up his routine and make an early exit.

"Is it because I'm talking about uncomfortable stuff?" he asked, not realizing that he was about to experience his own struggle session.

"I think there's a distinction between being uncomfortable and being disrespectful," one of the group's student organizers said, to whoops and applause from the idiot audience.

"I think I'm being respectful," Patel said.

"I just don't think you're entitled to certain jokes you're making, and I don't think it's appropriate," the student replied.

"Why?" asked Patel, still not fully aware that this was not a debate—it was a public flogging.

"I think the comments you were making about being gay and black is very disrespectful."

---

449   Shubham Saharan, "Student organizers boot former SNL from stage during standup routine for jokes deemed offensive," *Columbia Spectator*, Dec. 1, 2018: https://www.columbiaspectator.com/news/2018/12/01/student-organizers-boot-snl-writer-from-stage-during-standup-routine-for-jokes-deemed-offensive-2/.

Patel tried in vain to explain that the joke had actually been provided to him by a real, living gay black man. "This is strange," he said. And then, in the most depressing and embarrassing moment of the entire incident, he tried saving himself with an attempt at pulling rank on the intersectionality scale.

"Look, it's a strange time to be an Asian person in this country," he said. "I'll give you that much, because it feels like there's a lot of racial tension. And at any moment black and white people are going to go to war and Indians are going to have to choose and Asians are going to have to choose." You almost wanted to hug Patel and tell him that it was too late. He had already been offered as a sacrifice to social justice and the church of intersectionality.

He went on to say that he was sure none of his material had been disrespectful and that he thought any offense taken was a matter of generational differences. He then finally left and the audience applauded his exit.[450]

A week later, Patel wrote a tepid op-ed for the *New York Times* criticizing the student leaders who had kicked him off the stage, while at the same time missing the point that his incident was not some bizarre mishap that he was unlucky enough to have stumbled into.

"I do not think we should let the actions of a small group—actions that get blown out of proportion because they feed a narrative many people want to hear—paint college campuses as bad places to perform and paint this next generation as doomed," he wrote, before naïvely theorizing that the episode was a symptom of "a 24-hour news cycle" that makes it "hard to sift through and find the signal and find what is really being said."

No, no, no, Patel. No, no, no, no, no.

This wasn't the action of a small group, and college students aren't victims of the news cycle. This is the new reality and it functions just as social justice dictates. Many college students have realized that they can

---

450 Veritech, "Nimesh Patel getting kicked off the stage at Columbia," YouTube.
       com, Dec. 6, 2018: https://www.youtube.com/watch?v=fN-3DByTq6k.

now gain privileges by being victims, and maintaining that status often means engaging and instigating confrontations just like the one Patel experienced. The purpose is to signal that there's a new order to the way things are done.

What happened to Patel has happened to countless others in the comedy field.

Steve Harvey in March 2015 told a joke on his morning radio talk show that he had told several times before, involving a fictional black church-lady character named Sister Odell and her annoyance at the special-needs daughter of a fellow churchgoer. The social justice mob immediately called for Harvey to be pulled from the air.

He apologized in a note on Facebook, explaining to the willfully ignorant that Sister Odell isn't real and no one else in the scenario of the joke is real, either.[451]

Though Harvey had bowed to the grievance gang, it seemed to go unnoticed that three months later on the Netflix show *Comedians in Cars Getting Coffee*, he admitted that his apology had been contrived and for all the right reasons.

"You know, I said she was thirty-four years old, sitting over there blowing bubbles," he said of the fake special-needs character in his Sister Odell joke. "Well, that was it. That was it. And boy, they went on Twitter, Instagram…. I apologized. I had to do it."

He explained that the apology had been required by radio executives to keep advertisers from fleeing his program. "Because I got a talk show," he said. "Because now here comes a sponsor—and now all the rest of them have to piggyback and act righteous, too. 'Oh, they're pulling their sponsorship; well we gotta act like we care, too.' They don't really care. They don't really care. It's the deal. We got to act offended."[452]

---

451   Steve Harvey, Facebook, March 27, 2015: https://www.facebook.com/ SteveHarvey/posts/to-everyone-please-accept-my-sincerest-apologies-it-was-not-my-intent-to-hurt-an/1553810864879773/.

452   Jerry Seinfeld, YouTube.com, Aug. 14, 2015: https://www.youtube.com/ watch?v=ZOSlYLdN0Wk.

That's the reality and it's entirely incompatible with what comedy is supposed to be.

In an interview with the *Wall Street Journal* in February 2019, popular stand-up comic Colin Quinn said it perfectly. "I feel like a lot of people now are saying, 'You know what? Comedy is supposed to be uplifting,'" he said. "It's like, what are you, the new moral majority all of a sudden?"

⌘　⌘　⌘

Like every other part of the culture, social justice has descended on Hollywood and wrecked the entertainment industry. Those in the business have two options: Buy into the social justice ideology as privileged victims or risk having their careers go up in smoke.

Most in the entertainment business aren't like Kevin Hart. Most aren't willing to resist the demands of the social justice mob if it means sacrificing their stardom.

And that's how we ended up with a mass entertainment industry that's less concerned with producing high-quality, enjoyable TV shows, movies, and celebrities than it is with reinforcing the importance of grievance, oppression, and victimhood.

Entertainment is now beside the point. Hollywood is now simply one more hub for social justice and a breeding ground for privileged victims.

CHAPTER 11

DEMOCRATS HAVE AN INTERSECTIONALITY REVOLUTION

If you buy into the social justice scheme, politics is the place for you—the Democratic Party in particular. Democrats competing for the party's 2020 nomination made it clear from the start that this wouldn't be a traditional political contest. It would be America's first intersectionality presidential primary. Two of their white male front runners introduced themselves with amends for being white.

Beto O'Rourke, who served for six years in the U.S. House as an unremarkable congressman from Texas before losing his 2018 Senate race, announced his run for president on March 13, 2019. Just two days later, he was pledging to be "more thoughtful" about "the way in which I acknowledge the truth of the criticism that I have enjoyed white privilege."[453]

Despite going by a Spanish nickname, O'Rourke is of course whiter than David Duke's cleanest sheets. And he has shown an uncanny

---

453   Eric Bradner, "Beto O'Rourke apologizes for jokes about wife, says he has benefited from 'white privilege'" CNN, March 17, 2019: https://www.cnn.com/2019/03/15/politics/beto-orourke-wife-white-privilege/index.html.

knack for saying precisely the opposite of what a party run by the social justice mob would want to hear, even as he tries so desperately to prove his "woke" credentials.

Demonstrating a deep connection to America's heartland, O'Rourke decided to roll out his campaign with a cover story in *Vanity Fair*, a magazine often referred to as "the common man's bible." In the article, he spoke as though his candidacy was a natural evolution in America's manifest destiny. "Man, I'm just born to be in it," he said.[454]

The day the *Vanity Fair* article came out, he told voters at a coffee shop in Iowa that while he's away, his wife cares for their three children, "sometimes with my help." The remark was innocuous, a clear attempt to graciously give his wife credit for the work she does, but the social justice mob that makes up much of the Democratic Party's base viewed it as a suggestion that childcare is a woman's job, while running for president is his.[455]

O'Rourke had been the darling of the news media when he challenged Senator Ted Cruz, the most reviled man in Washington. But after O'Rourke entered the crowded Democratic presidential primary, the national newspapers and cable and networks shrugged. He initially avoided doing TV interviews, which was probably for the best. The more voters saw of him, the further he sunk in the polls.

To remind people of who he is, O'Rourke agreed to appear on ABC's *The View*, where he got to experience his own personal struggle session.

O'Rourke apologized and atoned for his wrongs, confessed his sins, and checked the grievance boxes that the Democratic Party now

454 Joe Hagan, "Beto O'Rourke: 'I'm Just Born to be in It,'" *Vanity Fair*, March 13, 2019: https://www.vanityfair.com/news/2019/03/beto-orourke-cover-story.

455 Katie Kindelan, "Why it matters that Beto O'Rourke said he 'sometimes' helps his wife raise their 3 kids," ABC News, March 16, 2019: https://abcnews.go.com/GMA/News/matters-beto-orourke-helps-wife-raise-kids/story?id=61709626.

demands of its candidates. He told the ladies of *The View* that he was "meeting people where they are in their communities," then pandered in Spanish about how everyone in America is important. He admitted there's still much for him to learn and, because the segment wouldn't have been complete without it, he atoned for all of his privilege.

Cohost Meghan McCain asked him about the *Vanity Fair* spread and his solo cross-country tour that he embarked on while his wife cared for their children. "These are things in my mind that a female candidate wouldn't be able to get away with," McCain said.

O'Rourke assumed his default position, which is submission. "You're right," he said. "There are things that I have been privileged to do in my life that others cannot." He dutifully added that "the systematic, foundational discrimination that we have in this country in every aspect of life is something that I have not experienced in my lifetime, and I've had advantages that others cannot enjoy."

With that, O'Rourke summarized the point of this entire book. But keep reading because it's just getting good!

Asked again by Joy Behar if it was a mistake to appear on the magazine cover, O'Rourke said, "Yeah, I think it reinforces that perception of privilege," because "no one was born to be president of the United States of America, least of all me."

(O'Rourke might have tried to be a little more forthcoming. He posed on the cover of *Vanity Fair* to launch his campaign because his campaign was a literal vanity affair.)

After confessing those sins, O'Rourke was asked about criticism he had received for saying that he only "sometimes" helps his wife with raising their children. "Absolutely, and I deserved it," said O'Rourke, ever eager to talk about how wrong he is at all times. "So listen, in a real ham-handed way, I was trying to acknowledge that she has a lion's share of the responsibility during this campaign." It's like O'Rourke watched too many romantic comedies with sensitive male leads. Someone should tell him that those really are just movies.

To put a bow on it all, O'Rourke acknowledged he has his own "work cut out" for himself in order "to be a better person and ensure that I'm more mindful to the experiences that others have had different than the experiences that I've had."

Where is the joy in any of this?

At a campaign stop in Salem, New Hampshire, O'Rourke came ready as ever to check his privilege, and he did it in the most clownish way. At the event, hosted in May 2019 in the backyard of a former ambassador to Saudi Arabia, O'Rourke suggested that the tax code could be used to transfer wealth from whites to blacks. One attendee asked him whether he could, "as a privileged white man, kind of lead the racial healing that we need and withstand the rise of white supremacy."[456] O'Rourke's answer was a work of art. "I can choose to do this as a white man, to involve myself in this conversation," he said. And then, he awkwardly declared that he could "just as easily choose to back out of it." It was as if he thought it might have been a trick question.

But that's what happens when you try to operate under the absurd. You do the absurd.

Before former vice president Joe Biden even officially announced his campaign, he was prepping for what he knew he would have to do. At an event in January 2019, he said, "The bottom line is, we have a lot to root out, but most of all the systematic racism that most of us whites don't like to acknowledge even exists." Naturally, he said this at an event hosted by Reverend Al Sharpton's National Action Network, so that Biden might pay his respects and kiss the ring of virtue. "We don't even consciously acknowledge it," Biden continued. "But it's been built into every aspect of our system."[457]

---

456 Emily Larsen, "Beto O'Rourke suggests using tax system to transfer wealth from rich whites to blacks," Washington Examiner, May 10, 2019: https://www.washingtonexaminer.com/news/beto-orourke-suggests-using-tax-system-to-transfer-wealth-from-wealthy-whites-to-blacks.

457 John Verhovek, "Joe Biden: White America 'has to admit there's still a systemic racism'," ABC News, Jan. 21, 2019: https://abcnews.go.com/Politics/joe-biden-white-america-admit-systemic-racism/story?id=60524966.

Correctly anticipating that his party would demand that he account for his part in the 1991 Clarence Thomas Supreme Court confirmation hearings, Biden made preemptive amends for that, too. Twice.

"Anita Hill was vilified when she came forward by a lot of my colleagues," Biden said in September 2018, after Brett Kavanaugh's own confirmation was marred by sexual assault allegations. "I wish I could have done more to prevent those questions and the way they asked them.... [W]hat happened was, she got victimized again during the process."[458]

Disavowing his role as the chair of the Senate Judiciary Committee during the hearings was apparently not enough. Six months later, Biden condemned his Senate colleagues who had served the panel for their race.

"There was a real and perceived problem the committee faced," he said during remarks at an event raising awareness for sexual assault victims. "There were a bunch of white guys. No, I mean it sincerely—a bunch of white guys hearing this testimony." He added that the "white man's culture" has "got to change."[459]

Unfortunately for old-time Biden, he, like most people, doesn't understand the social justice movement. He isn't aware that it is never truly sated by apologies, even if that's what the mob is demanding. Nothing outside of complete submission is acceptable.

After having kneeled before the altar of grievance on race, Biden was then hit with a series of sexual misconduct accusations related to his years of well-known hugging, caressing, and cuddling, most or all of which takes place in public.

---

458 Adam Edelman, "Biden: Senate must treat Kavanaugh accuser Ford better than Anita Hill," NBC News, Sep. 21, 2018: https://www.nbcnews.com/politics/politics-news/biden-senate-must-treat-kavanaugh-accuser-ford-better-anita-hill-n911806?cid=sm_npd_ms_tw_ma.

459 "Joe Biden laments role in Anita Hill hearing," YouTube.com, March 26, 2019: https://www.youtube.com/watch?time_continue=147&v=aqonFjYjAGM.

On March 29, 2019, as Biden was prepping to officially declare his campaign, Lucy Flores, a former Nevada State assemblywoman, penned a piece for *The New Yorker* to say that she had—oh my God!—been kissed by Biden on the back of her head without her explicit consent.

The piece recounted a 2014 campaign stop that Biden made on behalf of Flores and other Democrats running for office in Nevada. "I found my way to the holding room for the speakers, where everyone was chatting, taking photos, and getting ready to speak to the hundreds of voters in the audience," wrote Flores. "Just before the speeches, we were ushered to the side of the stage where we were lined up by order of introduction. As I was taking deep breaths and preparing myself to make my case to the crowd, I felt two hands on my shoulders. I froze. 'Why is the vice-president of the United States touching me?'"

She said she was "mortified" when he "inhaled" her hair. "He proceeded to plant a big slow kiss on the back of my head," she wrote. And finally, "My name was called and I was never happier to get on stage in front of an audience." She described feeling "uneasy, gross and confused" by what was no doubt a deeply traumatic three seconds of the vice president touching her back.[460]

This wasn't a matter of sexual assault; it was an invasion of personal space. That can often be remedied by simply asking an individual to take a step back, or even—and I know this isn't okay to say—removing yourself from the situation. Who would think to write an op-ed in *The New Yorker* over this?

Flores was then featured on CNN's *State of the Union* and MSNBC's *Kasie DC*. Her story was covered multiple times in the *New York Times*, the *Washington Post*, and *USA Today*.

---

460   Lucy Flores, "An Awkward Kiss Changed How I Saw Joe Biden," *New York*, March 29, 2019: https://www.thecut.com/2019/03/an-awkward-kiss-changed-how-i-saw-joe-biden.html?mod=article_inline.

The outpouring of support for Flores led to another allegation. Connecticut woman Amy Lappos came forward in her local paper to say that during a fundraiser in 2009, Biden "put his hand around my neck and pulled me in to rub noses with me." She said she thought he was readying to kiss her on the mouth and that she was certain the encounter was rooted in "sexism or misogyny."[461]

A day after that, twenty-two-year-old Caitlyn Caruso told the *New York Times* that when she was nineteen, she had met Biden at an event in Las Vegas and that he placed his hand on her thigh and hugged her for an extended period.[462] Would somebody get Caruso a rape kit?!

DJ Hill, a fifty-nine-year-old writer, also told the *Times* that she met Biden at a fundraiser in Minneapolis in 2012, and that he made her "very uncomfortable" when he slid his hand down her back while posing for a photo.

In its story about both Caruso and Hill, the *Times* was sure to add that "touching someone you know is one thing; touching complete strangers, as Mr. Biden often does, is another."

True, but no one can honestly say that any of these are examples of sexual assault or harassment or abuse. Not that it matters, really. This is the reality of the Democratic Party that Joe Biden, Barack Obama, and the rest of the Democrats asked for by insisting that you must listen to and believe any woman for no other reason than that she's a woman. Hillary Clinton said it in 2015: "Every survivor of sexual assault deserves to be heard, believed, and supported."

---

461   Neil Vigdor, "Connecticut woman says then-Vice President Joe Biden touched her inappropriately at a Greenwich fundraiser in 2009," *Hartford Courant*, April 1, 2019: https://www.courant.com/politics/hc-pol-biden-grabbed-aide-20190401-vl7chim3hrdjtcwu2tszrhozzm-story.html.

462   Sheryl Gay Stolberg and Sydney Ember, "Biden's Tactile Politics Threaten His Return in the #MeToo Era," *New York Times*, April 2, 2019: https://www.nytimes.com/2019/04/02/us/politics/joe-biden-women-me-too.html.

A day after the *Times* story ran, the *Union* newspaper of California reported on Alexandra Tara Reade, who said that in 1993 she had worked as a staffer in Biden's office, when he was still a senator representing Delaware. She said that he "touched her several times making her feel uncomfortable" and that he "used to put his hand on my shoulder and run his finger up my neck."[463]

In a separate first-person op-ed for the *Union*, Reade wrote that her supervisor in Biden's office had asked her to serve drinks at a work event, supposedly because Biden "liked my legs" and thought that Reade was attractive. With great humility, Reade said that because she was a former model and actress, "such comments were of no consequence to me. I was asked to do many things based on my looks."[464]

Reade then said a legislative aide, who was a woman and also worked for Biden, told her to decline serving the drinks. So Reade said that she did and after that, she said, her role on the team was diminished and she was eventually told to look for another job. One minor detail: Reade said she didn't feel as though Biden's touching was a matter of sexual misconduct. Her story was nonetheless lumped in with all the others.

Biden went ahead and posted a two-minute video on Twitter wherein he vowed to change his touchy behavior to be more in line with modern "boundaries of protecting personal space."[465]

You could almost feel for him, naïvely explaining himself, promising to change his ways, as though any of it mattered. The day after the

---

463   Alan Riquelmy, "Nevada County woman says Joe Biden inappropriately touched her while working in his U.S. Senate office," *Union*, April 3, 2019: https://www.theunion.com/news/nevada-county-woman-says-joe-biden-inappropriately-touched-her-while-working-in-his-u-s-senate-office/.

464   Alexandra Tara Reade, "Alexandra Tara Reade: A girl walks into the Senate," *Union*, April 17, 2019: https://www.theunion.com/opinion/columns/alexandra-tara-reade-a-girl-walks-into-the-senate/.

465   Joe Biden, Twitter.com, April, 3, 2019: https://twitter.com/JoeBiden/status/1113515882960052224.

video posted, the *Washington Post* reported on yet three more women accusing Biden of misconduct.[466]

Vail Kohnert-Yount said that in 2013, when she was a White House intern, Biden introduced himself by pulling her in and putting their foreheads together. She remembered that he called her a pretty girl, and she felt that the gesture was inappropriate in a professional setting.

Ally Coll said she was helping organize an event for Democrats during the 2008 election and that when she was introduced to Biden, he complimented her smile while holding her shoulders, which, Coll said, lasted "a beat too long."

Sofie Karasek said she was twenty-two when she met Biden at the 2016 Academy Awards ceremony, where she shared a story with him about a college student who had committed suicide after experiencing a sexual assault. As with Kohnert-Yount, Biden grabbed the back of Karasek's head and pulled her forehead toward his. The moment was caught in a photo and, ironically, the *Post* published it at the time and called the image "powerful." Karasek herself had the photo framed and preciously positioned it on a shelf for display. But after the #MeToo movement gained steam, she said, she decided to take it down.[467]

Funny how Karasek found the interaction with Biden inappropriate only after the social justice mob told her it was.

If you laughed at any of the claims against Biden, it's okay. They're laughable. But this is the culture that Democrats asked for.

---

466   Elise Viebeck and Matt Viser and Colby Itkowitz, "Three more women accuse Biden of unwanted affection, say apology video doesn't quell concerns," *Washington Post*, April 4, 2019: https://www.washingtonpost.com/politics/biden-says-hell-adjust-his-physical-behavior-as-three-more-women-come-forward/2019/04/03/94a2ed2c-5622-11e9-8ef3-fbd41a2ce4d5_story.html?noredirect=on&utm_term=.5dc38d88fe11.

467   Colby Itzkowitz, "There's a moving story behind this powerful photo of Biden and a sexual assault survivor at the Oscars," *Washington Post*, March 7, 2016: https://www.washingtonpost.com/news/inspired-life/wp/2016/03/07/the-amazing-story-behind-this-photo-of-a-sexual-assault-survivor-and-joe-biden-at-the-oscars/?noredirect=on&utm_term=.77d8bc2eaa05.

Predictably, the Anita Hill hearings would continue to haunt Biden throughout the early weeks of his campaign. The *New York Times* on April 25, 2019, reported that Biden had called Hill to express his "regret for what she endured" nearly thirty years before, referring to her testimony in front of the Senate Judiciary Committee, which Biden had presided over at the time.[468]

"I cannot be satisfied by simply saying, 'I'm sorry for what happened to you,'" said Hill. "I will be satisfied when I know that there is real change and real accountability and real purpose."

Further, she said, there "needs to be an apology to the American public because we know now how deeply disappointed Americans around the country were about what they saw" at Hill's hearing. "And not just women. There are women and men now who have just really lost confidence in our government to respond to the problem of gender violence."

With that, Hill had officially left the reservation. Her old allegations against Thomas had nothing to do with violence. She never testified that he had so much as laid a finger on her. Her testimony was only that when she worked for Thomas, he had made inappropriate remarks to her about pornography and pubic hair.

Comments about a sex movie, assuming they ever happened, are now considered gender violence, according to privileged victim Anita Hill. Deconstruction of the language is a permanent feature of social justice.

Biden can never be sorry enough for having presided over the committee that so brutally victimized Hill, who is now an esteemed professor at Brandeis University and is to this day lauded by glossy magazines and portrayed as an irreproachable feminist hero in sympathetic TV movie specials.

What precisely is Biden supposed to have done during the hearings that he didn't do? He permitted Hill's testimony right before

---

468 Sheryl Gay Stolberg and Carl Hulse, "Joe Biden Expresses Regret to Anita Hill, but She Says 'I'm Sorry' Is Not Enough," *New York Times*, April 25, 2019: https://www.nytimes.com/2019/04/25/us/politics/joe-biden-anita-hill. html?emc=edit_cn_20190426&nl=politics&nlid=7020910720190426&te=1.

Thomas was scheduled for his confirmation vote, and then Biden voted against the confirmation. Yes, Republicans on the committee cross-examined Hill on the bizarre details of her claims—why did she remain in Thomas' employ for so long? Why did she lie about not knowing other witnesses who had been called forward to testify?— but that's how a hearing works. No one gets to make an inflammatory accusation against someone who is up for one of the most powerful jobs in American government and then walk away without scrutiny. As a law professor, Hill knows that. She was simply using her status as an oppressed figure—a privileged victim—to advance a political agenda.

In Biden's first national interview after his campaign launch, the dejected women of ABC's *The View* asked Biden again to apologize for Hill's hearing, and he was understandably confounded at the request to address the issue one more time. Was he supposed to have physically shielded her from questioning? We know what happens when Biden so much as touches a woman on the shoulder.[469]

It's never enough, and Hill is living proof.

In an op-ed for the *Times* in May 2019, after her phone call with Biden, Hill attempted one more time to portray herself as a victim of sexual assault. She wrote in her column that her 1991 Senate testimony against Thomas could have been the beginning of the #MeToo movement. If only, she said, the Biden-led Senate Judiciary Committee "had done its job and held a hearing that showed that its members understood the seriousness of sexual harassment and other forms of sexual violence."[470]

469   Caitlin Yilek, "'The View' hosts confront Biden about
       apologizing to women he touched," *Washington Examiner*,
       April 26, 2019: https://www.washingtonexaminer.com/news/
       the-view-hosts-confront-biden-about-apologizing-to-women-he-touched.
470   Anita Hill, "Anita Hill: Let's Talk About How to End Sexual Violence," *New
       York Times*, May 9, 2019: https://www.nytimes.com/2019/05/09/opinion/
       anita-hill-sexual-violence.html.

There was that word "violence" again. In addition, Hill had elevated herself to take the throne of the #MeToo movement. It can't be said that she doesn't know how to work the social justice angle.

⌘ ⌘ ⌘

Pete Buttigieg, the Whoville-like mayor of South Bend, Indiana, was in some ways a natural fit for the 2020 Democratic primary race. He's gay, which automatically earns him a near-top ranking on the intersectionality grievance scale. But he also happens to be white, financially well-off, and he has an elite educational background, all of which would be liabilities in a party that puts a premium on oppression.

When Buttigieg decided to run for the Democratic nomination, he must have known he'd have to make amends for the time he violated social justice doctrine, uttering the ultimate blasphemy.

It was during his State of the City address in 2015 when Buttigieg said that "there is no contradiction" in acknowledging the risk police take in overseeing their communities while granting that there are some racial biases in certain areas of law enforcement that need to be addressed. "We need to take both those things seriously, for the simple and profound reason that *all lives matter*," Buttigieg said.[471]

To run in the Democratic primary, he needed forgiveness.

Buttigieg disavowed his use of the "all lives matter" obscenity when he spoke at Al Sharpton's National Action Network in April 2019. He said that he hadn't understood when he said it that the phrase would come to be "viewed as a sort of counterslogan to Black Lives Matter."

It wasn't so much a genuine apology for saying something offensive as it was a recognition by Buttigieg that he was ready to pledge allegiance to the social justice movement.

---

471   Kyle W. Bell, "FULL TEXT: Mayor Buttigieg's State of the City Address 2015," *South Bend Voice*, March 11, 2015: http://southbendvoice. com/2015/03/11/full-text-mayor-buttigiegs-state-of-the-city-address-2015/.

He reaffirmed his loyalty over and over again by saying what he knew the movement would need to hear.

In January 2012, at the start of Buttigieg's first term as mayor, federal authorities informed him that his city's chief of police, a black man named Darryl Boykins, was under private investigation for accusations that he had wiretapped the private phone calls of other police officers.

Boykins' office had secretly recorded the calls of a few officers, and Boykins allegedly confronted any officer he perceived to have been disloyal. The police officers who had been recorded further accused Boykins of threatening to demote or fire them over things they had allegedly said on the recordings.[472]

Just two months after Buttigieg took office, he asked for Boykins' resignation and received it, igniting an immediate backlash from blacks in the community who believed they had not been given an adequate explanation for the firing of their first black police chief. Boykins shortly thereafter attempted to withdraw his resignation, and he sued the city.[473] The officers whose phone calls he had allegedly recorded filed lawsuits as well, and all parties reached settlements with South Bend.[474]

Buttigieg got rid of a police chief who was no longer respected by his underlings. Boykins had lost their confidence by allegedly spying on them and intimidating them with threats. Far easier decisions have been made in the history of local government, and yet running up to

---

472 Kelli Stopczynski, "Officers: Former chief intimidated & threatened them over wiretap," WSBT.com, Aug. 13, 2014: https://wsbt.com/news/local/officers-former-chief-intimidated—-threatened-them-over-wiretap.

473 Erin Blasko, "Former chief Boykins sues city, claims racial discrimination," *South Bend Tribune*, June 3, 2013: https://www.southbendtribune.com/news/former-chief-boykins-sues-city-claims-racial-discrimination/article_ac265141-ca82-5da4-b4fc-aa3cacf318ee.html.

474 Erin Blasko, "South Bend settles wiretap claims for $575,000," *South Bend Tribune*, Dec. 18, 2013:https://www.ndinsider.com/south-bend-settles-wiretap-claims-for/article_9019e762-6f00-5d85-a024-0038de0976b4.html.

his presidential campaign, Buttigieg apologized for firing Boykins. In his February 2019 autobiography (which portrays Pete on the cover rolling up his sleeves, presumably so he can get into the hard work of mayoring), Buttigieg calls his firing of the shady police chief "my first serious mistake as mayor," noting that the reaction to his decision from blacks in the city was "instant and fierce."[475] That's just what America needs—a president who starts shaking when the reaction is "instant and fierce"!

Buttigieg has perfected the art of groveling, but no matter the number of apologies, it's always hunting season.

A May 2019 story in the *New York Times* said that one of Buttigieg's "biggest vulnerabilities" running for the nomination is that he is "a white man who has led a life of relative privilege."[476]

Antjuan Seawright, a Democratic strategist based in South Carolina, groaned to Politico that the news media were dedicating too much coverage to the mayor at the expense of other, presumably more aggrieved candidates. "What I hear from people [about Buttigieg] is that they see the epitome of privilege."[477]

In an interview on Comedy Central's *Daily Show*, host Trevor Noah asked Buttigieg if the mass-media attention on his unlikely campaign was because he was "benefiting from white male privilege." Noah added that other candidates "of different skin colors" might not "get the same level of coverage."[478] Perhaps Noah had never heard of Barack Obama, Alexandria Ocasio-Cortez, Kamala Harris, and Cory Booker, all of

---

475 Pete Buttigieg, *Shortest Way Home: One Mayor's Challenge and a Model for America's Future*, Ch. 16.

476 Jeremy Peters, "Pete Buttigieg Confronts Race and Identity in Speech to Gay Group," *New York Times*, May 12, 2019: https://www.nytimes.com/2019/05/12/us/politics/pete-buttigieg-speech-2020.html.

477 Noland McCaskill, "'The epitome of privilege': Booker supporters seethe over Buttigieg mania," Politico, May 13, 2019: https://www.politico.com/story/2019/05/13/cory-booker-pete-buttigieg-2020-1317660.

478 *The Daily Show*, Comedy Central, April 29, 2019.

whom have enjoyed exclusively positive, outsize coverage from the starts of each of their political careers. Buttigieg nonetheless knew what he had to do. "I try to check myself," he said. "I do think it's simply harder for candidates of color or for female candidates, and I'm very mindful of that."

Submission to the oppressed? Check. Assumption of victimhood for nonwhites? Check. Deference to the oppression of women? Check.

If someone wrote a sketch comedy about the intersectionality competition that was the early days of the 2020 Democratic presidential primary, Senator Kirsten Gillibrand of New York and Representative Eric Swalwell of California would be the stars. No other candidate sweat as hard as they did to win the grievance vote.

Gillibrand wasn't even subtle about her strategy to win the nomination. She would rack up as many intersectionality points as possible and leverage that superior level of "woke" all the way to victory. She started early, a month before her official campaign launch, tweeting in December 2018, "Our future is: Female, Intersectional, Powered by our belief in one another. And we're just getting started."[479] The term "intersectional" is pretty much recognized exclusively by adherents of social justice. She knew exactly whom she needed to speak to for the primary.

At a campaign event in May 2019, Gillibrand vowed that should she be elected, she would find a handicapped person and ensure they got an important role. "I will commit to making sure someone with disabilities is part of my administration and in my cabinet," she said.[480] (She could have quickly checked that box plus a few more by selecting

479   Kirsten Gillibrand, Twitter.com, Dec. 4, 2018: https://twitter.com/
        sengillibrand/status/1070106980298186753.
480   Rachel Frazin, "Gillibrand pledges to have person with disability serve in
        Cabinet," TheHill.com, May 4, 2019: https://thehill.com/homenews/
        campaign/442130-gillibrand-i-commit-to-having-person-with-disability-in-
        my-cabinet.

Representative Maxine Waters as her running mate, but I think she may have been referring to physical handicaps.)

A few days later, she posted a video on Facebook of a man dressed in drag, thanking Gillibrand for "sitting with a queer person, [and] talking about queer issues."[481] Poor Gillibrand. She had the right idea about her party, but her overtures were so cool-mom desperate.

In June 2019, she was roundly mocked on social media after a video clip surfaced showing Gillibrand in a gay bar, shimmying from side to side with a shot in her hand and wearing a tucked-in white T-shirt that said, "Love is rave." As though meeting a gay man for the first time, she looks at the camera and belts out, "*Gay rights!*"[482]

Back at ya, Kirsten!

Her appeals were agonizing. In an interview with the *Des Moines Register* on June 10, 2019, she said that as president she would only nominate candidates for Supreme Court who would rule in favor of abortion rights, because to not do so would be the same thing as appointing a judge who doesn't like blacks or Jews. "Imagine saying that it's okay to appoint a judge who's racist or anti-Semitic or homophobic," she said.[483] It's a wonder she didn't throw out her back with the extreme reaching.

Eric Swalwell's early campaigning was like the political version of male bondage but without any pay off. He was eagerly submissive to the social justice movement and tried to prove it in every way possible, lest he get spanked too hard by his dominant. Swalwell proudly tweeted in April 2019 that as a white man, he's fully aware that he "can't speak to someone else's experience," so therefore, he made the sacred promise

---

481   Kirsten Gillibrand, Facebook.com, May 5, 2019: https://www.facebook.com/ KirstenGillibrand/videos/594106034442823/.

482   "Kirsten Gillibrand Cuts Loose In Iowa Gay Bar, Sipping A Shot And Modeling Her Pride Month T-Shirt," June 9, 2019, YouTube.com: https:// www.youtube.com/watch?v=-pXNKbBFrdE.

483   Alexandra Desanctis, "Gillibrand Compares Being Pro-Life to Being Racist," *National Review*, June 11, 2019: https://www.nationalreview.com/corner/ kirsten-gillibrand-compares-being-pro-life-to-being-racist/.

that as the nominee, he would select a woman as his running mate. How big of him. The tweet included a video clip from an MSNBC interview wherein he says it's important to "recognize where you can't speak for someone's experience and pass the mic to someone who can." [484] (What better way to "pass the mic" than to appoint a woman to one of the least consequential jobs in Washington?)

Swalwell ticked off the social justice requirements one by one. He checked his white male privilege; he asserted his belief in the higher "truth" that comes with being oppressed; and he honored the authority of intersectionality.

A few days later, Swalwell posted another tweet, this time smartly observing that women were conspicuously absent from the nation's founding governing document. "Do you know how many times the word 'Woman' is mentioned in the Constitution?" he wrote. "Zero. That is unacceptable. Women must be equally represented and equally protected." [485] Either Swalwell was counting on his followers being idiots or he doesn't know that the word "man" is also not included in the Constitution. The phrase "we the people," however, is found at the very beginning.

Proving that Swalwell and Twitter were never a good combination, he posted another missive in June 2019, boldly declaring: "If you're Hispanic, there's nothing @realDonaldTrump wont do to break up your family, cage your children, or erase your existence with a weaponized [U.S.] census." [486]

Someone on his staff might have let Swalwell know that there are a plenty of Hispanics in the country residing here legally, and that not a single one of them is in jeopardy of having his family molested by

484 Eric Swalwell, Twitter.com, April 23, 2019: https://twitter.com/ericswalwell/status/1120889884737249281?ref_src=twsrc%5Etfw%7Ctwcamp%5Etweetembed%7Ctwterm%5E1120889884737249281.

485 Eric Swalwell, Twitter.com, April 30, 2019: https://twitter.com/ericswalwell/status/1123408951075397637.

486 Eric Swalwell, Twitter.com, June 22, 2019: https://twitter.com/ericswalwell/status/1142436739476312064.

Trump. Being Hispanic is not synonymous with being an illegal immigrant, but it was apparently all the same to Swalwell.

All of the party's leading privileged victims gathered on one stage for a two-part debate in June 2019. From the start, it was a race between all of the candidates to see who aligned themselves the most with the social justice cause. The candidates checked them all: illegal immigrants, women, gays, trans people, blacks. Even trans people who are black.

Senator Booker aimed high, declaring, "We do not talk enough about trans Americans, especially African American trans Americans and the incredibly high rates of murder right now."[487] As though it were a natural transition, Booker made that observation immediately after he had paid tribute to the civil rights movement and recalled the dark era when blacks were lynched by whites for sport. MLK's successor was named that night. (By the way, there is no serious data suggesting that trans people, or even specifically black trans people, are targeted for murder because of their being transgender. As covered in the chapter of this book dealing with the trans issue, the assaults and murders of trans people are often, if not mostly, traceable to drug dealing, prostitution, and muggings.)

Earlier in that same debate, former Housing and Urban Development secretary Julián Castro paid his own respects to any trans female who wants an abortion. "[J]ust because a woman, or let's also not forget someone in the trans community, a trans female, is poor, doesn't mean they shouldn't have the right to exercise that right to choose," said Castro.[488] To be sure, a trans female is a man attempting to live as a woman, so perhaps having access to uterine-related medical services

---

487   Julio Rosas, "Cory Booker: We don't 'talk enough' about 'African American trans Americans,'" *Washington Examiner*, June 26, 2019: https://www.washingtonexaminer.com/news/cory-booker-we-dont-talk-enough-about-african-american-trans-americans.

488   Julio Rosas, "Julián Castro: Reproductive justice includes abortions for the trans community," *Washington Examiner*, June 26, 2019: https://www.washingtonexaminer.com/news/julian-castro-reproductive-justice-includes-abortions-for-the-trans-community.

wouldn't be at the top of that person's concerns, but apparently Castro couldn't afford to take any chances.

Tributes to social justice replaced the more traditional and more fun debate "zingers." Asked about economic justice and whether it was enough to drive up Latino votes for Democrats, Castro changed the topic. "I also think that we have to recognize racial and social justice," he said to thunderous applause. He then ticked off the names of black people who had been shot dead by police officers in recent years.[489]

New York Mayor Bill de Blasio got in on the Black Lives Matter action by reminding everyone that he has a half-black son. Booker and Castro, as well as O'Rourke, used the national broadcast to speak to voters in Spanish. It went on and on.

The second night of the debate was the same. Buttigieg had just taken several days off from his campaign schedule because a black man in South Bend, fifty-four-year-old Eric Logan, had been shot dead by a white police officer. At the time of the debate, very little was known about the circumstances of the shooting. The county prosecutor had said that the officer, Ryan O'Neill, responded to a call about a suspicious person who may have been trying to burglarize empty vehicles in the middle of the night. O'Neill approached Logan, who the prosecutor said had wielded a large knife. O'Neill fired his gun twice, with one bullet piercing Logan. O'Neill, contrary to police rules, did not have his body camera on to record the encounter.[490]

There was nothing to be said about it without knowing exactly what happened, and a special counsel had been appointed to hopefully find out. But Buttigieg couldn't help taking the blame for a black man who had been shot by a white police officer. During the debate, he was asked

---

489 "Julián Castro Names Unarmed Black Victims of Police Brutality at First Democratic Debate," YouTube.com, June 27, 2019.

490 Tom Davis and Sara Burnett, "Buttigieg goes home to South Bend after man killed by police," Associated Press, June 17, 2019: https://www.apnews.com/a127b524a1374ad5aa4ecbbc251cc488.

270

why the South Bend police force wasn't more demographically in line with the city at large, a question that ignores the possibility that maybe most black people in South Bend simply aren't interested in working as cops. It's not practical to assume that the demographic makeup of every profession should be closely aligned with the immediate surrounding population. Buttigieg was nonetheless eager to submit. "Because I couldn't get it done," he said. He also asserted that law enforcement needed to be brought "out from the shadow of systemic racism" and that there was a "wall of mistrust, put up one racist act at a time" that "threatens the well-being of every community."[491] For that harrowing effort of social justice appeasement, Buttigieg's national support among Democratic voters dropped. Before the debate, he was at 5 percent. After, he fell to 4 percent, according to a CNN poll.

It was like a sadistic game of Twister. Who will be next to collapse after stupidly trying to put their left foot in front of their right hand while trying to get a hug from Al Sharpton?

To secure the social justice nomination, the party's candidates will all have to take a knee. It's absurd to watch the presidential candidates for one of our only two major political parties behave this way, but also sobering upon realizing that none of it is by accident. Much of the country, from coast to coast, is operating the same way.

⌘　⌘　⌘

Submission to the grievance mob is mandatory for Democrats and the lower they can kneel, the more promising their political careers within the party. Representative Alexandria Ocasio-Cortez has mastered the art, earning her full privileged victim status.

Her entire platform and persona are based on the various types of oppression she enjoys: She's a woman, she's Latina, and her campaign

---

491　CNN, SSRS, July 1, 2019: http://cdn.cnn.com/cnn/2019/images/07/01/rel8a.-.democrats.and.healthcare.pdf.

for the House in 2018 centered on her biography as a bartender from a modest background.

With her place on the intersectionality hierarchy high and firmly in place, any criticism of her is instantly framed by adoring culture fascists in the national media as Ocasio-Cortez the victim against yet another oppressor.

In November 2018, a friend of mine who works on Capitol Hill spotted Ocasio-Cortez, Washington's newest and cutest celebrity, walking through one of the hallways of a congressional office building. He took a photo as she passed by and sent it to me. Ocasio-Cortez was sharply dressed for someone who had branded herself as a no-frills, poor bartender. To be sure, she has humbly donated a pair of busted old shoes that she says she wore while knocking on doors for her campaign to be put on display at Cornell University.[492]

Just days before the photo was taken by my friend, Ocasio-Cortez had indignantly claimed that she had been mistaken for an "intern/ staffer."[493] I tweeted the photo with the caption, "Hill staffer sent me this pic of Ocasio-Cortez they took just now. I'll tell you something: that jacket and coat don't look like a girl who struggles."

Within twenty minutes, my Twitter feed had exploded with replies from journalists and the Ocasio-Cortez fans bitching at me about the "creeper" tweet. Like the privileged victim she is, Ocasio-Cortez shared my tweet with her hundreds of thousands of followers with the suggestion that the photo I had published was a form of harassment. "If I walk in with my best sale-rack clothes, they laugh & take a picture of my backside," she wrote, as though her ass were the focus of a photo that showed her from head to toe.

---

492 Marie Solis, "Ocasio-Cortez's Beat-Up Campaign Shoes to Be Featured in New Fashion Exhibition," Vice.com, Nov. 28, 2018: https://www.vice.com/en_us/article/nep37x/alexandria-ocasio-cortez-campaign-shoes-fashion-exhibition.
493 Alexandria Ocasio-Cortez, Twitter.com, Nov. 20, 2018: https://twitter.com/AOC/status/1062923224336531462.

CNN media correspondent Brian Stelter, who essentially functions as a very wide buffer for the Democratic Party, called the photo a "creep shot," because it showed Ocasio-Cortez from the back.[494] NBC also called it a creep shot.[495]

The online mob didn't bother me. But I'll never get over the journalists who routinely claim that the White House is curtailing their freedoms now gleefully criticize another journalist for publishing a photo of an elected official in a public place—her work place, no less. But Ocasio-Cortez is a privileged victim, and the culture fascists in the national media are less interested in news than in reinforcing the importance of grievance and oppression.

The controversy over the photo was covered by the *Washington Post*, *USA Today*, the *New York Post*, *Atlantic* magazine, *Harper's Bazaar*, and the BBC, as well as dozens of websites. Some of them wrote about it multiple times, including the *Washington Post*.

The sour women of ABC's *The View* took turns one by one to offer their world-renowned insights, attributing different motives and meanings to my tweet. Ana Navarro and I are acquainted and once met for breakfast. Despite knowing full well that I'm half Mexican, Navarro suggested on *The View* that I might have published the tweet because I'm intimidated by a "brown" woman.

Whoopi Goldberg looked into the camera to say, "Hush, boy," something that she couldn't say to my face, since I hadn't been invited to defend myself.

On MSNBC, Stephanie Ruhle anchored a segment wherein one of her guests questioned whether my name was real and said I should have

494   Brian Stelter, Twitter.com, Nov. 15, 2018: https://twitter.com/brianstelter/status/1063240107464056833.

495   Allan Smith, "'Creep shot': Firestorm over photo of Ocasio-Cortez posted on Twitter," NBC News, Nov. 15, 2018: https://www.nbcnews.com/politics/congress/creep-shot-firestorm-over-photo-ocasio-cortez-posted-twitter-n936906.

been fired.[496] Ruhle, who looks like she's constantly having hot flashes, looked into the camera to ask me (I wasn't invited to defend myself on her show, either), "Would you like us to criticize what you look like?" Talking out of the side of her mouth, MSNBC contributor Elise Jordan described my tweet as a "dog whistle" on "class and misogyny."

The Atlantic's Megan Garber wrote that my tweet was "a bad thought, posted in bad faith." She didn't explain exactly why she believed my tweet was "in bad faith,"[497] but reinforcing social justice doesn't require explanations. The only thing that matters is reducing those who are deemed to have privilege. Garber wrote that it should never have been an issue that Ocasio-Cortez wore "a well-cut jacket rather than a dirt-streaked potato sack," (Garber engages in a stupid false dilemma and yet it was *me* who had acted "in bad faith.")

Other news writeups described my comment as "clothes shaming," which might make this the first time in history that describing a person as well dressed is a form of "shaming."

The point of all of this was to get me to apologize and appropriately reduce myself in front of the oppression fetishists. But I wasn't sorry. My one regret is that I deleted the tweet with the photograph of Ocasio-Cortez, knowing that it would only start another round of hysteria. And of course it did. After I deleted the tweet with the photo, I noted in a separate tweet that, if anything, I had actually paid the congresswoman a compliment.

Ocasio-Cortez noticed that tweet too and she once again shared it with her followers, this time saying that I should apologize for my "misogyny."[498]

---

496 *MSNBC Live with Stephanie Ruhle*, Nov. 16, 2018.

497 Megan Garber, "How Alexandria Ocasio-Cortez's Plain Black Jacket Became a Controversy," *Atlantic*, Nov. 16, 2018: https://www.theatlantic.com/entertainment/archive/2018/11/alexandria-ocasio-cortezs-clothes-a-tedious-backlash/576064/.

498 Alexandria Ocasio-Cortez, Twitter.com, Nov. 15, 2018: https://twitter.com/Ocasio2018/status/1063240055236501505.

Emboldened by her champions in the media, she became obsessed with my tweet.

The next day, she posted an additional two tweets related to my tweet with the photograph, name-checking the place where I worked, the *Washington Examiner*. "The reason journos from @FoxNews to @ dcexaminer can't help but obsess about my clothes…is bc as I've said, women like me aren't supposed to run for office - or win," she prattled in one tweet. In another, she quoted Megan Garber's piece in *The Atlantic*, tweeting, "It is never, really, about the clothes. It is about belonging. It is about power."[499]

Four days later, she said in yet another tweet, "The actual fear driving the attacks on my clothes…isn't that these folks are scared that I shouldn't represent people in Congress. It's fear that they've allowed their riches, their privilege, + their bias to put them to a point where they can't." It remains a mystery as to what gave Ocasio-Cortez the impression that I was rich.

Still, two months later, in an interview with CBS' *60 Minutes*, she carried on as a victim of misogyny. "Would you be taking a creep shot of [Democratic House Leader] Steny Hoyer's behind and sharing it around?" she said.[500]

Alexandria from the block should understand something, though. She could successfully present herself as a victim and get backing from the media, but if I played the intersectionality game, I would win. I'm Latino. I'm from a working-class family. I grew up in the South. And I'm gay. Checkmate! My experience—my truth—is no more privileged than hers. For every man who has complimented her wardrobe, there are a dozen more who have done far worse to me. (In hindsight, I may have even liked some of it.) The key difference between me and

---

499   Alexandria Ocasio-Cortez, Twitter.com, Nov. 16, 2018: https://twitter.com/ AOC/status/1063611599351672834.

500   Jordan Uhl, Twitter.com, Jan. 6, 2019: https://twitter.com/JordanUhl/ status/1082069983801364481.

Ocasio-Cortez is that I don't use my race as a discount card like she does and I don't use my sexuality to advance through life as she does with her gender.

Putting all of that aside, the congresswoman is a half idiot who routinely embarrasses herself in her interviews and public remarks.

I know the word "dumb" is supposed to be racist anytime President Trump applies it to a black person,[501] but if it weren't for Ocasio-Cortez being an attractive minority, the media would have been comparing her to Sarah Palin from the moment she won her district primary in 2018.

Ethnic Democrats who look good on TV can expect one question from the press: "Are you running for president?" It's the sole reason Senators Kamala Harris and Cory Booker were ever considered top contenders for the 2020 Democratic presidential nomination, without having done anything of substance in Congress.

After a breezy interview in August 2018 with CNN's Chris Cuomo, the *New York Times* might have transitioned from describing Ocasio-Cortez as a "political rock star" to describing her as "kind of slow."[502] Cuomo asked Ocasio-Cortez basic questions about her political positions, like whether she supported Representative Nancy Pelosi for House speaker—answer: "We gotta take a look at what's going on"—and how the U.S. would pay for multitrillion-dollar universal health insurance. To that end, she questioned why we don't consider "the cost of all the funeral expenses of those who died" because they lacked insurance when considering the true cost of healthcare. Instead of asking if Ocasio-Cortez was sober, Cuomo pensively nodded along.

---

501 "With LeBron James comments, is Donald Trump catering to racist base?: Today's talker," *USA Today*, Aug. 5, 2018: https://www.usatoday.com/story/opinion/2018/08/05/lebron-james-comments-donald-trump-catering-racist-base-todays-talker/910323002/.

502 Andy Newman, Vivian Wang, and Luis Ferre-Sadurni, "Alexandria Ocasio-Cortez Emerges as a Political Star," *New York Times*, June 27, 2018: https://www.nytimes.com/2018/06/27/nyregion/alexandria-ocasio-cortez-bio-profile.html.

We don't include funeral expenses in the cost of U.S. healthcare for the same reason that we don't incorporate the cost of the gas it takes to drive to a physician. At that point, it's no longer healthcare. It's welfare. But privileged victims can rest easy that they will rarely be challenged on the details.

Conservative commentator Ben Shapiro in August 2018 invited Ocasio-Cortez to debate him after her upset primary victory in New York. She responded and, on brand as ever, played the victim, likening the challenge to being catcalled.[503] (Just two months prior she had accused her primary opponent of being sexist—for not showing up to debate her.[504])

Nearly every public utterance by Ocasio-Cortez is a tragic reminder that in some districts around the country, pretty much anyone can run for office and win.

At a conference in March 2019, she said that "people can't afford to live." She claimed that the American economic system is not sustainable and that all of the public "should be scared right now, because corporations have taken over our government."

She said in February 2019 on her Instagram page that the effects of climate change make it a legitimate question for potential parents to ask, "Is it okay to still have children?" A month before, she had forecast the coming apocalypse. "The world is going to end in 12 years if we don't address climate change, and your biggest issue is how are we gonna pay for it?"[505]

---

503 Alexandria Ocasio-Cortez, Twitter.com, Aug. 9, 2018: https://twitter.com/ AOC/status/1027729430137827328.

504 Alexandria Ocasio-Cortez, Twitter.com, June 18, 2018: https://twitter.com/ AOC/status/1008876093653348353.

505 William Cummings, "'The world is going to end in 12 years if we don't address climate change,' Ocasio-Cortez says," *USA Today*, Jan. 22, 2019: https://www.usatoday.com/story/news/politics/onpolitics/2019/01/22/ ocasio-cortez-climate-change-alarm/2642481002/.

President Trump points at the hundreds of thousands of migrants from crime-ridden, impoverished countries flooding into the U.S., and the media call him a racist hate monger. Ocasio-Cortez imagines that the world is going to combust in a ball of flame, and journalists can't get enough of the little tyke!

Ocasio-Cortez is never asked to account for her warped, dark view of the world. That would require TV news anchors' doing something other than squinting thoughtfully at each of her painfully ignorant blurbs. Magazines would have to run something about her other than spreads that glamorize her in designer clothing.

Ocasio-Cortez has also claimed that $2 trillion spread out over ten years would cover the cost of universal health insurance. The true price tag would be closer to $18 trillion, by the *Wall Street Journal*'s estimate,[506] and double that by others' estimates, and yet Ocasio-Cortez is treated like a thought leader.[507] She has also alleged that the Defense Department's 2018 budget was increased by $700 billion, which in reality reflected the department's total budget, not an increase in its funding.[508] She claimed that the reason Amazon pulled out of a deal to build another headquarters in New York is that "a group of dedicated, everyday New Yorkers & their neighbors" quashed it, when, more accurately, it was Ocasio-Cortez and far-left activists who pressured Amazon

506 Laura Meckler, "Price Tag of Bernie Sanders's Proposals: $18 Trillion," *Wall Street Journal*, Sep. 14, 2015: https://www.wsj.com/articles/price-tag-of-bernie-sanders-proposals-18-trillion-1442271511?ns=prod/accounts-wsj.

507 Ricardo Alonso-Zaldivar, "'Medicare for All' Would Cost $32.6 Trillion Over 10 Years, Study Says," Associated Press, July 30, 2018: https://www.bloomberg.com/news/articles/2018-07-30/study-medicare-for-all-bill-estimated-at-32-6-trillion.

508 Katelyn Carelle, "Alexandria Ocasio-Cortez falsely claims military increased funding by $700 billion last year," *Washington Examiner*, July 27, 2018: https://www.washingtonexaminer.com/policy/budgets-deficits/alexandria-ocasio-cortez-falsely-claims-military-increased-funding-by-700-billion-last-year.

to drop the planned operation. The new headquarters would have brought thousands of jobs to the area. Her approval numbers in the state immediately tanked after that smash hit.[509]

This was her record less than a year in office. Give Anderson Cooper credit, though, for somehow summoning the great courage on CBS' *60 Minutes* in January 2019, putting forth to Ocasio-Cortez the truth that some people had noticed her "factual mistakes."

In his distinct, hold-'em-accountable style, Cooper said to the congresswoman, "One of the criticisms of you is that your math is fuzzy." (Yes, and one of the criticisms of Jeffrey Dahmer was that his extracurriculars rubbed some people the wrong way.) There was no question from Cooper, just an underhanded toss for Ocasio-Cortez to give her best swing. Even so, her reply was a gem. "I think that there's a lot of people more concerned about being precisely, factually and semantically correct than about being morally right."[510]

Ocasio-Cortez may not have all the facts down, but her personal morality is intact, so what's everyone so concerned about?

This is the person whom liberal *New York Times* columnist Michelle Goldberg has described as "charismatic and rousing" rather than the more accurate "arrogant and ignorant."[511]

---

509   Jacob Pramuk, "Alexandria Ocasio-Cortez's approval rating in New York declines following Amazon deal collapse, while Trump hammers Democrats over 'socialism,'" CNBC, March 19, 2019: https://www.cnbc.com/2019/03/19/aoc-approval-rating-falls-after-amazon-deal-collapse-as-trump-hammers-democrats-over-socialism.html.

510   Ian Schwartz, "Ocasio-Cortez: People More Concerned About Me Being 'Factually Correct' Than 'Morally Right'," Real Clear Politics, Jan. 6, 2019: https://www.realclearpolitics.com/video/2019/01/06/ocasio-cortez_people_being_more_concerned_about_me_being_factually_correct_than_morally_right.html.

511   Michelle Goldberg, "The Pragmatic Left Is Winning," *New York Times*, Aug. 9 2018: https://www.nytimes.com/2018/08/09/opinion/columnists/left-sanders-ocasio-cortez-primaries.html?rref=collection%2Fsectioncollection%2Fopinion&action=click&contentCollection=opinion&region=rank&module=package&version=highlights&contentPlacement=2&pgtype=sectionfront.

⌘　⌘　⌘

Minnesota representative Ilhan Omar, who was elected at the same time as Ocasio-Cortez, holds the same privileged-victim status, but on steroids. Her precious identity—a woman, a Muslim, a Somali refugee—makes her a social justice triple threat.

Her election was a tribute to intersectionality and she is very aware of the gifts that come with oppression and grievance.

No matter what Omar says, no matter how outside the mainstream or even antithetical to American tradition, the culture fascists in the media can explain it away. Her most horrific statements are excused and skirted.

During a speech at an event hosted by the Council on American-Islamic Relations (CAIR) in March of 2019, Omar wallowed in grievance and victimhood.[512] She said that Muslims "for far too long have lived with the discomfort of being a second-class citizen" and that every Muslim "should be tired of it." She called on them all to "raise hell" and "make people uncomfortable." (Because if there's one thing Muslims haven't yet mastered, it's how to make people uncomfortable.)

She offered no example of what gave her or any other Muslim second-class-citizen status, but she weighed in on the 9/11 terrorist attacks, observing that CAIR had been created after "some people did something," and that as a result of that something, "all of us [Muslims] were starting to lose access to our civil liberties." (CAIR was actually created in 1994, well before 9/11, but that's a minor detail that didn't pique the interest of any of the two thousand fact checkers dedicated to Trump anytime he mistakes a zero for the letter "o.")

Again, Omar gave no example of Muslims having been denied any civil liberties, but her flippant description of 9/11 as "some people did something" didn't go unnoticed.

512　"Omar: 'Raise Hell, Make People Uncomfortable,'" YouTube.com, April 8, 2019: https://youtu.be/3OprxD5njXo.

Conservatives on social media picked up the clip of Omar's comments and passed it around, and it made its way onto right-leaning news sites like the Daily Caller and Fox News.

With haste, in swooped the guardians of all things decent. Glenn Kessler of the *Washington Post*'s fearless "Fact Checker" column wrote with sensitivity that Omar's remarks "may lack context." He opted against doing any actual fact-checking, instead deciding to "leave it to readers" to determine whether Omar had caused any offense.[513]

CNN's Brian Stelter defended Omar's comments as "probably not the best choice of words." The real story, he said, wasn't that Omar had spoken pertly about the deadliest attack on America ever, but that her remarks were noticed at all by conservatives.[514] Stelter invited Democratic activist Waleed Shahid on his show to fault the "alt-right far-right" for noticing Omar's remarks to begin with; the ultimate goal, Shahid said, was "to defame and destroy the character of Ilhan Omar."

Really? Maybe the goal was to put a check on anyone who might trivialize what happened on 9/11, but that's just a thought.

Trump dove into the controversy, posting a video on Twitter that spliced Omar's "some people did something" comment with images of the Twin Towers burning on 9/11. "WE WILL NEVER FORGET!" read Trump's caption.[515] It's a brilliant video, and it exquisitely captures the raw emotion and pain still felt by 9/11 victims, their families and friends, and anyone who is alive to remember it, as contrasted with Omar, an irreverent refugee.

After Trump's tweet, culture fascists in the national media and Democratic Party kicked into full #Resistance mode.

---

513 Glenn Kessler, "'Some people did something': Rep. Omar's remarks in context," *Washington Post*, April 11, 2019: https://www.washingtonpost.com/politics/2019/04/11/some-people-did-something-rep-omars-remarks-context/?utm_term=.8dbe9e13ad03.

514 *Reliable Sources*, CNN, April 14, 2019.

515 Donald Trump, Twitter.com, April 12: https://twitter.com/realDonaldTrump/status/1116817144006750209.

The Associated Press ran interference for Omar, bleating in a report that "Neither Trump's tweet nor the video included her full quote or the context of her comments."[516]

The context of Omar's full quote is worse! Trump in his tweet didn't include the parts where Omar had said Muslims should "raise hell" and "make people uncomfortable." If only Trump *had* used the context. She was *lucky* he didn't.

The *New York Times'* Charles Blow reasoned that Omar "could have used different, more severe language" to describe the 9/11 tragedy, but that the attention she received was the result of "a conservative peculiarity." Predictable as ever, he went on to attribute Trump's criticism of Omar to "white supremacy."[517]

Masha Gessen of *The New Yorker* described the criticism of Omar as "bullying and political violence."[518]

Omar features all of the hallmarks of a privileged victim. Because Omar claims to be oppressed on multiple fronts, she is automatically endowed with a higher morality than those with privilege. It's taken for granted that her detractors are inherently inferior and morally corrupt. The culture fascists in the media inoculate her against criticism and aid her advancement.

Sensing that Trump wasn't backing down, Omar broke the emergency glass and did what perpetual victims in politics do. She claimed that the video he posted had inspired threats against her life.

Whining about a death threat is now the highest form of humblebragging for Democrats in Congress and liberals in the national media.

516 "Dems defend Omar after Trump retweets video against her," Associated Press, April 13, 2019: https://www.apnews.com/5d866c967f7c4db8a98e980bce2b5a38.

517 Charles Blow, "Demonizing Minority Women," *New York Times*, April 14, 2019: https://www.nytimes.com/2019/04/14/opinion/ilhan-omar-minority-women.html.

518 Masha Gessen, "The Dangerous Bullying of Ilhan Omar," *New Yorker*, April 15, 2019: https://www.newyorker.com/news/our-columnists/the-dangerous-bullying-of-ilhan-omar.

The second any one of them gets a threatening tweet from some nameless, unknown person on the internet, we're all expected to drop what we're doing and lament the state of our politics—bonus points if you can blame some Republican, preferably President Trump, for "inciting violence."

Omar said in a statement that since Trump's tweet about her 9/11 comments, she had "experienced an increase in direct threats on my life—many directly referencing or replying to the president's video." She pointedly accused Trump of violent rhetoric and hate speech.

It's one of the many cards privileged victims play when they sense they're losing a fight. They complain about "rhetoric" (in this case, "rhetoric" refers to a video of Omar's own words), they claim to have been targeted by death threats, and then they sit back as the news media do the rest.

Rolling Stone magazine had the congresswoman's back, stating that, "It shouldn't be surprising that the smear campaign [against Omar] has led to death threats."[519] The *Washington Post* followed suit with a story about Omar's "hundreds" of death threats.[520] The BBC wrote that Omar had seen a "rise in death threats" following the Trump video.[521]

A day later, while Trump was in Burnsville, Minnesota, a local reporter asked him if he had any second thoughts about the video

---

519 Ryan Bort, "Trump's 9/11 Tweet Caused Death Threats Against Ilhan Omar to Spike. Of Course It Did," *Rolling Stone*, April 15, 2019: https://www.rollingstone.com/politics/politics-news/trump-9-11-tweet-death-threats-ilhan-omar-822225/.

520 Michael Brice-Saddler, "He easily found hundreds of death threats against Rep. Ilhan Omar. He wants Twitter to stop them," *Washington Post*, April 16, 2019: https://www.washingtonpost.com/technology/2019/04/16/he-easily-found-hundreds-death-threats-against-rep-ilhan-omar-he-wants-twitter-stop-them/?utm_term=.318c29a31a1e.

521 "Ilhan Omar: Muslim lawmaker sees rise in death threats after Trump tweet," BBC, April 15, 2019: https://www.bbc.com/news/world-us-canada-47938268.

with Omar and the Twin Towers.[522] Trump said no. Thank God. There was nothing wrong with the video, and it contained nothing untrue. There's nothing unfair about highlighting a newly elected official and a pattern of remarks that demonstrate a creepy view of the country. The Democrats' leader in the House, Speaker Nancy Pelosi, had indicated her own displeasure with Omar at a news conference just days before, stating that she had been trying to speak with Omar about the matter but had been unable to reach her.[523] If the leader of Omar's own party was concerned, why should the subject be off limits for anyone else?

And by the way, anyone with even a modest public profile in politics or the media has received death threats. It comes with the territory and Omar isn't special for having received them, too.

Ask the White House how many death threats the president has received.

At a Trump campaign rally in June 2016, a British man was arrested after trying to grab a police officer's gun with the intent to use it to assassinate then-candidate Trump.[524] Like most would-be assassins in American politics, the man had a history of mental illness.[525]

I don't seem to recall Trump releasing a statement about it and I certainly don't recall anyone in the news media asking Democrats or

522 Dave Orrick, "Trump continues feud with Ilhan Omar, says she doesn't understand 'real life,'" *Pioneer Press*, April 15, 2019: www.twincities.com/2019/04/15/trump-came-to-minnesota-feuding-with-ilhan-omar-but-never-mentioned-her-when-he-got-here/.

523 Susan Ferrechio, "Nancy Pelosi: Ilhan Omar, call your office," *Washington Examiner*, April 12, 2019: https://www.washingtonexaminer.com/news/congress/ilhan-omar-call-your-office.

524 "British Man Who Was Arrested At Trump Rally Sentenced On Weapon And Disruption Charges," Department of Justice District Attorney's Office District of Nevada, Dec. 13, 2016: https://www.justice.gov/usao-nv/pr/british-man-who-was-arrested-trump-rally-sentenced-weapon-and-disruption-charges.

525 Ken Ritter, "British man pleads guilty in Trump attack case in Las Vegas," Associated Press, Sep. 13, 2016: https://www.apnews.com/a6581ad3b3e747e4a5c831e26eea230d.

other liberals to cool it with the accusations of racism, sexism, and every other kind of bigotry. Of course not. To them, rhetoric is only problematic when it's directed at a privileged victim.

Threats against Omar aren't any more remarkable than threats against Representative Steve Scalise, Republican of Louisiana.

Wait, I'm so sorry. Scalise wasn't even given the courtesy of a threat. He was simply given a shotgun blast to the hip by a disgruntled Bernie Sanders supporter. Poor comparison. My mistake.

Death threats received by public figures are, unfortunately, a fact of life in a free country. Omar doesn't deserve deference because she gets them, too.

This is to say nothing of her blatant anti-Semitism. There's a sensible position anyone can understand when it comes to criticizing Israel, the only democracy in the Middle East, and yet Omar is curiously unable to articulate it without using explicit stereotypes about Jews.

In her short political career, she has claimed that the people of Israel have "hypnotized" the world (she apparently thought "scammed" might have been too obvious), she has referred to the "apartheid Israel regime,"[526] and she has asserted that Republicans in Congress depend on Jewish wealth. (It's noteworthy that Democrats received more money than Republicans did from pro-Israel groups in the 2018 campaign cycle.[527])

There is no denying that Omar is an anti-Semite, and there's no reason anyone in the Republican Party, the Democratic Party, or the media should be confused about it.

Omar was born in Somalia, lived much of her childhood there, and then moved with her family to a neighborhood in Minnesota

526 Ilhan Omar, Twitter.com, May 31, 2018: https://twitter.com/IlhanMN/status/1002295140172664832.

527 Heather Timmons, "The numbers behind Ilhan Omar's AIPAC tweet," Qz.com, Feb. 11, 2019: https://qz.com/1547435/the-numbers-behind-ilhan-omars-aipac-tweet/.

full of other Somali refugees. Somalia is 100 percent Muslim,[528] and I'll assume I don't need to get into the longstanding conflict between Muslims and Jews. The Somali communities in and around Minneapolis are insular, with little overture to the mainstream, and so it's not a shock that Omar, having been enmeshed in that culture, absorbed a lot of sentiments that are anathema to American tradition.

In a story published in August 2018, the Minneapolis *Star Tribune* quoted Hassan Mursal, a small-business owner in a city outside Minneapolis, as saying that the locals have "realized" that their new Somali neighbors retain "a different culture."[529]

You don't say.

In that different culture, you can expect views that are exotic, even abhorrent, to take hold. Federal data shows that people leave or attempt to leave Minneapolis in the hope of joining Islamic terrorist networks abroad more than people in any other city in the U.S.[530]

Omar comes from the same dregs. Her antipathy toward Jews are, for her circumstances, normal.

⌘　⌘　⌘

America's culture fascists insist you either sit there and pretend to be confused about something obvious, or you blame yourself for not *getting it*.

528　"The Global Religious Landscape," Pew Research Center, December 2012: https://web.archive.org/web/20130309232303/http://www.pewforum.org/uploadedFiles/Topics/Religious_Affiliation/globalReligion-full.pdf.

529　Ibrahim Hirsi, "Somali immigrants find growing acceptance in Minnesota," Associated Press, Aug. 25, 2018: http://www.startribune.com/somali-immigrants-find-growing-acceptance-in-minnesota/491700881/.

530　Hollie McKay, "How Minneapolis' Somali community became the terrorist recruitment capital of the US," Fox News, Feb. 16, 2019: https://www.foxnews.com/us/how-rep-ilhan-omars-minnesota-district-became-the-terrorist-recruitment-capital-of-the-us-officials-highly-concerned.

This is social justice, and it's the foundation of the modern Democratic Party. If you're a Democrat with aspirations for the White House, the primary campaign is no longer a deliberative process. It's an intersectionality contest. Advancement depends on acknowledging grievance and checking privilege.

It will either kill the party or it will kill the country. As of this writing, the 2020 election has not been decided. But it's not looking good for the country.

CHAPTER 12

FIGHT OR FLIGHT

Don't ever mistake the privileged victims or their enforcers—the culture fascists—for a blip in history. They're not an extreme version of political correctness. They're not a symptom of some new kind of hypersensitivity. They're not a random mutation that we'll one day look back on with wonder and amusement.

They are the product of a deliberate and complex ideology.

It's systematic, coordinated, and calculated.

Social justice might not be so bad if it were quarantined to college campuses or if it were merely the pet project of neurotic Hollywood celebrities. But the ideology is now taking deep root in each and every one of America's cultural hubs and not for nothing. There's a purpose. It's meant to spread and upend every American tradition, convention, and institution. It's meant to erase the meritocracy and our way of life. It's a complete reordering of the country. It's an attempt at replacing talent with mediocrity, fairness with grievance, and merit with intersectionality.

In politics, it's a knife trained on the throats of those deemed to have privilege. In academia, it's a shakedown tactic used against anyone on campuses who transgresses its dogma. In Hollywood, it's a machine pumping out movies, TV shows, and celebrities dedicated to proliferating and reinforcing its doctrine. And in the news media, it's a mandate that the narrative—the privileged vs. the oppressed—supersedes all else.

We're all simply expected to accept the new reality.

Social justice is the pursuit of absolute power as it corrupts absolutely. It seized the #MeToo movement, hijacked the Democratic Party, distorted the meaning of words, perverted the concept of victimhood, and elevated everything else that sucks.

Social justice is a shortcut to the top. Claiming victimhood on account of race, gender, or sexuality opens doors everywhere. It's a subversion of the social order, a demand that those deemed to enjoy "privilege" submit to those who claim to have been aggrieved.

Social justice is the new way to fight. He who can lay claim to the highest form of grievance, victimhood, and oppression on the intersectionality scale wins.

Intersectionality. Grievance. Oppression. Victimhood.

Social justice and the privileged victims are everywhere, reinforced by the culture fascists in academia, political Washington, the national news media, and the entertainment industry.

For those yet untouched by the disease, there are only two options when it finally reaches their doors: submit as required or fight back.

Acknowledgments

So as to not inadvertently render anyone close to me unemployable, I unfortunately have to leave out a lot of names and identifiers when paying out my immense gratitude to the ingenious and endlessly patient people who helped with this book. But here is a desperately incomplete attempt to thank everyone who suggested ideas, offered advice, and gave me their time. Thank you to my publisher, David Bernstein, for his enthusiasm in putting this book to print; to Theodore and Bear for some help editing; to Michael and Matilda for a lot of ideas that made the cut; to the brilliant Michael Rectenwald for walking me through the history and neurosis of social justice (be sure to buy his latest book, *Google Archipelago: The Digital Gulag and the Simulation of Freedom!*); to Ashe Schow for doing God's work in debunking campus "rape culture"; to Andy Ngo for diving face-first into hate-crime hoaxes and victim culture so that most of the rest of us will never have to; to Ryan Anderson for pointing me in the right directions; to Ann Coulter for her encouragement; and not least of all, thank you to my loving family for making sure I would never become a privileged victim.